Chicken Soup for the Soul.

Miracles, Angels & Messages from Heaven

T0191039

Chicken Soup for the Soul: Miracles, Angels & Messages from Heaven
Amy Newmark

Published by Chicken Soup for the Soul, LLC www.chickensoup.com
Copyright ©2024 by Chicken Soup for the Soul, LLC. All Rights Reserved.

The publisher gratefully acknowledges the many individuals who granted Chicken Soup for the Soul permission to reprint the cited material.

Front and back cover photo of sky courtesy of iStockphoto.com (bgton)
Interior image generated using Adobe Firefly from the prompt "mountain with heavenly light behind it"

Photo of Amy Newmark courtesy of Susan Morrow at SwickPix

Cover and Interior by Daniel Zaccari

Publisher's Cataloging-in-Publication data

Names: Newmark, Amy, editor.
Title: Chicken soup for the soul : miracles, angels & messages from heaven / Amy
    Newmark.
Description: Cos Cob, CT: Chicken Soup for the Soul, LLC, 2024.
Identifiers: LCCN: 2024938949 | ISBN: 978-1-61159-116-3 (paperback) | 978-1-61159
    351-8 (ebook)
Subjects: LCSH Angels--Literary collections. | Angels--Anecdotes. | Miracles--Literary
collections. | Miracles--Anecdotes. | Self-help. | BISAC SELF-HELP / Motivational and
Inspirational | SELF-HELP / Spiritual | SELF-HELP / Personal Growth / Happiness
Classification: LCC BL477 .C457 2024 | DDC 202/.15--dc23

Library of Congress Control Number: 2024938949

Miracles, Angels & Messages from Heaven

Amy Newmark

Chicken Soup for the Soul, LLC
Cos Cob, CT

Changing your world one story at a time®
www.chickensoup.com

Table of Contents

❶

~Miracles Happen~

1. Miracle Outside the Happiest Place on Earth, *Christy Hoss* 1
2. The Sweetest Reunion, *Nancy K. S. Hochman* 4
3. Chance Encounters and Open Doors, *Ruth Rogers* 8
4. Heartbeats, *Shannon Shelton Miller* 12
5. Beach Blessings, *Patricia Senkiw-Rudowsky* 16
6. A Walking Miracle, *Claudia Irene Scott* 20
7. A Perfect Photographer and $10,000 Prize,
   Christina Ryan Claypool 23
8. The Holy Rosary, *Patricia Senkiw-Rudowsky* 27
9. You Can Run... But You Can't Hide, *Merry Broughal* 30
10. The Bracelet, *Cj Cole* 34

❷

~Comfort from Beyond~

11. The Photo, *Tara Flowers* 38
12. Tiny Visitor, *Debbie LaChusa* 41
13. Touched by an Angel, *Jasmine Hart* 44
14. The Power of Moms, *Jodi Renee Thomas* 47
15. A Message from Dad, *Nan McKernon* 51
16. Butterflies and Believers, *Linda Zelik* 56
17. The E-Mail and Voice of Innocence, *Deborah Tainsh* 60
18. Searching for Mom, *Christy Heitger-Ewing* 64
19. A Blue Bird Day, *Sarah Asermily* 68
20. On the Wings of a Luna Moth, *Suzanne Garner Payne* 72

3

~Guardian Angels~

21. Turn Here, *Barbara D. Duffey* 76
22. The Spirit of an Old Building, *Marie Largeant* 79
23. Ever Thankful, *Shirlene Joan Raymann* 82
24. Mama's Secret, *Elizabeth A. Atwater* 84
25. Do Not Open That Door, *Pastor Wanda Christy-Shaner* 87
26. When Guardian Angels Sit Watchful on Your Shoulder,
    Toya Qualls-Barnette 89
27. Divine Direction, *Dee Dee McNeil* 92
28. Double Protection, *Pastor Wanda Christy-Shaner* 94
29. Love Never Dies, *Karen Blair* 96

4

~Answered Prayers~

30. Even the Small Prayers, *C. Durand* 101
31. Unlocking a Blessing, *Joanna McGee Bradford* 104
32. Case of the Missing Glasses, *Melinda Pritzel* 107
33. How God and My Angels Saved Me, *Sarina Byron* 111
34. An Unexplained Happening, *Maureen Slater* 114
35. The Convoy, *Elton A. Dean* 118
36. The Miracle of Tanka, *Michelle Jackson* 121
37. Vanished, *Molly Mulrooney Wade* 125
38. Divine Deer, *Debbie Prather* 129
39. God Cares for Piano Players, *Betts Baker* 132

5

~Miraculous Coincidences~

40. A Blue Wall Beneath the Ocean, *Karen Storey* 137
41. Finding Fred, *Elisa Yager* 141
42. A Celestial Wrong Number, *S.R. Karfelt* 144

43. Laurie and the Yellow Curtains, *Deborah Guilbeault* 148
44. Ten Long Weeks, *Kristen Schad* 152
45. The Power of a Wish, *Judy Bailey Sennett* 155
46. The Rich Uncle in Orlando, *Laura Bentz* 158
47. Christmas "Myrakle" *Mary Ellen Angelscribe* 161
48. The Book, *Karleen Forwell* 164
49. Flight Home, *Jennifer Kennedy* 166
50. Heaven's High Five in a Hotrod, *Diane Young Uniman* 170
51. The Miracle Gift from Heaven, *Erin Pfeifer-Andrin* 174

❻

~Messages from Heaven~

52. Dad and Beyond, *Anne E. Beall* 178
53. The Puzzle Piece of Love, *Priscilla Dann-Courtney* 180
54. I Don't Believe in Signs, *Jennifer Stults* 182
55. Ciao Bella, *Cindy Horgash* 185
56. The Pigeon, *Shelby Harrell* 187
57. Messenger in My Driveway, *Luanne Tovey Zuccari* 190
58. Goodbye from Beyond, *Freddy B. Nunez* 194
59. Birthday Greetings, *Erin Kani* 197
60. My Two-Year-Old Delivered a Message, *Kendra Phillips* 201
61. A Missed FaceTime Call, *Tess Clarkson* 204

❼

~Angels Among Us~

62. Garden Center Angel, *Patricia Rossi* 208
63. Double Play, *Jacqueline Ford* 211
64. An Angel in Uniform, *Susan Allen Panzica* 213
65. A Lost Faith Found, *Nanette Norgate* 217
66. A Fluffy Little Angel, *Patti Alexander* 220
67. A Miraculous Healing, *Christine Trollinger* 222
68. Angel in the Desert, *Rick Kurtis* 224

69. The Butterfly People, *Billie Holladay Skelley* 227
70. 200 Pounds of Comfort, *Sarah Criswell Guldenschuh* 230
71. Visits with Mom, *Cheryl Potts* 232

❽

~How Did That Happen?~

72. Cancellations I Can Live With, *Jill Burns* 237
73. A Good Life After All, *Maureen Ryan Griffin* 241
74. Last-Minute Change of Plans, *Dawn Smith Gondeck* 245
75. A Little Dip of Comfort, *Beverly F. Walker* 248
76. Alan's Heart, *Judith Jackson Petry* 250
77. Safely Home, *Hana Haatainen-Caye* 254
78. Faye Day, *Melinda White* 257
79. Did You Hear About Paul? *Kristine Ziegler* 260
80. Bearing the Load, *Judy Salcewicz* 262
81. A Miracle Hello, *Mónica Moran González* 265

❾

~Divine Intervention~

82. Listen, You Will Hear a Voice, *Barbara Jackman* 269
83. Look Down, *Anneice Chapple* 272
84. Lord, Help Me Make It to Lordsburg, *Story Keatley* 275
85. A Joyful Shopping Encounter, *Ferida Wolff* 279
86. This Happened, *Thomas Brooks* 281
87. A Mother's Message, *Susan Wilking Horan* 285
88. The Timely Warning, *Sergio Del Bianco* 288
89. Pinned Under an Excavator, *Laurie Spilovoy Cover* 290
90. Expect the Unexpected, *N. Newell* 294
91. From a Distance, *Rochel Burstyn* 296

⑩

~Listen to Your Dreams~

92. The Second Cup of Coffee, *Sharon Johnson* 302
93. Get Ready, Daddy. I'm Coming! *James R. Coffey* 305
94. Love Survives, *Ruth L. Wallace* 309
95. One Last Goodbye, *Rachel Chustz* 312
96. Finding the Courage to Take Action,
    Barbara Dorman Bower 315
97. Absolutely, No Parking, *Kristi Adams* 318
98. My Mother's Earring, *J. Lynn Benkelman* 322
99. Big Ol' Bear, *Tea Railene Coiner* 325
100. Dot Matrix Dreams, *Kristine Benevento* 329
101. Taking Mom's Travel Advice, *Lisa Marlin* 332

Meet Our Contributors 335
Meet Amy Newmark 349
Thank You 351
About Chicken Soup for the Soul 352

Miracles Happen

Miracle Outside the Happiest Place on Earth

*Believe in miracles. I have seen so many of them come
when every other indication would say that
hope was lost. Hope is never lost.*
~Jeffrey R. Holland

W hen we arrived at LEGOLAND in Southern California after a ninety-minute drive, we discovered that the gates were closed and locked. We knew that wildfires had been burning all over the area, but none were near our destination. We'd scrimped and saved so we could afford a trip to this theme park that the kids had been begging to visit. But because it's tucked in a valley, smoke blown in from the fires made it dangerous for visitors.

I now had to explain to four disappointed children that the highlight of the trip we had planned for weeks was canceled. It had already been a hard year. My nine-year-old son had been diagnosed with diabetes and my husband had emergency open-heart surgery and was out of work for months.

We were living on a shoestring budget when our cousin announced she was getting married in Southern California. Nevertheless, we wanted to celebrate with her, so we began to plan how we could pull off the trip.

Our solution: We'd drive, stay with family, and use a coupon for discount tickets to go to LEGOLAND the day after the wedding.

Now, we had to improvise. We asked God to help us because we had no idea what to do with a van full of sad children. Then, we brainstormed. Disneyland was out of reach financially, but outside its gates was a massive LEGO store. We decided to take the children there and let them pick out LEGO sets to take home and build. They could spend as much time as they wanted exploring the store.

Driving another ninety minutes on the freeway, we could see smoke clouding the sky, getting thicker by the minute. Arriving outside Disneyland, the kids were excited to shop and see all the life-sized things built to decorate the LEGO store. While the children and dads shopped, my sister Cindy's phone rang. It was our mother in Minnesota, wondering how we were faring with all the fires raging around us. We went outside to take the call. Cindy was updating our mother about our revised plans when she felt a tap on her shoulder. Another tourist had overhead the conversation.

"My name's Patty, and I have tickets to Disneyland," the woman said. "We're not going to use them, and I couldn't help but hear your story. I've been praying for the right people to give them to."

While the rest of the family was still shopping, we went with Patty to the big hotel where she was staying. She explained that her daughter had just gotten married at Disneyland, and some of the guests hadn't used the passes they were given as thank-you gifts. But then, up in her room, she discovered only two valid tickets were left. Patty took us back down to the hotel's front desk. Cindy and I were not sure what Patty was doing, but we waited at a table in the lobby for her to finish talking to someone.

When Patty returned, she handed us eight tickets to Disneyland and said, "Have the best day ever!"

I'd heard of random acts of kindness, but those type of things happened to other people, never to us. I couldn't believe that this wonderful, generous woman was sending all eight of us to Disneyland!

With tears of joy spilling down our faces, my sister and I hugged Patty, exchanged personal information, and took her picture. As we parted ways, Patty was no longer a stranger but forever a part of our family. God had answered Patty's prayers and ours, too.

Anyone who has visited Disneyland knows how long the lines are. It was already 2:00 in the afternoon, and I was certain we wouldn't have enough time to do much but walk around and maybe get on a couple of choice attractions.

However, because of the smoke in the air from the fires, Disneyland looked like a ghost town. There were no lines at the most popular rides, and the children enjoyed riding them over and over without waiting.

At the end of the day as the park was closing, we knew we had had "the best day ever." We will never forget the miracle given to us by Patty, who would be called, in Disney terms, our "fairy godmother."

— Christy Hoss —

The Sweetest Reunion

We cannot destroy kindred: our chains stretch a little
sometimes, but they never break.
~Marquise de Sévigné

When my mother was in her late seventies, I hesitantly asked whether she knew anything about her half-siblings. They were among the few family topics we had never discussed.

"I have three half-sisters and one half-brother," my mom volunteered, while staring down at a file on her lap.

"I hired a detective many years ago to find them," she added. "I planned to contact them but decided against it. She paused, and in almost a whisper said, "They probably never even knew about me."

Sensing her fear about chancing a meeting with her father's children, of opening Pandora's box only to be rejected, I hugged her gently and shut the lid on the subject.

Her mother had died from post-delivery complications when my mom was two days old. Her grieving father, Henry, took her to a woman who cared for orphans in her home. During a visit, Henry became concerned that the baby girl was malnourished. He asked his in-laws, with whom he was on poor terms, to take her. He told them his goals were to build his sign-painting business and to marry a woman who would help raise his daughter.

When he had accomplished both, he sought to bring his daughter home. But her grandmother, Dora, was unwilling to relinquish her three-year-old granddaughter. An extended custody battle between my father and his mother-in-law ensued. Close to four years later, the judge awarded the grandmother custody. The courtroom was the last place my mom saw her father.

Sadly, my mom continued to face loss. Her grandmother Dora passed away from heart disease when Mom was eleven. Mom was forced to shop, cook and clean for the household. Not long after, her grandfather fled to Florida, leaving my mother in the care of an emotionally abusive uncle and aunt.

Years later, my mother met a podiatry student at a dude ranch. When they ran into each other again, in the New York City subway, he asked for her phone number. My father was the most nurturing and sensitive person my mother ever met. When he proposed marriage, my mother felt deeply blessed. With renewed hope and confidence, she tracked down her father's phone number to share the good news and ask him to walk her down the aisle. She wanted to welcome him into her now happy life.

"Hello. I'm your daughter Mary," my mom said into the phone. She heard a woman's voice in the background. Then her father's: "Please don't call me again. No one knows about you." It was one of many times my mother cried on her husband's broad shoulders.

My mother passed away at age ninety-one. Several months afterward, I considered searching for her half-siblings, but felt torn. Was I being disrespectful to my mom's memory and wishes by pursuing the search?

As it turned out, a year-and-a-half later, I was contacted by a cousin on my mother's side who was researching family genealogy. He sent me copies of two local newspaper articles from the early 1930's about the custody battle. He also sent names and contact numbers for my mom's half-siblings and their families. I felt that I now had permission to reach out to my mother's siblings.

The following week, my adult son visited. I told him about the cousin.

"Wow! This is an amazing coincidence," Jonah replied, before telling me his story. Around the same time our cousin contacted me, a woman on the Ancestry.com chat reached out to Jonah. The DNA they shared suggested they were distant cousins.

While exploring the connection, I reminded Jonah of my mother's maiden name. He promptly typed it into the chat.

Jonah received a response several hours later.

"I'm in awe," said his contact, Jamie. "We've been trying to find your grandmother since the late 1970's. But no one knew her married name."

Jonah gave Jamie my phone number. Within a few moments, Jamie launched a three-way phone call with her mother, Bobbie, my mom's youngest half-sibling, and me. Jonah listened on the speaker.

Bobbie cried over having missed the opportunity to meet her older half-sister. She said that it was likely her own mother, Henry's second wife, who kept him from visiting his daughter.

Despite my voice being choked with tears, I did my best to encapsulate my mother's life: to introduce her to a lovely half-sibling. I told Bobbie that despite her challenging childhood, my mother used her deep determination to become a prize-winning artist, and a studio art teacher. She was also a loving mother, a deeply cherished wife, and a nurturing woman who rescued animals and provided sage advice to anyone in trouble.

I don't know whether kindness is inherited, but all my mother's half-siblings recognized my mother's willingness to help others in themselves. Bobbie told me that she and her older sister Elaine sat on park benches as young children, looking for people who were alone in order to provide them with some company. Elaine, who spent most of her career as a cardiology and school nurse, provided solace to students, teachers, and even administrators. I also learned that Elaine found herself in the right place at the right time, saving the lives of several strangers on the subway.

Finally, Bobbie spoke about her brave-hearted big brother, David. When his father Henry was on his deathbed, he asked David to find my mother, the child he had unwillingly abandoned, in order to give her his meager life savings. Elaine and Bobbie joined the search. David placed ads in newspapers, and even reached out on the Bernard Meltzer radio show.

Days later, I received calls from Uncle David and Aunt Elaine. They both deeply regretted having missed getting to know their half-sister. Still, they were happy to have learned about their sister's life. And to welcome me, their newest niece.

My Aunt Elaine and Uncle Isaak live in Brooklyn, an hour's drive away. My husband and I have shared deeply satisfying visits with sweet Uncle Isaak and Aunt Elaine — now a wonderful friend and mentor. My husband and I felt fully at ease with Aunt Bobbie and Uncle Danny's visit from California. During our trip to South Carolina, we enjoyed Uncle David and Aunt Marilyn's hospitality and warmth. We gained new insights into the grandfather I never met.

I'm sorry my mother was afraid to take the chance of meeting her half-siblings, but it's perfectly understandable given her father's rejection of her when she called him. Somehow, I feel that she engineered this from beyond and that she, too, is enjoying the miracle of our warm, welcoming, extended family.

— Nancy K. S. Hochman —

Chance Encounters and Open Doors

Don't give up before the miracle happens.
~Fannie Flagg

My lifelong dream job seemed to have finally arrived right after graduate school. I was thrilled to begin teaching in November at a highly rated neighborhood school. My assignment was to take over a recently promoted teacher's sixth-grade class—one with some discipline issues.

No problem, I thought when the principal warned me about them. As the greenest of graduates with not one college lesson on classroom management, I naively assumed that if learning was fun and children were treated with respect, behavioral problems simply wouldn't exist.

As it turned out, I barely made it through the year. Four preteen boys astutely assessed the situation and tested every boundary. My second class the following year was, thankfully, an engaging group of highly cooperative students. But there was still a problem. The school's strict rules and rigid structure began to drain me.

A hard truth slowly hit home. Teaching, after many years of dreaming about and preparing for it, was not a good fit for me.

After considerable thought, my husband and I took a financial leap of faith and decided I would not sign another contract. It was one of the toughest decisions of my life, because we needed two incomes.

I had to move fast.

After weeks of soul searching, tears, and reading every career book available, an old conversation drifted into my mind late one summer night as I lay in bed unable to sleep. While in grad school, I'd attended an open house at the public television station near the university and toured their state-of-the-art facility.

Intrigued by the infinite job possibilities, I'd asked the guide, "What does it take to get a job here?"

"Go out and teach a couple of years," she advised. "Then come back and apply in our Education Department."

I had the requisite two years of teaching! Energized by this realization, I practically leapt out of bed the next morning. My resume got a quick makeover before I drove to the station a couple of miles away, brimming with fresh hope.

Those high hopes hit a brick wall abruptly on encountering the station's intimidating Human Resources Manager. After a cursory glance at my resume, she coldly informed me, "There are no openings that fit your work experience."

Deflated but not defeated, I resolved to stop by her office monthly — armed with a sunny, upbeat demeanor — to check on new job postings. This was before the Internet, so that was the most efficient way to seize an opportunity before it was gone.

In the meantime, my application at a temp agency landed me in a mind-numbing job at a Fortune 100 insurance company — pulling staples out of files in a chilly, cavernous basement lined with tables of silent workers. Sometimes, I had a little cry in my car before going inside.

After six months of checking in at the TV station, I was on the verge of giving up. But on impulse, one day I entered through the station's back door and encountered a favorite grad-school professor whom I hadn't seen in two years.

Surprised, he asked what I was doing there. I briefly explained and asked him the same.

"I'm an educational consultant for a current series they're producing. If you want, I'll introduce you to some people who might help you get a job here."

I could hardly contain my excitement.

The chance to interview for three entry-level positions came rapidly. They weren't dream jobs but, potentially, a "foot in the door." My hopes were dashed each time, though, when I was notified that the job had been given to a candidate with significant experience in that area.

My heart said I was supposed to work at the station… yet no door opened.

The last interview was for a tape librarian position. I hit it off well with Kevin, the department manager, but that job, too, went to another applicant. The news was crushing. My once-promising plan now seemed like an impossible dream.

After two grueling months of full-time staple pulling, Tracy, my temp supervisor, mercifully reassigned me to a small insurance company on the outskirts of town where I answered phones.

Because of its location, I joked with friends, "Only God, Tracy, and my husband know where I am."

Tracy called one day and put me on the spot with an invitation to a kitchen-housewares party at her apartment. I was not a fan of these parties and had successfully avoided them until then. I groaned inwardly and accepted.

It was a small party with eight people packed into a cramped living room. I quietly chatted with Tracy's good friend, Lisa.

"Where do you work?" I politely asked.

She smiled and replied shyly, "I just started a job as the tape librarian at the public TV station."

"Oh, no! You're the one who got that job!" I blurted out, completely caught off-guard.

She looked stricken. I instantly apologized, sharing the backstory. She told me that she had been the tape librarian at another TV station, and the public station had approached her.

At home that night, I shared my frustration with my husband. "I now know that to get a job there, they have to come looking for you."

Surprisingly, the very next morning, Kevin, the last manager who had interviewed me, called the insurance company. I answered, and he shared that there was another opening at the station. He asked if I was interested.

Shocked by his call and a little irritated, I boldly inquired, "Are you offering me the job or is this just another interview?" Clearly, my bruised ego wasn't up to more rejection.

"I am offering it to you," he stammered, taken aback.

When we met at the station two days later, I apologized for my bluntness and quickly explained my frustrating job search there. He appreciated my honesty and laughed when I asked, "How on earth did you find me?"

His response blew me away.

The morning after the party, the woman I met, Lisa, relayed our conversation to her office mate, Caroline. Five minutes later, Caroline walked downstairs to Kevin's office and, totally unrelated, asked if he had hired someone for a brand-new job posting.

"No, but I know exactly who I want," he answered. "Her first name is Ruth, but HR has lost her resume, and I have no idea how to find her!"

Caroline's face lit up. "I know exactly how you can locate her."

Contact was made… a position was offered and humbly accepted… and a new career was launched. I worked there happily for three years before moving to a station in a larger market.

With tremendous gratitude, I enjoyed a career in public television for almost thirteen years. And I always kept in mind that it was an opportunity made possible by two chance, maybe miraculous, encounters—in a hallway and at a party—that opened doors and enabled a seemingly impossible dream to come true.

— Ruth Rogers —

4

Heartbeats

The child must know that he is a miracle,
that since the beginning of the world
there hasn't been, and until the
end of the world there will not be,
another child like him.
~Pablo Casals

W e started getting the questions soon after our son's first birthday. Family, friends, coworkers, and acquaintances all wanted to know if we were going to have another child.

No one was asking more than I was. With my thirty-seventh birthday looming and a husband six years my senior, I could see the baby door creaking shut with every passing year. I cherished the bond I had with my younger brother, especially as we tackled our aging parents' health concerns, and I hoped my son could have the same connection with a sibling one day. I didn't want to feel as if I'd be leaving him alone in this world.

Still, seeing that second telltale line on a pregnancy test in early December, three months after our son turned two, didn't result in the same exhilaration I felt the first time I was pregnant. We'd taken precautions and put the "baby talk" on the back-burner, so I worried about my husband's reaction. He liked planning and order, while I sometimes preferred living by the seat of my pants.

I took another test two days later, splurging on one of those electronic deals that offered an immediate response and guaranteed accuracy. "Pregnant" flashed back at me, and all I could think about was the cost of daycare for two children and cobbling together sick days and vacation time for a semi-paid maternity leave.

When my mother called two days later, I wanted to tell her. That decibel of excitement I hoped to hear in her voice would ease my fear and make everything okay. But her mind was elsewhere. My seventy-one-year-old father, a type 2 diabetic, had gone to the operating room at a suburban Detroit hospital for yet another procedure related to his end-stage kidney failure.

Dad was the eternal optimist, even in the face of routine hospitalizations that increased in frequency following his heart attack at sixty-five. Still, with every emergency visit — sometimes for pneumonia or infections that in healthy people would have been easily treated — our family hoped he'd walk away with a cleaner bill of health. No one wanted to voice the obvious: Dad, an Air Force veteran, a thirty-year teacher and lifetime sports enthusiast, was in his last days. His smooth, dark brown, wrinkle-free skin hid narrowing arteries, an oxygen-starved heart, and failing kidneys forced to depend on thrice-weekly dialysis for survival.

"The surgery went well," Mom said. She said those same words after every procedure; I almost expected that response. I decided to hold off on the pregnancy announcement until she told me that Dad was resting in the ICU and I could talk to him later that night or the next day. I'd tell them together in a few weeks, maybe at Christmas.

I didn't get that chance. The next morning, my husband called when I was at work.

"I'm here," he said. "Come outside."

I walked toward him in the parking lot where he was waiting outside his car.

"Your mother didn't want to bother you at work, so she called me," he began. "Your father had another heart attack last night." Dad was alive, he said, but comatose.

I wasn't ready for him to die, and I sobbed with the realization that our Thanksgiving visit weeks earlier might have been our final goodbye. He'd probably never meet his second grandchild.

Child. It was the first time I had used that word and considered my pregnancy as more than a disconnected mass of cells and tissue that I wouldn't have noticed if not for the confirmation of a pee stick.

"I have something to tell you," I blurted suddenly. "It's good news."

"We won the lottery? You got a promotion? You're pregnant?"

My grin after his last guess confirmed it.

"It's the circle of life," he said, as his slight smile grew into a laugh, and he hugged me tightly.

We had thought we weren't ready for a second child, not yet at least, but maybe it was never a question about what we wanted, just a fear of upsetting a tenuous balance in our marriage that we'd struggled to achieve after parenthood. We also thought we were prepared to say goodbye to my father at some point in the near future, but as I felt Dad's life slipping away, I clung to the promise of new life emerging.

That afternoon, before we started the four-hour drive to Michigan from our home in Southwest Ohio, I called the practice I had used for my first pregnancy and scheduled an evening appointment for January 22 when I'd be slightly more than ten weeks along.

Machines kept my father alive for seven more weeks, through Christmas and the dawn of a new year, but he never regained consciousness. He died on a Thursday morning, and I canceled that day's appointments—except one. It was January 22, and I had a 6:00 PM meeting with my midwife.

As I filled out paperwork that night in the waiting room with my husband by my side, I marked the usual boxes about my health history. I paused when I reached the section for my family.

Mother, alive. Father...

My pen moved to the box under "deceased." Check.

Soon, it was my turn to see the midwife.

"You're pregnant again. Congratulations! How are you feeling?"

"Well, my father died this morning," I said. I felt like I could throw up at any moment.

The smile left her face. "I'm so sorry," she said. "We could have rescheduled your appointment. It wouldn't have been a problem."

"Thank you, but I needed to be here today."

Ten hours after my father took his last breath, I heard our baby's heartbeat for the first time. My husband recorded the sound on his iPhone, and we e-mailed it to my mother as we held hands. I cried—both for my loss and for the promise of a brand-new life.

— Shannon Shelton Miller —

Beach Blessings

Faith is unseen but felt, faith is strength when we feel
we have none, faith is hope when all seems lost.
~Catherine Pulsifer

My family and friends gather every Fourth of July at the Jersey Shore in Bradley Beach. The water has warmed enough to make swimming comfortable. Southside Johnny performs a concert at The Stone Pony. Fireworks illuminate the night sky.

During the year in question, after four days of basking in the sun, dipping in the water, and sharing Lay's potato chips, the long, festive weekend is drawing to an end.

My friend Gail's sister is the first one to break from our circle. She has a long ride home and doesn't want to contend with holiday traffic. She says goodbye and heads back to take a shower at the family cottage.

We continue to lounge outside, talking and playing a trivia game. Within a half-hour, Lisa returns. She looks panicked. The platinum diamond ring that she inherited from her mother is missing. Between the ninety-degree weather, staying up late, and drinking, she can't remember if she wore the ring to the beach or left it at the house.

We all rise and check the perimeters of our blankets. A few casual friends join in the search. We come up empty-handed.

Lisa returns to the house praying that she somehow overlooked the ring. It is not there. She is bereft. The jewelry is not only valuable, but meaningful to her. We all promise to continue looking.

As an educator, I have the entire summer off. Each day, I join my friends in the same spot. We scour the beach for the precious diamond. It is nowhere to be found.

In the ensuing week, a nor'easter batters the coastline. The wind blows so hard that trash bins have to be secured from blowing away. The odds of finding the ring become even slimmer.

Once the sun emerges, the public-works employees arrive with their trucks to rake the sand. They ride up and down the shoreline attempting to flatten the warped, uneven sand. They remove anything in their path to ensure the beach is clean for tourists.

Following a week-long hiatus due to the stormy weather, my husband and I return to our group. The sun is hot. The conversation is flowing. Our long talks provide therapy. We have all suffered from significant losses, including Gail, whose twenty-one-year-old daughter has recently passed away. The death has left her doubting her faith.

We hang out until the sun exhausts us. My husband folds the beach chairs and our umbrella. He squeezes them into our sand wagon. We slowly proceed off the beach.

Our condo is directly across from the beach entrance. I pour some olive oil into a frying pan and add some onions and chopped hotdogs. The smell is potent, so I slide open my balcony doors. I love to hear the sound of children laughing and people enjoying the sunny day.

Jay jumps in the shower. My phone rings. It is the curator from a gallery where my watercolors are displayed.

"You had a good day," the curator says. "I sold the marina scene. Come by and get your check. I'll be here for another hour."

Before I can respond, I view my upstairs neighbor exiting the building. His young daughter is beside him. He is carrying a metal detector. I feel a jolt of electricity run through me. I am prone to guidance from an unknown source.

"Okay, that's great," I respond. "I'll be over soon."

I hang up and rush to my terrace in an attempt to catch my neighbor. He has already crossed the street.

"Hey!" I call out, trying to grab his attention. It is too late. He has vanished down the entrance ramp. I return inside to stir my dinner.

My husband appears from the bedroom. He is refreshed. I share my good news.

"Roddy called. I sold a piece. He will be there for an hour. Let's hurry and eat so we can pick up my money. We can celebrate! I will buy you the biggest ice cream in Asbury Park."

"Sounds good to me," he agrees.

My intuition will not rest. I dial Gail.

"My neighbor just went to the beach with his daughter, and I got the strangest sensation. I can't go out because I have some business, but I think you should take a look."

"Really?" she says unenthusiastically. "I am so tired and hungry. We just got the sand off everything."

"I know, but I definitely felt something," I add.

"Okay," she agrees, but I am not sure if she is just humoring me.

The gallery owner has my check. I keep my promise to Jay. We drive over to Asbury Park to purchase some malts. We locate an open bench to devour our treat.

We people-watch and then amble back to the car. I have left my phone in the console. When I retrieve it, I see there is a voice mail. It is Gail. She is barely audible. It sounds as if she's been crying.

"Call me," she pleads.

"Is she okay?" Jay asks.

"I dunno. Let's just go to their house."

We rush back to Bradley Beach. As soon as I step onto Gail's driveway, she rockets off the porch. She wraps her arms around me and begins to sob.

I embrace her. "What's going on?"

"I went out, Patti, although I really didn't feel like it. I was so tired, but I know you get those feelings. There were three people with metal detectors, but somehow I knew it was him. I introduced myself as your friend and told him about the ring. We started looking, but we weren't finding anything. I was really hot, hungry and skeptical, so I left."

Her tears are overflowing.

"It's okay." I attempt to soothe her.

"He and his daughter continued searching, but then it started to get dark. He wanted to leave, but she insisted on staying. There was one big family remaining, and the little girl wanted to look under where they were sitting. He started getting really frustrated, but he said she gets those feelings like you, so he stayed. Finally, the group left, and they went over to that spot. She put her hand into the sand and dug. On the first try, she plucked up the ring."

"What?"

"You weren't home, but he remembered that I mentioned I live on the lake, so they all came over here and were calling my name. I saw them and ran out. They told me the story. I can't believe they've found my mom's ring after all these weeks. I wanted to give the little girl a reward or something, but she refused."

She breaks down. "Patti, do you know what her name is?"

I realize I don't.

"It's Joanna."

That's the name of Gail's deceased daughter.

"That's crazy!" I exclaim.

"Right. What are the odds?"

Joanna returned the ring to Gail that day. More importantly, she restored Gail's faith. Gail finally began to accept that her daughter was at peace and they would be reunited one day.

— Patricia Senkiw-Rudowsky —

A Walking Miracle

Every day holds the possibility of a miracle.
~Author Unknown

I'd headed to the mall one sun-drenched spring afternoon in Florida because I was feeling depressed over some recent hurtful situations. Meandering down the aisles of Books-A-Million was one of my favorite things to do whenever I felt bored or blue. I scoured the shelves for a book that might lift my spirits. I didn't find anything, but as I passed the magazine rack near the exit, an unfamiliar magazine caught my eye.

It was called *Spirituality & Health*. I picked it up, flipped through the pages, returned it to the rack and left the store. When I got to the car, I felt my inner voice whispering, "Go back and buy that magazine." I had long ago learned not to ignore that gentle voice.

I went back and bought the magazine for what seemed like an exorbitant price: $4.95. I had never spent as much on a magazine.

That night as my husband of thirty years and I lay in bed — he doing his crossword and I reading my new magazine — I came to an essay called "What Goes on There, Really?" After reading the half-page essay, I knew in a moment that I had been invited to take a special journey.

The piece was about walking the labyrinth at Grace Cathedral in California. It was long before they became as popular as they are today, so I was unfamiliar with spiritual labyrinths.

"Barry, I don't know when, but I am certain that one day I will be walking in this labyrinth." I showed him the photo of the maze-like circle based on the famous medieval one at Chartres Cathedral in France. "I just know it." No matter that it was three thousand miles away.

He uttered his typical response, "Whatever you say, honey," and went back to his crossword. We both laughed, and that was that.

Three weeks later, Barry came home with a cat-that-ate-the-canary grin. I could tell he was bursting to share some happy news.

"What?"

"Well," he began in his usual low-key manner, "the bank wants me to go to San Francisco in a couple of weeks. I have no idea why as I'm not a conference meeting guy; I'm a techie. And, oh yeah," he nonchalantly added, "they said that you can tag along too if you pay your own airfare."

I was stunned. Traveling had never been part of Barry's job description. He even questioned their decision to send him all the way to California for this particular meeting.

"But I'm the guy they want to go out there for some reason. Beats me," he said, laughing.

I was thrilled. I had never been to San Francisco. I asked for the specific dates and ran to my appointment calendar. As a workshop presenter, I would not be able to cancel any workshops that I had booked for that week on such short notice.

Phew! There was one scheduled for two days before and one for the day after the trip dates.

Then I checked to see how many frequent-flyer miles I had accumulated. I had just qualified for a free trip, so I made my reservation immediately. The universe was telling me to proceed.

Then it hit me. *San Francisco? That's where Grace Cathedral is!* Barry said he was astonished that I had not thought of it sooner because he remembered my recent prophecy, which was why he was grinning so much when he came home. He joked that he actually did listen occasionally. And we would be staying at a hotel within walking distance of that church!

Four days into our trip to San Francisco, my husband had seen no one from corporate headquarters because the managers kept canceling the meetings. Meanwhile, we were told to continue to enjoy the sights, and I got to go to the cathedral.

On the fifth day, the manager whom Barry was finally scheduled to meet called the hotel and said that he did not think Barry needed to come to the offices after all. It would be just as efficient to discuss the matter over the phone.

So, my husband sat in our hotel room on a conference call with a man only a few miles away. Business was accomplished exactly as it could have been if Barry had stayed in Florida. Barry never traveled for the bank again.

For me, the golden hours spent walking the labyrinth of this wondrous cathedral will stay with me forever. It was mystical how deep sorrows came to the surface as I began the walk.

Tears flowed as I followed the path to the center. On the way out of the maze, I felt the release of some deep emotional scars. I am certain, twenty years later, that I was meant to be there at that time.

I will never understand it. First, the magazine article (which I still have) calling to me "you must come." Then, almost immediately, the business trip that made no logical sense. The fact that my work schedule fit perfectly around that window in time. And finally, the free trip I had just qualified for with my frequent flyer miles.

Was it all just so that I could walk the labyrinth? Maybe. I do know it was an extraordinary example of how life often offers us the most wonderful serendipity. And, yes, I call them miracles.

— Claudia Irene Scott —

A Perfect Photographer and $10,000 Prize

Every happening, great and small,
is a parable whereby God speaks to us,
and the art of life is to get the message.
~Malcolm Muggeridge

A s a freelance journalist with several decades of experience, my career has been spent reporting inspiring or faith-filled stories for regional magazines, Christian television, and newspapers. A forty-nine-year-old local woman's brutal slaying at the hands of a young neighborhood man — whom she had only ever tried to help — certainly didn't fit into the inspirational category.

It seemed cruel and insensitive to ask the murder victim's heartbroken parents if they wanted to recount their tragic tale. But the thought that I should contact Debra Henderson's family wouldn't go away. Through the years, I have interviewed numerous grief-stricken individuals. It amazes me how publicly sharing about the good or purpose resulting from their loss frequently comforts the loved ones left behind.

Truthfully, though, I couldn't imagine anything good or purposeful coming from Debra's heinous slaying. She was a middle-aged, bubbly blonde with a vivacious personality and a kind heart for everyone.

Having personally spoken with Debra on various occasions, I couldn't fathom how anyone could perpetrate such a gruesome crime against her.

Yet I desperately desired to ease her family's sorrow because I had attended church with them prior to my move to a nearby city. A decade before Debra's death, I'd met her parents, Dale and Nancy Henderson, while compiling our church's history for a newspaper feature. We chatted for hours in their living room, looking through their vast collection of clippings and keepsakes from their decades as Lima Community Church members.

After Debra's passing, the small voice inside urging me to contact Dale and Nancy finally won out. Reluctantly, I phoned them, quickly explaining my intention not to intrude or add to their trauma but that I couldn't shake the unrelenting almost supernatural sense that they might want to share something concerning the tragedy. Debra's murderer was already serving a life sentence, and details about the crime had been reported by the media on numerous occasions.

There was silence on the other end of the line. Finally, seventy-two-year-old Dale began recounting what he had said to the twenty-five-year-old killer during the sentencing hearing.

"...I forgive you. I can't explain... how God makes it possible for me to forgive you, but He did."

Dale said that for almost seven months before his daughter's death, he was driven to say "The Lord's Prayer" every evening. Then, in the courtroom, the grieving father read the famous prayer to the attacker, including the words, "...and forgive us our debts (sins), as we also have forgiven our debtors (those who sin against us)" (Matthew 6:12 NIV). He explained how he came to comprehend the prayer's meaning concerning forgiveness. "Wow, I did not know what all this meant. Even murder, murder, even murder."

As Dale related his riveting courtroom message to me over the phone, I realized that this story needed to be told. The lifestyle editor at *The Lima News* where I freelanced agreed that the article would be a fit for the newspaper's Sunday edition, along with a couple of photos taken by a staff photographer.

I set up an evening meeting with Debra's parents, siblings, and adult children. Not all of them had achieved Dale's level of forgiveness. Still, they wanted to share their collective story, about what it was like to lose someone so precious in such a cruel fashion.

The chief photographer at the newspaper was a seasoned, award-winning photojournalist, the one I assumed would be taking the pictures. Then I received word that Craig wouldn't be coming. Rather, the newspaper would be sending a young intern named Justin, whom I had never met. I debated canceling the interview.

Debra's family was fragile and broken by grief, and I wanted to protect them from more hurt. This wasn't a typical news story, and I wasn't sure a young intern had enough experience to be sensitive to their trauma. Inwardly, I panicked. Still, it would be unprofessional to cancel the meeting on such short notice without a legitimate reason. I had to trust that God was sending the right photographer, even though it seemed wrong.

Sitting in Debra's parents' living room that evening, a place I had been during happier days, I turned on my recorder and began the interview. As I asked my questions, Dale poured out his story of forgiveness. For Debra's sister, part of her forgiveness journey included sewing a blanket for the convicted killer. Yet there were family members who admitted they were struggling.

Debra's loss was a senseless injustice perpetrated by a young man who had frequently abused drugs and alcohol. The compassionate, middle-aged victim had only tried to help the intruder from the time he was a boy growing up with her own son.

"I knew this boy. Our whole family knew this boy," Dale said. Debra had fed the young man on occasion, given him clothes, and taken him to church. For her efforts, her attacker broke in and killed her. I listened to their various accounts and sympathized with their heartbreak and trauma, but not being a trained counselor, I didn't know what to say.

The young photographer sat quietly. Then, without warning, Justin began to tell his own story in an effort to comfort a family grappling with the enormity of the gruesome offense. Justin's brother had also been murdered, and the short sentence his brother's killer received had seemed grossly unfair.

Despite his grief, Justin walked his own road to find forgiveness and peace. There had been no need for me to be frantic about the intern's ability to be compassionate. Justin had lived through the same circumstances and come out stronger and wiser. I was awed by his empathetic words of understanding.

Miraculously, out of about 700 entries from mainstream media, my newspaper feature, "Finding Forgiveness," won the first-place $10,000 prize in the former national Amy Foundation Writing Awards in 2011. I hadn't made much money during my career nor had any success in moving up from being a small-market journalist. Nearing retirement age, I had been secretly wondering if my work mattered or if I was any good at my craft. Winning the national award somehow solidified that I had chosen the path that my Creator intended.

To this day, I hold Debra's family close in my heart. Her mother has passed on, but I like to think of Nancy being gloriously reunited with her daughter in Heaven. As for me, the privilege of telling Debra's story taught me to trust in the miracle of God's provision—not because of the prize money but for His gift of sending a grieving family the perfect photographer.

—Christina Ryan Claypool—

The Holy Rosary

The relationship between parents and children, but especially between mothers and daughters, is tremendously powerful, scarcely to be comprehended in any rational way.
~Joyce Carol Oates

The day after my mom died, I drove out to Pennsylvania to the quaint country town where she was born. My brothers and I sat discussing arrangements with the funeral director. One of our topics was what to do with the last articles that were in her possession when she passed. She had always worn a rosary and never went anywhere without her chunky, over-stuffed pocketbook.

We decided that the rosary should be buried with her. My eldest brother rummaged through her wallet. I asked if I could keep her purse because it reminded me of her. She often sat at my table talking with me as I cooked, and that pocketbook was always right beside her.

My brother agreed and picked through the pocketbook in a businesslike fashion to ensure that he had all the money and insurance cards. I gazed in at the other contents. The purse contained typical items: a shopping list, a compact, a small bag with a nail file, a little bottle of perfume.

When my eldest sibling was certain that there was nothing else of financial value, he handed me the pocketbook. I was happy that I would still be able to plop that pocketbook right in her spot at my kitchen table. In a sense, we would still be having our morning coffee together.

On the day of the viewing, Mom looked beautiful. She was laid out in the dress that she had worn to my wedding twenty-six years earlier. That purchase was the one time when she had splurged. Money had been tight in our family, and she had always placed everyone else's needs before her own. Her sacrifices never embittered her, though. My mother was a devout Catholic who believed that being of service to others was the right way to live.

The funeral was going smoothly. People flowed in and out of the parlor. They acknowledged the old photos and Mom's peaceful appearance. Then someone mentioned that there was no cross on her rosary. I stepped up to the casket and realized that it was true. The crucifix on her rosary beads was missing.

I had brought my own rosary and clutched it in my pocket for strength. It was a well-crafted, baby-blue crystal rosary, imported from Italy, which my aunt had given to me. When I faced tough situations, I'd carry it in my pocket.

I struggled for a second. Should I put my own rosary within her grasp? I would never get it back. It would be buried with her. I hesitated, trying to think of alternatives.

Then I thought of my mother and felt ashamed. Material things never mattered more to her than I did. She would offer me anything in her house if I complimented her on it. I felt ashamed for even questioning whether to replace the broken version.

I wanted her to have something beautiful with her on her final journey, so I placed my rosary within her grasp. It was not easy to let go of that rosary because it had seen me through some dark days, but if anyone deserved it, my mom did.

After the funeral, I went home and plopped that pocketbook on the kitchen table. I lit a Blessed Mother candle. For weeks, I let the condolence cards collect on the table, creating a memorial until there was nowhere left to eat.

Finally, after a month, when my son was returning from college, my husband Jay gently suggested it might be time to pack up the memorial. I knew he was right. It was time to take a step forward. But all the cards comforted me, and putting them away seemed to acknowledge the finality of my mother's death.

I re-read each card and then packed away all the items with the exception of the pocketbook. Jay agreed the pocketbook was kind of cute and not an issue because it didn't take up much room.

One early December morning, I lit my candle, put on "Mother and Child Reunion" to play, and sat alone at the table. Who would ever care about me as much as my mother? Who would listen to me as I rambled on about my dreams and problems? I felt so alone.

Christmas was coming, and I was struck with an atypical moment of doubt. How would she ever be restored? How could I have possibly believed that I would ever see her again? I was angry at the magical thinking on which she had raised me. Practicality left no room for miracles. Being dead was final.

Suddenly, I felt an urge to rummage through Mom's pocketbook. I found the compact, her lipstick, the shopping list and something we hadn't noticed before: a small, plastic case. I unscrewed the box's top and peered inside.

White tissue paper was crumpled over an item. I pulled apart the paper with my fingertips. At first, I couldn't believe what I had found. Inside the paper was a rosary identical to the one that I had placed in the casket with my mother. Perhaps my aunt had given her one as well.

I felt a rush of warmth. Had we overlooked the item before? Was it a coincidence? Could it be a miracle? I could hear my mother's voice: *When we give to another, it always returns to us when we need it most.*

I felt my mother at my kitchen table once again. It was the best gift I could receive during that first Christmas season without her. Somehow, I knew my mother would always be with me, and I didn't feel alone any longer.

— Patricia Senkiw-Rudowsky —

9

You Can Run... But You Can't Hide

Faith is not only daring to believe; it is also daring to act.
~Wilfred Peterson

I'm not fussy when it comes to what I drive. I have only four requirements: It must have a radio, air conditioning, and fabric seats, and people won't point and laugh at it.

I did have a car that we bought used and that was so wonderful that I thought I would never need another one. It was a white Toyota Corolla. White wouldn't have been my first choice since I'm not good at keeping it washed, but what's a little dirt? It had a radio, air conditioning, and fabric seats, and it didn't look as old as it was. To me, it was perfect and fit all my requirements.

I drove that car for several years and had zero mechanical issues. I was thrilled knowing that I would never need to buy another car.

Unfortunately, that would not be the case.

On a nice, clear morning, I was driving to work when I was rear-ended.

I was stopped at a four-way stop about three cars from the intersection. I was in the downtown area, so traffic was fairly heavy and slow-moving to get up to the corner.

Next thing I knew, I was hit from behind. I was knocked into the steering wheel, and my car was pushed forward and crashed into the one in front of me. It was a hard hit. My foot was on the brake when the driver crashed into me, so I knew he had to be flying to shove my car forward so far.

I felt kind of shaky, so I didn't get out of my car when the young man from the car in front of me and the young driver from the car behind me came up to my window to ask if I was okay. I said I didn't know.

We all agreed to pull off the road into an empty parking lot right on the corner.

We did, except someone went missing. The young driver who had started this chain reaction was gone!

The other driver and I exchanged our insurance information. He said his car wasn't damaged, and he needed to leave for a meeting.

I didn't think I was hurt, but since this was now a hit-and-run, I called 911 to report it. I knew I needed a police report for the insurance company. I told them I was fine.

Minutes later, I heard sirens coming closer… lots of sirens. I don't like to draw attention to myself, so I started praying the sirens weren't for me.

They were.

Fire truck! Paramedics! Police! Yikes! I wanted to slide down in my seat and hide.

After I assured them several times that I didn't need an ambulance, they all left except for the officer to take the report.

I wasn't much help making the report since I never got out of the car to see the car that hit me.

I remembered the young driver. He looked like a high-school student. Other than the sequence of events, there was nothing else I could add.

The officer admitted there wasn't anything that could be done with so little information.

At that point, I still had not gotten out of my car.

"Can you tell me how much damage there is?" I asked.

"None," he said.

How could that be? I was hit hard enough to push my car forward a few feet while my foot was on the brake.

It didn't make sense. The first responders must have thought I was some kind of nut for seeing no damage to the car and calling for help.

The officer gave me his business card in case I had any questions later, and I drove off to work.

My car felt like it was driving off-kilter, but it seemed okay otherwise. (Later, the repair shop totaled the car because the chassis was cracked.)

I found an open spot in the employee parking lot, ran into the office, put down my belongings, and checked in with my boss. I told her what had happened, but I still couldn't believe there was no damage to my car. I went back out to take a look.

The officer was right. I didn't see any damage either.

As I turned to walk back into the office, I noticed something on the bumper. I looked closer. There, in the dirt on my white bumper, was an outlined impression of a license-plate number. Could it be?

I went back into the office, grabbed a coworker to look at it (just to make sure I wasn't seeing things), and then called the officer.

"You won't believe this," I told him, "but it looks like the license-plate number of the car that hit me is outlined in the dirt on my back bumper!"

At first, he just chuckled but said he would check it out. I could tell he was skeptical.

I told him where to find my car in the parking lot. A few minutes later, he called back to say I was right. It was exactly what I had described: the outline of a license plate, number and all.

Since the high school was just a few miles away and he had some evidence, the officer said he'd go see if he could match the license number on my dirty bumper to a student's car. Shortly afterward, he called to say he had found the car and talked to the student.

"I was going to call you," the student said when he was called out of class. "I panicked when the lady in the car said she wasn't sure if she was hurt or not, so I left."

If the driver had stayed on the scene, the accident would have been dealt with between insurance companies. But because he had fled the scene, he got a juvenile record that would stay with him until he was an adult.

I'm thankful the officer found the guilty party so I wouldn't be left to pay for another car. His insurance company picked up most of the cost for a replacement.

Whenever I tell this story to others, they can't believe it. *What? Really? Whoever heard of such a thing?* are the responses I get.

As for me, the white car was replaced with a black one, and I'm still not great at washing it. Whenever I'm asked if I want my car washed at the gas station, it doesn't take a second to turn it down.

After all, you never know!

— Merry Broughal —

10

The Bracelet

*We are each of us angels with only one wing, and we
can only fly by embracing one another.*
~Luciano De Crescenzo

The year I was born, the Vietnam War had been underway for eight years. Many of the men and women who served in that conflict never came home. In an effort to promote awareness for those missing or suffering in captivity, a group called VIVA began the POW/MIA bracelet campaign.

The original, simple cuff bore the name/rank/date of loss of a serviceperson who was missing or possibly captive. They were solemn reminders of empty places at the dinner table, beloved family members unable to return home. They were seen on the wrists of nearly everyone — famous people and regular people alike — hoping the servicepeople would never be forgotten.

***

At eleven years of age, I was bored. We had been on the road to the annual family reunion, several states away from the Kansas farm where I lived, for what seemed like days. It was hot, and the road looked endless. We pulled into a roadside station for gas and to stretch our legs. I managed to talk my grandmother into getting me a frozen slushy, and I wandered over to the yard-sale items to wait for everyone to finish up.

Just as I was turning around to head to the car, a bracelet, sitting alone on a shelf, caught my eye. I leaned down to try and read it as I was taught not to pick up things. All I saw was a name, and I was curious.

From behind me, a gruff voice greeted me. The proprietor of the station, walking with a cane, put out his hand to shake mine. I pointed to the cuff and asked him what the bracelet was for. He picked up the bracelet and held it up, reciting the name engraved there: CWO Bobby L. McKain. He was a Kansas boy, lost in 1968 at the age of twenty-two.

His voice cracked a bit as he explained there was a bracelet in the world for every missing soldier left behind. When I asked him why we didn't just go and bring them home, he leaned down and put the cuff on my wrist. He closed it and stepped back carefully. He cleared his throat and nodded his head once to acknowledge the gift as being right and truly given.

"He goes home with you now, little girl. See that you don't forget him."

With that, he walked slowly back inside the garage and vanished into the cool darkness.

I made a promise that day that I would not forget this man, and he would be like family to me for the rest of my life. As the years went by, I was true to my word. I wrote letters to the Army to see if there had been any update on Bobby. I was given the option to leave my information for his family to contact me and was able to speak with his mother. She sent me the occasional note, honoring me with stories of her son.

With the advent of the Internet, I was able to learn more about Bobby. I located his younger brother, still in Kansas, and talked with him. He sent me photos of his wall of pride: medals and photos of McKain men all the way back to World War I, standing for their country. I heard more stories: that Bobby was a bit of a jokester, that his big, wide grin was infectious, and that he was well liked.

A couple of years later, out of the blue, I received a letter from the Army. Bobby was coming home. Bundles of bones returned to the U.S. in 1985 were finally yielding DNA matches. Among those identified were Bobby and his co-pilot, Arthur Chaney. They were being laid to rest in Arlington.

In the years since his return, Bobby has been visited by so many people in my name. I am of Diné (Navajo) descent, so my friends and family have left flags, wreaths, roses, an eagle feather, and tobacco at Bobby's gravestone to honor him for me. He has been remembered as I promised.

I carried Bobby's bracelet for fifty years. To be honest, I thought this was the end of our story. I was wrong. An article I wrote about him appeared as part of his "legend" on the Vietnam Veterans Memorial wall page, a great honor. I left my e-mail address for others to share stories with me.

Checking my e-mail one morning, I saw many unfamiliar names. For a moment, I was ready to delete them as junk e-mail, but a small voice whispered in my head, "Look closer." I opened one and spied the name McKain. As I opened e-mail after e-mail, I began to cry until the words were unreadable on the screen. A new generation of Bobby's family had found me.

Cousin after cousin had written to tell me that they had read my words. They wanted to thank me for keeping Bobby alive in my heart and the hearts of my readers. They invited me to be an "honorary cousin" in Bobby's family.

They are part of my life now, and I am hoping to go back to Kansas this coming year. I want to give my bracelet to my cousin so that it can be passed down through his family for many more people to hear of Bobby's bravery.

If you visit Washington, D.C., you can find our Bobby on panel 54E, Line 027, on the Vietnam Veterans Memorial wall. He is there along with more than 58,000 others who were killed, captured, or are still lost.

Our tribal customs say that when we take our final journey, every single ancestor is there to greet us and welcome us to then stand and watch over the generations to come.

I have a feeling that a handsome, young man with a big, goofy grin will be right up front.

— Cj Cole —

Chapter

2

Comfort
from Beyond

11

The Photo

Mother, the ribbons of your love are
woven around my heart.
~Author Unknown

My mom kept a box of mementos in the bottom drawer of her bureau. From time to time, she would take it out and share the stories behind each item. There was the ticket stub from the first date she had with my father, a promise ring he gave her before enlisting in the Army, love letters, souvenirs, and countless photos. An item that continually captured my attention was a black-and-white image of my mom as a teenager. She was the typical 1950s teenybopper, with a poodle skirt, saddle shoes and high-perched ponytail, laughing with another girl outside her high school. The girl was her best friend, Maria. I learned that they were inseparable and shared the type of bond that is hard to find these days.

Unfortunately, Mom lost touch with Maria shortly after she married my dad. This was long before Facebook and social media, so tracking her down was not a viable option. Over the years, she would comment to me about how much she missed her dear friend. But, of course, life moved on.

I think I was fascinated with this picture due to the innocence and pure joy it represented. Mom had faced many challenges, from very young widowhood to losing a child to suicide. I would return to this photo because it stood as a reminder that, at one time, she truly did have the gift of a carefree existence.

Years later, after my mom was no longer with me, I found myself in a perpetual stage of grief. She had been my everything, so the void of not having her in my daily existence was paralyzing. At the same time as when she passed, my son, my only child, started school, and I realized that the only way to begin to move forward was to go back to work. I believed that keeping busy would lessen the pain.

I missed my mother terribly, and my well-intentioned friends would tell me, "Look for the signs." There were none. Believe me, I tried to see them in everything. A red cardinal? A sudden breeze on a still day? A rediscovered long-lost item? Nope. Nothing.

So I powered on at my new career and with raising my son. I did not interact socially with my colleagues. I had no desire to make any new connections. I'm pretty insular, and, to this day, my two best friends are the same ones I have had since I was twelve years old. I was simply there to do my job and focused on getting my projects finished.

After a couple of months, I received an e-mail from my employer. A colleague had just lost her mother, and he shared the funeral details. I did not know this individual, but, likely associating it with my own experience, I felt compelled to pay my respects.

Upon entering the funeral home where the viewing was being held, I noticed two long tables in the foyer. One displayed a book to sign, and about twenty photos were arranged to the left of it. I glanced at them while waiting in the receiving line. They were mostly what I assumed were her family, children and grandchildren at various stages of her life.

However, wedged in the back, a 5"x7" picture in a black-lacquered frame captured my attention. I did a double take. How was it possible that right in front of me was the same photo of my poodle-skirt-clad mom that had fascinated me all those years ago?

I do not know why, but I turned around and said to no one in particular, "That's my mother in that picture!"

I spent the next ten minutes in line in a daze. When I finally reached my co-worker, I offered my condolences but could not help blurting out, "You have a picture of my mom on your table."

She looked at me as though I was a bit crazy. Then, after a pause — as if she knew — she asked, "Was your mom named Lucia?"

After confirmation, we hugged one another for what seemed like an hour. We briefly shared the history between our mothers and learned that they both had spoken wistfully of one another quite often.

I remember driving away that night with an overwhelming sense of peace. Here was my sign. Mom was telling me without question that she was always with me and had always been.

My colleague has now become one of my dearest friends. We bonded over our grief, our mutual love for our moms, and the beauty of how that relationship shaped the women we are today.

That serendipitous encounter opened my eyes to the possibilities. That cardinal in the garden and that unexpected cool breeze on a hot summer night are and always have been Mom telling me, "You are going to be okay."

— Tara Flowers —

12

Tiny Visitor

The pain passes, but the beauty remains.
~Pierre-Auguste Renoir

Four months before Dad passed away, I went to San Diego to visit him. He was eighty-nine, his health was declining, and I wanted to spend time with him before it was too late.

One afternoon, when Dad and I were talking, he suddenly asked, "Where do you think we go when we die? I don't believe in all that heaven and hell stuff the church teaches."

My parents were Catholic and had gone to mass every Sunday until they moved into assisted living. Mom often commented how much she missed going. Dad never mentioned it.

Having recently watched a documentary on death and dying, I decided the best way to answer Dad's question was to share what I'd seen in the film. "People report seeing a bright light when they die and being greeted by loved ones who've already passed."

Dad's face brightened. "I want to see my dad," he blurted out. "I have so many questions. I don't know why I never asked my mom about him." Dad had never known his father — he died when Dad was eleven months old — and he seemed excited at the prospect of reuniting. He almost seemed to be looking forward to it. From that day on, Dad referred to death as the next phase.

When I got word that Dad was nearing the end, I got on a plane back to San Diego. By the time I arrived, he was unconscious. As I sat in the chair next to Dad's bed, holding his swollen hand, I heard birds singing outside the open window.

"Do you hear the birds, Dad?" I asked, knowing he couldn't answer. "When you get to the other side, will you send me a sign to let me know you're okay? That you're at peace?"

In the documentary, a woman reported being visited by a cardinal after her mother died. Perhaps Dad could send me a cardinal.

He died the following afternoon. I wasn't with him. I'd stepped out to get some fresh air in the courtyard, a quiet space with green grass, patio tables, and chairs padded with sun-faded cushions. I sat down beneath an umbrella and immediately noticed I had company. A hummingbird had flown up to a feeder twenty feet away. Mesmerized, I watched the tiny bird drink the red liquid. I wasn't in the courtyard for more than five minutes when my sister-in-law came running toward me and shouted, "He's gone!"

"What?" I replied. "I was just with him!" As it turned out, everyone except my brother and niece were out of the room when Dad took his last breath. I learned later that dying people often choose to spare loved ones from witnessing their death.

I hurried back inside. When I got to Dad's room, my entire family had returned, and Mom was sitting in the chair next to Dad's bed, holding his hand. I burst into tears and fell into my brother's arms.

"The hummingbird! It was Dad! He was letting me know he's okay," I choked out between sobs. Then I told my family how I'd asked Dad to send me a sign and about the hummingbird in the courtyard. When I regained my composure, I walked over to the bed, leaned down, kissed Dad on the forehead, and whispered, "Thank you for sending me the hummingbird."

The next day, the visits began.

I woke up early and headed out for my morning walk. As I passed a neighbor's house, I noticed a flag waving in the breeze with an image of a giant hummingbird staring back at me. I'd walked by that house many times and had never seen the flag. I continued walking, listening to music through my earbuds. I had just turned the corner and was heading back to my parents' house when my phone rang. When I answered, a familiar voice asked, "Hey you, how are you doing?" It was my friend Amy.

"I'm just finishing up my walk," I replied. Then I told her about the hummingbird in the courtyard. "Oh my god! There's another one!" I exclaimed when I noticed a hummingbird in a lavender plant next to the sidewalk. "Amy, I've been seeing hummingbirds everywhere!"

When I got to Mom and Dad's house, I opened the gate, walked into the backyard, and sat down on the patio. "You're not gonna believe this," I told Amy, who was still on the phone. "There's a hummingbird wind chime hanging right above my head."

"Of course, there is," said Amy. Then she texted me a meme that read: *A hummingbird can be a sign that a loved one is near.*

For the next two weeks, I was greeted daily by hummingbirds. Inside a curio cabinet, a photo of Mom and Dad in a frame adorned with colorful flowers revealed a hummingbird sitting just above Dad's head. A bejeweled hummingbird perched proudly on a side table in the living room. A delicate, hand-carved wooden hummingbird was suspended from the bottom of a birdhouse hanging in the sunroom. I'd spent weeks in that house and had never noticed any of them.

Every evening as I relaxed in the backyard, a pair of hummingbirds came to visit. They'd zoom in, land in a tall tree in the corner of the yard, and, after resting a spell, fly down and dance around the lilies, orchids, blooming cacti, and Matilija poppies in Dad's garden. They looked to be having a grand time together.

When I returned to North Carolina, they followed me home. One evening, I was sitting in my living room when two hummingbirds flew up to the window, paused, peered in, and darted away. It was the first time I'd seen hummingbirds at my house in the five years I'd lived there. Lately, I've noticed a hummingbird flitting from flower to flower in the orange jewelweed that popped up next to the fence. I watch him through the window as he lingers among the blooms.

Dad never got the chance to visit me in North Carolina. He was too feeble to travel after I moved. But every time my tiny friend stops to drink from the small, spotted flowers, I feel like Dad's here, stopping by to let me know he's okay and at peace.

— Debbie LaChusa —

13

Touched by an Angel

The bond between friends cannot be broken by chance;
no interval of time or space can destroy it.
Not even death itself can part true friends.
~Saint John Cassian

I t was a cool February evening in our cozy neighborhood. Mike and I picked up Tom and Linda, our longtime friends and neighbors, to have dinner at our favorite Chinese restaurant. After dinner, we bought a pie and returned to Tom and Linda's house to have dessert. As always, our conversation was filled with laughter, but then it got more serious.

It turned out that Tom and Linda had quite the repertoire of stories about their encounters with spirits. Tom in particular had many profound experiences. There was the time he had a spiritual connection with his younger brother, who'd tragically lost his life in a plane crash along with his two-year-old son. Tom also talked about seeing his grandmother after she passed away.

Listening to Tom and Linda's stories, I couldn't help but marvel at these experiences. I lamented over never having the experience of seeing a "spirit" myself and wondered how I would react if I did. I said I was envious and hoped that I would also get a visit from a friendly "ghost" someday.

Little did we know that this conversation would set the stage for something both eerie and heartwarming.

Three months later, right before Memorial Day weekend, the

unexpected happened. Tom and Linda, known for their adventurous spirits, typically embarked on thrilling escapades whenever the urge struck. They were a very active retired couple, always on the go, either flying their plane, taking off on their two-seater Harley, enjoying weekends at their lakefront second home, four-wheeling with their off-road Jeeps, or traveling to foreign countries.

This time, they surprised us by announcing they'd be staying home for a change. We were going away that weekend, so they offered to take care of our mail and newspapers.

The night before we left for our getaway, Tom casually mentioned his plan to fly over to their second home to mow the lawn but said he would be home the rest of the weekend.

When Mike and I returned from our getaway we were slammed by shocking news. After Tom had mowed his lawn a friend had stopped by to show off his new boat. Tom agreed to take a quick cruise around the lake with him before he flew back home. Tragically, they were involved in a freak accident, making it Tom's last boat ride ever.

A few days later, something inexplicable happened. I was alone in our bedroom when, suddenly, I saw Tom standing there, his gaze fixed on me. The encounter lasted for only seconds, but during that time, it felt as though he was trying to convey something to me. It was almost as if he was letting me know without verbalizing it, "You wondered what it's like to see a spirit? Well, here you go!"

At that moment, I was reminded of our conversation just three months prior. It would be just like Tom to go out of his way to provide me with this experience! I was surprised that I wasn't alarmed or frightened by his presence. It all felt very natural and real.

I shared this uncanny encounter with Linda, who then relayed to me that Tom had also visited another neighbor. He had offered her comfort with his presence and inquired about "his little girl." The neighbor was confused as to who the little girl was. Linda told the neighbor that "little girl" was the nickname Tom affectionately gave her when they were high-school sweethearts.

Linda confided that she was disappointed that Tom hadn't visited her, too. But the neighbor told Linda that Tom said he would not be contacting his wife anytime soon as he thought it would be too difficult for her.

That was so typical of Tom. Not only was he thoughtful and kind, but he was always willing to go the extra mile. Although Tom didn't talk to me like he did with the other neighbor, in that fleeting moment Tom had fulfilled my curiosity about the afterlife by giving me that brief visit.

Seeing Tom brought me comfort and closure, confirming that the bonds of friendship transcend the boundaries of life and death.

— Jasmine Hart —

14

The Power of Moms

Music is well said to be the speech of angels.
~Thomas Carlyle

"It's Mother's Day, so you can have anything you want," my husband told me over our morning beverages. "Shopping spree, fancy dinner, you name it."

"Thank you, sweetheart." I teared up, not wanting to ruin his incredible gesture by telling him that he could not give me what I wanted that day. My mother had passed away years before, so spending time with her was not an option. And my adult daughter was away for work. The two people with whom I wanted to spend my day were not available. But I did appreciate his thoughts.

As the day passed, I kept myself and my morose mood in my office, wishing for something that would lift my spirits. As the afternoon approached, I got a phone call from my "adopted mom," Sandy. My ex-boyfriend's mother had been kind enough to take on the role of my matriarch after my own was no longer with us. It had been so long that I no longer thought of her as my "bonus mother." She was just "Mom."

"Hi, Mom," I answered. "Happy Mother's Day!"

"Well, I just wanted to call and tell you how much I love you, and I am so lucky to have you as a daughter. I thought I would call and tell you how very special you are to me and everyone else."

Again, I held back tears, not only for her gesture and sentiment but in gratitude for how lucky I was to have this incredible woman in my life. "Well, thank you for being my mom in my mommy's stead," I said, choking on my emotions. "Do you have any plans for the day?"

"No, both of my sons are busy," she said, sounding upset.

Hoping to lift both our spirits, I said, "There's a movie I wanted to see. Would you like to go? It could be a mother-and-bonus-daughter day."

"Thank you so much for the offer," she said, "but I am just not in the proper headspace."

"I feel you, Mom. Just know how much I love and appreciate you," I said as we got off the phone.

As soon as I hung up, I burst into the ugly sobbing that one can only do alone. Once I felt better, I pulled myself together and went about my day, with no one the wiser.

An hour later, my phone rang, and it was Sandy again.

"Hey Mom, is everything okay?"

"Yes. I was just wondering if the offer for the movie is still open," she said sheepishly.

"Of course! But it starts in thirty minutes. I will meet you there!"

It was a date for two women feeling alone on the holiday.

"Why are you putting on pants?" my husband asked as I hurried.

"Mom wants to go see a movie," I explained while rushing to wash my face and get out the door.

"Can I come?" Johnny asked timidly because of my mood for most of the day.

"Of course, but we are leaving in five minutes," I said.

We had a lovely day, watched a movie, and had lunch. Then my husband took me shopping, mostly for things we needed for the house, but the thought was there.

Despite the lovely time, I came home still in a funk. I grabbed all the snacks I could from the pantry and went to bed to lose myself in comfort food. Then, my phone rang.

"Hello?" I answered, with a mouth full of cookies.

"Mom, I just wanted to tell you Happy Mother's Day!" I could barely hear my daughter over the background noise on her side of the call. "I can't talk. I'm working. I just wanted you to know that I love you. Gotta go! See you when I get home."

Despite all the wonderful things that had happened that day, I lost it. I missed my daughter. I missed my mother. I would have given a limb to spend an hour with either of them, but I couldn't. I suddenly realized why my adopted mom had agreed to go to the movie. Being the mother of adults on Mother's Day can be lonely, especially when your own mother is no longer around.

Surrounded by junk food, I put on one of my mother's favorite movies and dove into my self-indulgent longing for those who were not around. Hearing my sobs, my husband came in to check on me. I didn't want to discuss it. Instead, he held me while I cried and ate my weight in potato chips.

"What is that noise?" my husband asked quietly.

"It's just the movie," I said through my overload of emotions.

"No, it's not. It's something different. I've seen this movie every time you get upset. This sound is different."

"I don't care about the noise. I just want my mom back!" I snapped at him.

"Babe, it's coming from this," he said softly, coming from our bathroom.

"This" was a wooden music box. It had been on my mom's dresser for as long as I could remember. But it never actually played music. It was just this thing that my father had given her. It was also where she kept all the important things like her wedding ring, some of my baby teeth, and the #1 MOM necklace I had saved up to buy her with all my babysitting money.

The "music box" that had been sitting quietly on my windowsill was suddenly working. It was playing music. For me. On Mother's Day. I hugged it until it stopped playing. My husband tried to wind it, but it no longer played. And, months later, it still doesn't.

But on that one day, when I felt like my family was not with me, they were, all in their own ways. My adopted mom had changed her mind and enjoyed a movie with me. My daughter had taken time out of her busy schedule to call me. And my mother, Bonnie, had come by to send me love.

As I was writing this, I opened that music box. Nothing played. But the memories stored there will last forever.

—Jodi Renee Thomas—

15

A Message from Dad

She did not stand alone, but what stood behind her,
the most potent moral force in her life,
was the love of her father.
~Harper Lee, Go Set a Watchman

I was shopping for my daughter's twelfth birthday in a local store when I spotted an older woman pushing an empty shopping cart following me. I tried to outmaneuver her through women's shoes, bath and body, and housewares until we came face-to-face in the lamp aisle.

"Can I help you with something?" I accused more than asked. "Do I know you?"

"Please don't be afraid," she said. "I am not a stalker. But I do have a message for you if you're open to it."

"A message?" I chuckled, looking past her. "What, am I being punked or something?"

"No," she replied. "I am a medium, and I have a message for you from the other side."

My mouth fell open as I considered the offer. She looked normal enough. She was probably in her mid-sixties, makeup-free with bobbed, salt-and-pepper hair that brushed her shoulders. She wore jeans, sensible shoes, and a knee-length puffer coat, and she had a Coach purse nestled safely in the shopping cart seat.

My own mother had "the gift," as she called it, claiming to see and receive messages from the dead, something she inherited from her mother. Since I grew up with a dining room table covered in astrological charts, I was probably more open to this stranger's request than the average person.

"Okay," I said. "I am not sure I believe, but…"

She approached me head-on, her arm out slightly in front, waist high, palm down, bobbing something invisible. She inhaled deeply through her nose — what yoga instructors call a "cleansing breath" — and closed her eyes with the exhale.

"It's an older man, but he's coming through in mid-life. He has dark hair and clear blue eyes. It's someone you were very connected with in this life, and his end was quite painful for you both. You feel abandoned by him?"

Intense heat ran up my chest to my face. I gripped the handle of my shopping cart for stability.

"Yes," I choked. "I know who he is."

It was my father who'd died ten months earlier from prostate cancer. He had managed the disease successfully for decades with surgeries and medications, but when the cancer metastasized to his bones, he was dead within six months.

Dad's end of life was agony for us both. My mom was in extreme denial and approached his diagnosis by exerting excessive control in ways she wouldn't, or couldn't, see were cruel.

Dad's access to pain medication was limited; she felt it made him "loopy" and that he simply needed to tolerate pain better. (Like someone smuggling contraband into a jailed inmate, I eventually stashed some in a Baggie in my pocket and slipped them to Dad when she wasn't looking.)

Visitors were limited and often turned away at the front door, and conversations were closely monitored. Once he became paralyzed and bed bound, the phone was kept just out of his reach when she ran errands, to prevent unauthorized phone conversations.

For two months, I snuck over to my parents' house on Sunday mornings, waited in my car out of sight until I saw Mom's Lexus pull away for church, and visited with Dad, both of us noshing on his favorite donuts over the deepest conversations we'd ever had. I recorded them on my phone — although, nearly ten years later, I still can't bring myself to listen to his voice — and cherished the eight times we talked openly about life, regrets, children and grandchildren, and what he hoped my own future might hold.

Our secret visits ended one Sunday with Mom arriving home early from church in a blind rage at our "betrayal." The consequence was that Dad spent each Sunday morning alone, with the cordless phone just out of reach, and my phone calls and visits were denied for several weeks.

Two months before he died, Dad asked me to kill him with morphine, which sat in the untouched hospice "comfort pack" intended to ease suffering at the end of life. Mom believed morphine use would kill him immediately and repeatedly declared, "We aren't there yet."

"I can't do this anymore," he said, "and you can help me."

I stashed one of the small morphine vials in my nightstand while I pondered his request, praying night after night for God's guidance. While I never received the clear "Don't do this or you will go to hell" message I hoped for, I decided I couldn't kill my own father. He deserved better than he was enduring, but he'd had alternatives which he had declined — moving in with me and my family or an in-patient hospice unit — to spare my mother the anguish of not controlling his death. I returned the vial to the safety of the box stored in the back of my parents' fridge, no one the wiser.

Now, the woman in TJ Maxx waited patiently for me to tell her who the man was. I wasn't ready yet; I wanted her to tell me more so I could validate her story.

"He's referenced something about purple hair. Did this man have purple hair?" she asked.

"Oh, my God, he did for a bit, yes," I laughed. "He started dyeing it when he was going gray, and over time it developed a purplish hue. So, he stopped and embraced the gray."

She continued, "Well, he wants you to know that he is around you even though you think he's not. He just needs to be with her more right now, a woman. He says she needs him a lot more than you do. He knows you're strong so he's not worried about you, but he's worried about her. He wants you to know that if you need him, ask for him. And when you feel a chill over your left shoulder, it's him."

I wiped the tears, now falling freely, from my cheeks and told her about my father, how close we'd been, and how desperately I missed him. We just "got" each other like twins or soul mates of a non-romantic sort, and this unspoken understanding enraged my mother, so we had maneuvered around it. Mom claimed his spirit was living in their condo, and he'd been leaving coins in her path as reminders of his love for her, even in death. She believed that spirits could move metal and communicated with loved ones using spare change. A large photo of Dad adorning the entry hall was now surrounded by pennies, dimes, nickels and quarters, taped there as evidence of my father's devotion to her.

I felt slighted, I told the woman in front of me. "He's left me one coin. One. I'd like to believe I mattered, too. She's got a mortgage payment taped to her wall, and I have a dime in a dish on my dresser. Maybe I imagined how close we were. Maybe he didn't really care at all. I mean, what kind of father asks his only child to kill him because he couldn't stand up to his own wife?" I was ugly crying now.

She pulled some tissues from her purse and motioned for me to take them. "There are no accidents in life, which is why you and I are here right now, so I could deliver a message of hope to you. Your dad is telling you he loves you, and he knows you're strong. Is your mom really struggling with the loss?"

"She is."

"Dad sees you. He knows you. And he believes you are all right without him. He is not so sure about her. But he is checking in on you. Him and — there's another man with him — a blond."

"Could be Uncle Gary. His youngest brother. I took care of him when he was dying, too. Moved him from California to be closer to my dad while he was dying."

"Well," she put her hand on my forearm and squeezed, "your dad will come when you ask him to. It just may look different than it does for your mom. We get what we need, not what we want."

I took her calling card and tucked it in my purse, although I was never able to find it again when I searched for it. A few days later, I prayed for my father to send me a sign that he was around me when I needed him. I had been talking out loud to him about major, impending life changes, asking for guidance to no avail. I yearned for his wisdom, practicality, and unwavering belief in me.

That night, my father visited while I was sleeping. It was more than a dream because I could feel the calming remnants of his presence in our bedroom when I startled awake at 3:00 AM, shaking my husband to share the experience. In the dream, Dad was walking toward me, part of a group of professionally dressed men. I recognized my godfather, one of Dad's oldest friends, among them. Dad appeared to be in his mid- to late forties with sleek, jet-black hair, wrinkle-free skin, and a sun-kissed face. He was dressed like the powerhouse businessman he once was — in a charcoal suit and patterned tie, a camel cashmere coat and polished, tasseled, wing-tipped black loafers.

He broke free from the group for a few seconds and stopped in front of me on the cobblestone sidewalk, putting his hands on my shoulders. He looked me directly in the eyes and said, "It's in the letter. Remember, just don't ever settle for less than you deserve." After a gentle squeeze, he walked past me, rejoining his group, which continued up the sidewalk until they disappeared into a misty fog.

Soon thereafter, I found a box filled with my college memorabilia. Sifting through the photos, movie ticket stubs, and tchotchkes from what felt like another life, I spotted my dad's handwriting on a yellowing envelope stamped "9 March 1988." I pulled out folded sheets of the familiar notepaper that Dad always used to write me letters at school. I could almost smell the Old Spice as I scanned his heartwarming words of encouragement. The last lines of the letter contained the message I had been seeking: *You have the ability to succeed in anything you want or try to do. I love you dearly, Dad.*

I now have Dad's message tattooed on my left forearm, a forever reminder from the man who has never stopped believing in me, even when I can't.

— Nan McKernon —

16

Butterflies and Believers

*Butterflies are nature's angels. They remind us
what a gift it is to be alive.*
~Robyn Nola

Brokenhearted and in the depths of depression, I suddenly blurted out to my husband, "I can't stand being in this house another day. Let's take a road trip!"

Six weeks earlier, our young adult son had died in a senseless accident for which he alone was to blame. With a lot on his mind, including an upcoming civilian job in war-torn Iraq, as well as an ex-girlfriend who was messing with his emotions, he tried "huffing." This is a quick and cheap way the kids often use to get a brief feeling of euphoria. We were beyond shocked since Kevin had never used drugs, was an Eagle Scout, and had just graduated from college with plans of becoming a lawyer.

Our son had bought a spray can of computer keyboard duster at Office Depot on that fateful day. I'm sure he didn't think there was any danger since it was non-toxic compressed air. However, I later learned that the propellant in it is heavier than air. If enough is inhaled in a short time span, the lungs fill up, leaving no room for oxygen. The person suddenly dies from asphyxiation. Kevin had been alone in his room at the time as we were away on a short vacation.

After the funeral, our serious grieving began. Everything in our home reminded us of our kind and sensitive son. Pictures, his room, clothing, the table where we shared family meals — everything triggered our grief.

My husband, Joe, agreed that it might help if we had a change of scenery. Energized by this idea, I quickly put together a trip that included visiting our daughter in Nevada, two sets of friends in different parts of Colorado, and another couple in Flagstaff, Arizona. At least I had something else to focus on besides my pain. I made the calls, and the arrangements came together surprisingly easily.

Car loaded, we headed to our daughter's home in Las Vegas. Although subdued, the visit allowed us to have some private time to grieve and reminisce together. The day before we were to leave Las Vegas, I stood alone in the guest bedroom while absentmindedly thinking about packing.

That's when it happened.

I distinctly heard Kevin's voice behind me say, "I'm sorry, Mom." In that nanosecond, I reasoned that he hadn't really died, and it was all a huge mistake! I instantly spun around, fully expecting to see him, but sadly the room was empty. Crushed, with my flicker of hope dashed, I flung myself onto the bed, sobbing uncontrollably, while exclaiming, "Me too, honey, me too!" I later learned that this is not uncommon and is called an auditory after-death communication.

The next day, we continued on our three-week trip in hopes that beautiful scenery would help ease the searing pain. Although seeing the breathtaking mountains, sunlight filtering through the trees, and lovely streams was soothing, we still pulled that black cloud of devastating grief along with us.

While in Estes Park, Colorado, Joe and I decided to take a hike along a lovely, gurgling stream. Since we were in no hurry, we sat in the dirt to enjoy the area's serene beauty.

This is when the second inexplicable event happened.

A small monarch butterfly flew to within three feet of us and began staring at us as it flew back and forth between us. Dumbfounded, we stared back. After a couple of minutes, it landed in the dirt and continued staring as it walked the same path. Spellbound, we couldn't take our eyes off this butterfly's strange behavior. After a full ten minutes, it finally flew away.

My husband, who has a PhD in physics and never believed in any "woo-woo" nonsense, turned to me wide-eyed and asked, "Do you think that was Kevin?"

With tear-filled eyes, I responded, "Absolutely!"

In case those events weren't enough, I believe the entire trip had somehow been orchestrated by Kevin, leading us to the next and most astounding event in my life. I firmly believe my son wanted to apologize and explain things to me, which is exactly what happened next.

On our last stop before returning home, we stayed with some friends in Flagstaff. I felt comfortable baring my broken heart to Gail, a longtime friend. She asked if I'd ever consider seeing a psychic. I replied, "No, because I don't believe in them." Gail explained that her widowed sister had gone to a famous one in Sedona fifteen years previously and had gained a great deal of consolation.

I figured it couldn't hurt. Besides, what if she was the "real deal"? I called this psychic and, surprisingly, she agreed to see me the next day. All she knew was my first name and that I had lost a son two months prior. Joe refused to join me because seeing a psychic is against his religious beliefs.

I couldn't understand why my heart was pounding and my feet felt like lead as I walked up the steps to her front door. What was I afraid of? Tarra looked normal and greeted me with a hug. Once inside her den, she only wanted two things: a photo of my son and a personal item of mine to hold. I handed her a photo and my watch. She didn't ask me for any additional information.

The next hour and forty-five minutes were the most incredible of my life.

Tarra started with a prayer to essentially protect us from anything that was not of "truth, love and light." After pausing to stare off into the distance, she began. I sat in stunned silence as this complete stranger began relaying spot-on details about my son: things he loved to do, his relationship with each member of our family, names of friends, and especially how sorry he was for doing something so stupid. Kevin explained how much he loved his life and us. She relayed many specific details, like the exact amount of money we'd given him before leaving on our week's trip.

Throughout the reading, Tarra frequently coughed and complained that she felt a very heavy pressure on her chest, making it hard to breathe. After an hour, I finally confessed that he had died from "huffing." She nonchalantly retorted, "Oh, that's why I'm feeling this way."

I finally mustered the courage to have her ask him why. Kevin admitted that he had this dark side that he didn't want us to know about. He would sometimes "huff" when he needed to "calm" his mind.

I firmly believe my son, through that serendipitous trip, led me to Tarra. Additionally, I knew she was a gifted psychic/medium and that Kevin had truly been there with us.

Gratitude and joy filled my heart after experiencing this reading. I now knew that my son was happy in heaven. Additionally, I finally had the answer as to why he huffed that horrible day. The peace of mind I received from Tarra allowed me to begin the long and difficult journey of healing.

— Linda Zelik —

17

The E-Mail and Voice of Innocence

Miracles are not contrary to nature, but only contrary to what we know about nature.

~Saint Augustine

Before daylight on February 12, 2004, my husband, a retired U.S. Marine, and I received the knock that forever changed our lives. A U.S. Army chaplain faced us and said, "Sir, Ma'am, the Secretary of the Army sends his deepest regrets that your son, Sergeant Patrick Tainsh, was killed in action in Baghdad, Iraq, the night of February 11th."

The words were surreal. We couldn't process such an event. We had spoken with Patrick over the phone a few days earlier. After almost a year at war across Iraq, his unit, the 2d Squadron/2d Cavalry Regiment/Eagle Troop, was preparing to return to Fort Polk (now Fort Johnson), Louisiana.

Instead, Patrick returned directly to our community beneath a United States flag ten days after we received our notification.

On the morning of his memorial service, before we left for the chapel, I stepped onto our back porch into the February chill. I spoke out loud: "Patrick, please give us a sign. Let us know you're alright."

In the weeks that followed, my husband and I struggled with debilitating grief surrounding Patrick's death. There is no "readiness training" for such a traumatic life experience, especially when your child dies tragically in a war zone in a land over eight thousand miles away, and you haven't seen him in almost a year.

In the wake of the void left in our hearts and family, I sought signs from the universe daily that might let us know our son was at peace and still near in spirit.

A number of months after Patrick's military unit returned stateside, I opened my computer to discover an e-mail from one of his closest friends.

Dear Sergeant Major and Mrs. Tainsh,

I've something to tell you that I've been hesitant about because I fear you'll think I've lost my mind. But I've come to believe it's important to share as it might bring you some comfort. My daughter is three. Not long after I returned from Iraq, I took her with me when I went for a haircut. On the way back to my truck, she was sitting on my shoulders and rubbing the top of my head. She said, "Daddy, your hair looks like Sergeant Tainsh." I was taken back a bit but decided I hadn't heard her correctly. I knew she had never met Sergeant Tainsh. So, I let it go.

Not long afterwards, I was drying her off after a bath when she messed with my hair again and said, "Daddy, you look like Tainsh."

I said, "Who?"

She replied, "You know, Tainsh. Pat Tainsh."

I was shocked with disbelief. My heart started racing, and I had goose bumps.

I asked how she knew him. She told me that he comes to her when she's sad or lonely, and they dance and play together.

In the immediate moments of my silence, dumbfounded at what to say, she said, "He wants to let you know everything is okay. You don't need to worry about him."

It was all I could do not to cry after she said not to worry about him. But I was still stunned and unnerved with no under-standing of where this was coming from. I'm certain my daughter and your son have never met. I kept trying to think how she could know his name.

After my wife and I put our daughter to bed, I told my wife what had happened. She confirmed that our daughter and your son had never met in person at any time, and we were sure we hadn't spoken about the war or mentioned names in her presence.

I hope you don't think I'm totally crazy. But as strange as it sounds, I'm comforted by what my daughter said and hope the same for you. I'll never forget your son and our friendship. He became a true hero that night during an enemy ambush in Baghdad by "giving all" to save my life and others.

After reading the e-mail, I showed it to my husband. We held each other and cried with comforted hearts. We had received the sign we desperately needed.

I sent a return e-mail to the soldier expressing our gratitude for his bravery in sending the message, one that meant more than he could ever comprehend. I told him we had absolutely no doubt regarding an innocent child's ability to receive messages from "beyond the veil" in ways adults no longer could.

The soldier remained in contact with us through the years after the original e-mail and later shared another encounter between his three-year-old daughter and Patrick. It happened on a day he took her with him to the airport to pick up his mom who was arriving for a visit. While they waited, his daughter carried on a conversation with someone he couldn't see. When he asked who she was talking to, she simply said, "My friend, Tainsh."

His daughter, now in college, was six when he and his wife noticed she no longer had conversations with Patrick, conversations they never questioned or interrupted.

I have no doubt that Patrick found a way to bring comfort and peace to his friend, who had held Patrick as he succumbed to his wounds, and our family through the voice of a pure, innocent child. It also allowed Patrick to move forward peacefully on his new cosmic journey far away from the pain of war while knowing those he cared for and left behind had received needed comfort.

— Deborah Tainsh —

18

Searching for Mom

The dime came from heaven, an angel tossed it from above,
To let me know with each day that I am truly loved.
~Author Unknown

M y mother understood me in a way that no one else could. She comforted me no matter how heavy the world seemed at any given moment. She was my rock — my go-to person whenever I needed a hug, a laugh, or just a listening ear.

But when my precious mom slid into the depths of clinical depression, it was a battle. This surly beast refused to loosen its grip, and Mom went from bad to worse before I could access the proper resources to help her.

One day, my phone rang with news that would forever change me. When I got the call, my knees buckled, and I fell to the floor, horrified that my mom had been in such a deep, dark hole that she had felt this was her only way out. Now it seemed as if her darkness had transferred to me. Flattened by grief for the next several months, I existed in a fog, struggling to breathe, move, or function.

I felt as if some sinister force had beaten the living crap out of me. Broken and battered, I gasped and growled, flailed and fought, sputtered and screamed, lost in a pitch-black abyss where my world no longer made sense. I tasted nothing but intense bitterness. I smelled nothing but utter defeat. I heard nothing but eerie silence, save for that one nagging word that played over and over in my mind: *Why?*

I needed to find my way back to the land of the living, but how?

I did my best to get through each day by focusing on routine, but I'd have meltdowns when picking out bananas in the grocery store or I'd start sobbing while doing ab crunches on the medicine ball at the gym. I took baby steps forward, but an emptiness still consumed me. I wanted to feel my mom's presence so that I could inhale a moment of peace. But, try as I might, her presence eluded me.

Thankfully, I found a local support group for survivors of suicide that met twice a month. The moment I found them, I recognized that this was my life support. At group meetings, I felt understood at a time when even I couldn't comprehend the depth of my messed-up head and heart. In that room, I could cry, scream, curse, and vent without fear of judgment. I could hug others who felt, on a cellular level, the same kind of anguish that tortured me. Not that I would wish such agony on anyone, but that kind of unconditional support is necessary for healing to commence.

I also learned about the American Foundation for Suicide Prevention's annual Out of the Darkness Walks in which participants walk sixteen miles through the night, starting at sunset, and concluding at the break of dawn to signify the importance of bringing the stigma of mental illness out of the dark.

I loved everything about this and was eager to be a part of it.

Maybe, I thought, *if I do this walk, I'll feel Mom's presence.*

I registered for the following year's walk in Seattle.

I started my donation drive in January for the June event and ultimately raised more than $3,600. Raising money was cathartic. Every time a donation came through, I felt less lost, less scared, and deeply loved.

Armed with my decorated luminary bag, I flew across the country to participate in the walk. When I arrived at AFSP's registration table, I felt at ease. Seeing the other folks all milling around in the same light blue Out of Darkness T-shirts, a sense of solidarity set in.

I met so many wonderful people at the event, all of whom were walking to honor their mothers, fathers, sons, daughters, brothers, sisters, aunts, uncles, cousins, grandparents, and friends. I also talked to several people who struggled themselves with clinical depression.

At registration, participants dropped their luminaries with the AFSP staff, who, during the night, lit them and set them out along the path to the finish line. Participants reunited with their luminary at the event's completion.

I walked the entire sixteen miles with a woman named Deb. During our seven-hour walk, I learned that Deb's daughter, Liz, had taken her life five years earlier when she was just eighteen. I asked her if she still felt a connection to Liz, and that's when she told me that randomly finding dimes is a sign from a loved one saying, "Hey, I'm still here!" She told me that she finds dimes all the time now, and she never did before Liz died. I had to admit, I was envious. I desperately wanted to communicate with Mom. But in the past fifteen months since she died, I'd not come across a single dime.

Around 3:30 AM, the two of us wearily crossed the finish line.

Within a few minutes, Deb found her daughter's luminary, but I couldn't locate Mom's.

"Where are you, Mom?" I whispered into the wind. "I need to feel you, but I don't know where to find you."

Tears streamed down my face. My feet ached and my back stiffened as I kept searching. I hadn't flown 2,200 miles and walked all night long with nagging plantar fasciitis pain to be denied the emotional release of reconnecting with my mom. After thirty minutes of hunting, however, my hope waned.

Deb tried to assure me that my mom was still with me. I appreciated the pep talk but still left the grounds heartbroken. Defeated, deflated and depressed, I started the lone walk back to my hotel room with red, burning eyes. I wiped my cheeks with the sleeve of my jacket and prepared to cross the deserted road when I noticed something shiny lying on it. I squinted to make out the object and then gasped when I realized what it was. There, glistening in the streetlight, was a shiny, wet dime. I picked up the coin, ice-cold from the rain, and pressed it to my cheek.

I had found her. I could feel her. I clutched the dime to my chest and inhaled deeply. Then, I exhaled into a glorious moment of peace.

Ten years have passed since that Seattle walk. In the past decade, I've come across roughly 500 dimes, which I keep in a glass jar in my bedroom closet. Given that I'd never encountered a dime prior to Mom's passing, there's no doubt that Mom is sending these coins to me, not to fill up my piggy bank but to fill up my heart. It's comforting to know that she still cares and is looking out for me.

— Christy Heitger-Ewing —

19

A Blue Bird Day

Those we love don't go away,
they walk beside us every day.
~Author Unknown

We lost my grandmother on a Monday, just five days before the birth of my second son. Only two months later, we lost my father-in-law, and the world as I knew it was no more. A hole opened up in my new world, leaving each moment — waking and otherwise — feeling empty. Still, there was catharsis in remembrance. I could close my eyes and feel my father-in-law's hugs. I could hear my grandma's laugh dancing in the breeze if I took the time to listen.

I yearned for a sign to know that they were okay and still around. I even asked for it out loud once or twice.

And that was when I met the blue jays.

There is nothing quite like summer in New York. We'd spent months dreaming about days with warm breezes, clear blue skies and the blooming of perennials, and finally they arrived. Such days were deemed "Blue Bird Days" by my father-in-law.

For two young boys, fewer things are better than running around on pillowy green grass and pulling clean air into their lungs. One day, while I soaked in my sons' laughter and the sun on my skin, I noticed a blue jay perched on our fence, its azure feathers even brighter against the stark white vinyl it sat upon. It rested there, and it watched.

Something about the bird's presence propelled me toward it,

with both of my little guys in tow. We got so close that we could have touched it, but the blue jay didn't move. After saying "hello," we resumed our playing, although I could never quite keep my eyes from it. It remained there, sitting and staring, for nearly two hours before we went inside.

I asked several loved ones what they thought it meant. "Maybe someone's visiting you," they said. "Blue jays are just really social birds," said others.

I shoved the experience to the back of my mind and continued on with life as a wife and mama of two.

Except the blue jay showed up again. And again. And again.

It followed my husband around the neighborhood while he walked the dog. I'd find it perched in a tree, or on a post, or in the yard, staring up into the windows of the rooms in which I stood. Its gaze never faltered. It just watched, then watched some more. It was rare to see blue jays in other parts of our neighborhood, and yet there was always one hanging around our house. I'd never believed much in coincidence, but even if I had, it appeared too many times to be explained away that easily.

My in-laws had a hammock that my older son adored. He'd lie in it with his "Grandpie" — swinging back and forth, watching the sun glint through the tree's leaves above, singing made-up songs. After we lost my father-in-law, my husband and I brought the hammock home. It felt like a relic in which we could rest if ever we needed to feel close to him again. We did use it quite often, creating silly new versions of the songs he'd sing, keeping Grandpie's spirit alive in some small way.

Whenever my husband mowed the lawn, he'd move the hammock out of the way, toward the back of our yard. I'd been seeing blue jays often, wanting desperately to assign meaning to them. I longed to be able to look at them and say, "Hi, Grandma. Hi, Joe." They say that if something has meaning to a person, if it appears as a sign, then it likely is. I clung to that idea so much, smiling to myself each time a little blue bird found its way into my yard.

One summer morning, my husband had been outside mowing the lawn. The mower's rattling paused, and my phone vibrated from the kitchen counter. When I opened the message, it was a photo from my husband of a blue jay's feather. And not just anywhere. It was lying right beneath the hammock.

To me, it was a clear sign that seeing the blue jay was no happenstance. It felt as though I had guardian angels, as though all of my pleas to know that our loved ones were still around had been answered. And though that moment felt monumental, the blue jays didn't stop there.

Grief ebbs and flows, and there were days when I'd feel okay. Then there were others when the permanence of them being gone hit me like a truck. While I relished having them there with me somehow, it hurt. When my newborn was colicky and I couldn't calm him, I heard my grandmother's voice saying, "You can do this. You are doing an excellent job," as I danced around the kitchen with him in my arms. When either of my kids did something extraordinary — which, to me, was all the time — I heard my father-in-law saying, "They're perfect specimens," as he always did in life. It was painful, but it helped.

And ever since the blue jays arrived, I craved another visit. Another sign that they were still there.

Our sunroom had a metal roof. When it rained, or when the seeds of maple trees began to fall, a cozy pattering echoed through the room. It was loud enough that it would sound through the entire house sometimes, and it brought a sense of hygge that little else did. Months after we first met the blue jay, I was home with the boys one weekend morning. We were in the kitchen, dancing and laughing, munching on bits of breakfast between the fun. Suddenly, there was an overwhelmingly loud clacking coming from the sunroom's roof, so much that it startled the three of us. It'd been a sunny day, with not a hint of rainfall.

"What is going on?" I asked the question mostly to myself, standing in the sunroom and finding no clues as to what had been causing the racket.

As soon as I spoke, the noise stopped. Half a dozen blue jays flew from the roof, all landing in our backyard — in the trees, on the fence, in the grass. They looked at me and I at them, and a warmth grew from deep within my chest. I smiled and spun around, rejoining my boys in the kitchen.

—Sarah Asermily—

20

On the Wings of a Luna Moth

Between our birth and death we may touch
understanding, as a moth brushes
a window with its wing.
~Christopher Fry

"What's that?" I asked, sounding more like one of our fifth-grade students than a teacher. Janet, my teaching partner, was showing me her latest artwork, an illustration of a butterfly-like insect that I didn't recognize. Truthfully, I didn't know the names of many insects, birds, trees, and other living things. While I loved helping children with language arts, Janet was the scientist who guided our fifth graders to learn about our diverse natural world.

"A luna moth," Janet answered.

How had I never seen a luna moth? Janet's watercolor of the luna moth highlighted the moth's broad, lime-green wings, with a distinctive spot on each of the hind wings that looked like eyes. I would have remembered if I had seen one of these eerily beautiful creatures.

Janet shared that sightings were rare since luna moths tend to be seen only in the moonlight on warm, humid nights. Sadly, adult luna moths live only about seven to ten days. Living such a short life, flying only at night during the spring or summer, and needing to stay near their favorite food plants like persimmon trees — it was no wonder I had never seen one.

Janet shared that sightings of the luna moth are often thought to have special meaning. Since sightings are rare, luna moths are often considered to be good luck or a sign of hope. Some cultures believe that a sighting of a luna moth means that a soul has recently left its earthly body.

This elusive, spiritual creature captured my interest in a way I never expected.

Luna moths were only one of many new topics for me. Janet could turn a walk across the school's meadow and through the forest into an adventure just by pausing, pointing out something in nature, and asking questions that made our students think. Teaching with Janet, I was learning more about this wonderful world than I had ever known. I even developed a sense of wonder about what I used to call "creepy crawlies."

Janet appreciated beauty even in a dung beetle. I recoiled when I first saw her intricate painting of one, but Janet explained the ways the dung beetle recycles nutrients into the soil. Then I laughed when she shared that this one was the "splendid dung beetle." Her painting of the splendid dung beetle became one of my favorites.

Janet observed, questioned, and interpreted this world as a scientist. Even when she was diagnosed with cancer, she shared a concise, scientific explanation with me. She researched, formed a battle plan along with her oncologist, and fought her way through surgery and chemo treatments; yet the cancer found a way back into her system. She stepped down from her full-time teaching position to combat the cancer the second time, and she continued to celebrate the wonders of this world through her nature illustrations. A collection of seed pods, a branch of bleeding-heart flowers, and a brilliant blue morpho butterfly became the subjects of her watercolor paintings.

Early in the spring, Janet asked me to keep a watch on the bushes she had planted outside our classroom building. She was planning what she wanted to paint next, and she wanted clippings of pussy-willow branches, just as the ends of the branches began to look like fuzzy cat paws. About the time when the pussy-willow branches were ready to be cut, I learned that cancer had spread throughout her body, and Janet was dying. A fellow teacher and I spent precious moments at the hospital with Janet, reminiscing about our adventures together, while Janet listened with eyes closed but a smile on her face.

The next morning, my phone rang as I was heading out to school. Janet had passed out of this earthly world. For a brief moment, I thought about taking the day off from school. Janet and I had always agreed that there were no excuses for letting down our students, and that day was the first day of standardized testing, when our students needed me, not a substitute. With my students, I held myself together by reading the exact instructions, monitoring each student's progress, and giving each one a reassuring smile. Only after that day's testing session did I give my heart the opportunity to acknowledge that I had lost Janet, my dear friend.

As my students began their snack break, our school librarian came in the door, carefully holding a sheet of copy paper. "Look what I found outside on the sidewalk," she said. I looked at the paper, which held a lovely creature that had just passed away. To see that specimen at that very moment seemed to be more than a coincidence, but I knew Janet always looked for scientific explanations. Was it a chance encounter, or serendipity, or a sign from up above? Could this possibly be a special message from Janet? All I know for sure is that I suddenly felt hope, peace, and comfort.

It was a perfectly formed, iridescent green, beautiful luna moth, just like the one in Janet's painting.

— Suzanne Garner Payne —

Guardian Angels

21

Turn Here

One thing you can say for guardian angels: they guard.
They give warning when danger approaches.
~Emily Hahn

My parents were enjoying early retirement in Fort Lauderdale, but now my mother needed emergency heart surgery to replace a valve. I still lived in Maryland, where they had raised me, and so did my mother's mother, who was only in her seventies. My grandmother and I flew to Fort Lauderdale.

My dad met us at the airport and drove us to his office where he did some consulting two days a week. My grandmother and I took his car and set off for the hospital. On the way, we came to an intersection and stopped at a red light. I noticed a backhoe that was moving dirt across the way.

I also saw a strip mall on the left that appeared to be in decline. Half the stores were empty and had for-rent signs in their windows. The parking lot was empty, and the other stores appeared deserted.

"You need to turn left here so I can go to that cleaners. I need to take something to the cleaners," said Gram. There was a sign for Bayview Cleaners in large white letters on a blue background in the center of the strip.

"Gram, what do you need to take to the cleaners now? We just got here." I thought, *Why is she telling me this? This is very strange.* I didn't want to turn. We were in a hurry because I wanted to see my mother before she died. "Gram, I don't want to go to the cleaners. We can go later when we go home to Dad's house."

"Turn here," she said firmly. "I need to go to that cleaners. Turn now!"

Just then, the left-turn arrow went green on the traffic light, and I obediently turned left into the mall's parking lot. I didn't want to, but I did it because I wanted to obey my grandmother.

While I was turning, I heard a terrible crash. The traffic light behind us had plummeted to the road and exploded. There were shards of glass everywhere. Cars slammed on their brakes. People blew their horns and screamed. No one could move.

The entire road, four lanes, was covered in glass and other pieces of the traffic light. That huge stoplight struck the pavement in the middle of the lane that we would have taken if we had continued to drive straight.

What saved us was that left turn to go to a closed cleaners for no apparent reason. And because I hesitated before turning, debating whether I really had to obey my grandmother's urgent instruction, we delayed the car behind us a few seconds, so they were able to avoid getting hit, too.

I parked in front of the cleaners and took some deep breaths. Shaking all over from the experience, I tried to regain my composure.

"Gram, did you see that traffic light fall?" I said.

"No, I didn't. Is that what that crash was?" she answered. "I didn't see it. I was thinking about the cleaners and looking in that direction."

We both glanced back at the intersection to see the chaos the accident had caused. The car traveling in the opposite direction in the right lane had a shattered windshield. Dents and scrapes scarred the hood and side of a car that had been hit by the debris that we could see.

"Gram, that traffic light would have hit our car and killed us if you hadn't told me to turn. Why did you want to go to the cleaners?"

"I don't know. I don't have anything for the cleaners now. I don't know what made me tell you to do that," she said, shaking her head and patting me on the shoulder. "I'm so relieved you did what I told you to do. You are a wonderful granddaughter."

When I looked closely at the cleaners, I realized that it was closed. It looked like it had been out of business for some time.

"Gram, an angel must have told you to tell me to turn left to save our lives," I said.

"Yes, I think so, too. That was very strange. Very amazing," she said and reached over to hug me. "We have been blessed."

"I'm glad I followed your instructions. I didn't want to turn and really just wanted to go to the hospital," I said, still shaking, in shock, from realizing how close we had come to being harmed.

Later, we learned that the backhoe I saw on the right side of the road had cut the cable holding the traffic light, causing it to fall.

When we arrived at the hospital, we learned that my mother's condition had dramatically improved, and she was out of danger. She would survive her surgery. We were so happy to see her that we showered her with hugs and kisses, grateful that we were all still alive.

"Always obey your grandmother," I told my children when I got home.

— Barbara D. Duffey —

22

The Spirit of an Old Building

Angels are all around us, all the time,
in the very air we breathe.
~Eileen Elias Freeman,
The Angels' Little Instruction Book

I have worked as an environmental consultant for more than twenty-five years. In my line of work, I inspect properties and buildings — big buildings, little buildings, dilapidated buildings where you have to wear a hardhat and face mask, gorgeous buildings, new buildings, old buildings, buildings in areas where you wished you were carrying a double-barrel shotgun when you got out of the car, buildings where you just prayed your car was where you left it, and all buildings in between.

I remember every one of them. Some of the buildings were downright creepy — with no discernible reason as to why. They just felt "off."

A few years ago, I was conducting an inspection of an eight-story apartment building in Queens, New York. It was a typical apartment building, with typical amenities such as laundry facilities and a community room. But I was uncomfortable. Very uncomfortable. It felt as if I was carrying two concrete blocks, and it was difficult to breathe.

Thankfully, I had to step outside to feed the parking meter and felt instantly better. It was so much easier to breathe without the heavy weight I had been feeling in that building.

After the inspection was completed, I started the historical research as part of my investigation, which includes the history of a property back to its original use. According to the Sanborn fire-insurance maps, the apartment building and the surrounding area had been previously developed with a mental-health institution and tuberculosis sanitarium, which had been demolished in the early 1900s. Coincidence? Perhaps.

Last summer I had the pleasure of inspecting an iconic New York City hotel located in Midtown Manhattan. The art-deco–style hotel was designed and constructed in less than two years in the late 1920s, soaring forty-three stories high with over 2,000 guest rooms. A well-known inventor lived at this hotel for over ten years. He believed that the numbers 3, 6, and 9 were significant, and that they held the key to understanding the universe. His main room at the hotel was 3327, which is divisible by the number 3.

This hotel is massive. In addition to the forty-three stories aboveground, four sub-cellars (basements) are cut deep into the Manhattan bedrock, which would be no mean feat today, let alone 100 years ago. As part of my investigation, I needed to pay particular attention to the subterranean depths of the building, more so than the upper floors.

The deepest level, C-4, was not accessible. The first level, known as C-1, housed the offices, kitchens, housekeeping, fitness center, etc. It was a hive of activity. The second cellar, C-2, was poorly lit and used for storage and the old laundry rooms with the original dryers, which were so large that one could walk right into them. This level was constructed with a tunnel that permitted hotel guests to enter into the New York City subway lines located nearby without having to step outside, although it is closed off now.

Three of us were walking in the bowels of this iconic building during the inspection. On the third sub-cellar, C-3, we were in a very large room, not unlike a cavern, with 20-foot-high ceilings. The building was constructed with its own generator, a true engineering marvel for the late 1920s. It was massive, at least 40 feet long and 18 feet high.

I was admiring all the gauges, pulleys and wiring when I felt something tug on my left arm. I turned quickly to see if one of the others wanted to get my attention, but they were on the opposite side of the generator. I shrugged it off, thinking perhaps I had snagged my sweater on something.

A few minutes later, it happened again, but this time the tug was a bit more forceful. Again, no one was behind me, and I was standing in the center of the room and at least six feet away from any equipment. I admit to being a little unnerved, but I was not frightened. It didn't feel "off."

We continued the inspection of the third sub-cellar until we reached yet another exceptionally large room, which was even darker and so poorly lit that we were using flashlights. I had to go into an area where I would need to circumnavigate piping and some pits that had been covered over with plywood to confirm there was no staining around a vaulted heating oil tank.

Just as I was about to take another step, something grabbed my left arm again, with much more force than the two previous times. I was literally yanked backward.

Imagine my surprise when I realized I had been about to step into a four-foot deep concrete pit. The plywood that had been previously covering the pit had somehow shifted just enough to leave a gaping hole. Coincidence? I think not.

— Marie Largeant —

23

Ever Thankful

*The guardian angels of life fly so high as to be beyond
our sight, but they are always looking down upon us.*
~Jean Paul Richter

Fifteen years ago, I was driving in Germany, where I live. I was taking my son to a soccer game, and we were talking, laughing and listening to music. I am a confident driver, and as a mother of two sons, I am also a careful driver.

Germany is known for its beer and sausages, especially during Oktoberfest, but it is also infamous for its "no speed limit" on the Autobahn. I am used to driving on the German highway, and for most drivers, driving 100 miles per hour there is a common daily practice.

On this sunny day, as I headed to my child's soccer game an hour away, I had to merge onto the highway. I always check and double-check all my mirrors when doing so, and I always remember to turn my head and check that notorious blind spot as well. I clearly remember doing that and seeing that the road was clear.

I was ready to merge onto the highway. I wanted to move the steering wheel to the left, but something strange was happening. My arms did not move and turn the wheel. I was confused. Why was I unable to move my arms? Was I paralyzed? No, I knew I wasn't because I was still holding the steering wheel. So, why was I still driving straight ahead when I wanted to move to the left?

At that very moment, I noticed something out the corner of my eye. Then, I was startled by a loud noise and a flash. It was a motorcycle roaring by at top speed. Where the heck had this motorcycle come from? I had not seen it approach. As the motorcycle raced by and disappeared in the distance, my heart raced.

Suddenly, everything became clear. If I had merged onto the highway, we would have been in the direct path of the speeding motorcycle. I am convinced that it would have been a deadly accident for that rider, and maybe for my son and me as well. I gasped as I understood the gravity of the situation that we had just escaped.

Then, I understood why my arms did not follow my instructions and did not move. My guardian angel had protected me from a devastating accident by temporarily taking control of my body, immobilizing me.

As I processed what had just happened, I regained full control of my body. My arms once again obeyed my brain, and I was easily able to turn the steering wheel, as if nothing had ever happened. I merged onto the highway effortlessly, albeit in shock. The rest of our journey was uneventful.

That was the only time I have ever lost control of any part of my body. I had never realized that guardian angels can immobilize us, but then again they are in the business of protecting, guiding, and miracles.

I am tremendously grateful for the angel who took control of my body because I know that I would not have been able to forgive myself if I had caused the death of another person. I would have suffered emotionally the rest of my life. Instead, now I can live my life in peace, and focus on living my best and joyous life, ever thankful that someone was looking out for me and my son.

— Shirlene Joan Raymann —

24

Mama's Secret

*We should pray to the angels, for they
are given to us as guardians.*
~Saint Ambrose

The first time I saw the tall, thin man, I was three years old. Skipping down the front porch steps on short, chubby legs, I stumbled and felt my body pitching forward toward the concrete walk below. I remember the terror I felt, but, before I could cry out, a pair of strong, gentle hands grabbed me under the arms and lifted me to my feet. With tears flowing because the fear had not left me yet, I turned around, expecting a comforting hug from Mama.

But Mama wasn't there. I got a brief glimpse of a tall, very thin, pale man with a thick, black mustache. I ran inside, babbling about the strange man who had saved me from a bad fall. Mama hurried outside to take a look but he was gone.

After that, I saw the tall, thin man occasionally throughout my childhood. He always appeared just as an accident or a mishap was about to happen. I started to call him Hank for no particular reason.

When I was six years old, my friend Jane and I were swinging on the swing set in my backyard, trying to see who could go the highest. But then the chain on my swing broke, and I felt myself falling. Before I hit the ground, I felt arms wrap tightly around my middle and lower me gently to the ground. Mama, who had heard me scream, dashed outside and crouched down beside me, checking for injuries.

"You look fine," she said, with a mixture of surprise and relief in her voice. "I don't even see a bruise."

"Hank caught me," I said with conviction, even though I knew that she wouldn't accept my explanation.

Mama looked at Jane. "Did you see someone catch Libby?" she asked.

"No," Jane said. "But I saw her sort of float to the ground."

Mama shook her head. "Kids and their imaginations," she muttered.

Once, I heard Mama laughing with her friend Betty. "Most kids have imaginary playmates," she said. "Libby has an imaginary grown-up."

The last time I saw Hank, I was sixteen years old, an overconfident new driver. Driving home one night from a football game, I took a curve in the road too fast. I ran off the road and hit a large tree. I wasn't hurt, but I was too stunned to move.

Out of the corner of my eye, I caught some sort of motion. I turned my head to see Hank standing a few feet away, motioning frantically for me to get out of the car. Relief washed over me at the sight of him. I knew I would be okay. I pushed on the door, but it wouldn't budge. I could smell gasoline, and I looked at Hank, with panic welling up inside me. I reminded myself, *If Hank is here, I will not be hurt.*

I never saw him move, but suddenly Hank was on the other side of the door, pulling as I pushed. With a groan, the door swung open, and I tumbled out. Hank grabbed my hand and pulled me away from the car. I heard a loud boom and jerked around to see the car in flames.

I turned back to Hank to thank him for saving my life, but he was gone. I should have known he would be. Hank always appeared to me in a flash and left just as quickly. Once he had done what he needed to do, he vanished, sometimes leaving me to wonder if he was ever really there.

As I grew older, I sometimes doubted what I accepted without question in my innocent early years. Maybe that is why I didn't see him anymore. You can't see a miracle if there is doubt in your heart.

Many years later, I was helping Mama pack her things to move into a retirement home. I picked up one of her old picture albums and began to idly turn the pages. My breath caught in my throat as I gazed at a picture of a tall, thin, young man with a luxurious mustache.

"Who is this?" I asked.

Mama's eyes softened. "That's John Henry, my oldest brother. He always looked out for me." She smiled at the picture. "He mysteriously disappeared just before you were born. Suddenly, he was just... gone. The police didn't take his case seriously. John Henry was young and single, and they thought he had just gotten a case of wanderlust. We hoped that one day he would come home. We knew he would if he could, but he never did. I never told you about the wonderful uncle that you lost before you were born because I thought it would make you sad."

She looked at me wistfully. "When your father was killed while I was pregnant with you, John Henry assured me that he would always look out for you just as he had for me. That was one promise I knew he would keep. He would not have let anything stop him from keeping his word."

I swallowed hard. "He didn't, Mama," I said. "That is the man who was always there to keep me from harm when I was growing up."

Mama's eyes filled with understanding. Tears streamed down her face. She tenderly touched the photo.

"Of course," she said. "John Henry. Henry. Hank. You called him Hank."

— Elizabeth A. Atwater —

25

Do Not Open That Door

*It comes down to whether you believe in seven
miraculous escapes a week or one guardian angel.*
~Robert Brault

My husband had to run out to the grocery store one evening shortly after we moved into our new home. He planned on being gone for about ten minutes since the store was only a couple of minutes away. I was on the phone with my friend D.J. at the time.

About sixty seconds after he left, the doorknob began to move back and forth. I realized he had probably forgotten his keys again. He had been doing that a lot during that hectic time. I asked D.J. to hold on while I let my husband in.

I yelled that I was coming because he was still aggressively twisting the knob. As I reached for the door, I heard a voice. But the television wasn't on and my phone was back on the counter where I had left it.

"Do not open that door."

The command rang in the air and sent me into shock. I dared not move, but my hand was still resting on the knob.

I heard it again. "Do not open that door."

I pulled back and shakily spoke in the door's direction.

"Brandon, did you forget your keys again?"

The door movement became even more violent. I repeated the

question with the same results. Stunned, I ran back to the phone and told D.J. what was going on. Then, I hung up to call the police, although I knew it would take a while for them to arrive in our small town.

While I waited, the doorknob stopped turning and someone started pounding on the door. My saving grace, I believe, was the fact that the door was steel and not wood. It still has dents in it to this day. And what was the most frightening was that I had called out more than once. The person on the other side knew that someone was home and didn't care. They were still determined to get inside.

Finally, after about ten minutes, everything stopped. I was still in front of the door in complete shock when the doorknob moved again. I grabbed it. This time, I was determined to have it not move. In the darkness on the other side, I heard a familiar voice.

"Babe, what are you doing?"

At that point, I opened the door and pulled my husband inside. I hastily locked the door again. In tears, I told him the whole story. When I got to the point about being told not to open the door, he stopped me.

"Who told you not to open the door?"

I made my way to the couch and sat down. The reality of hearing a voice in an empty house finally dawned on me. I recalled its firmness and command but not harshness. Instead, it felt like protection. I thought I was alone in my ordeal, but I wasn't. I had an angel with me, protecting me. That evening could have been my last, but instead I was spared by a Heavenly voice.

And while the intruder was never caught, I still slept soundly that evening because of the knowledge that something larger than all of us is out there protecting us.

— Pastor Wanda Christy-Shaner —

When Guardian Angels Sit Watchful on Your Shoulder

There are no ordinary moments, ever, anyplace.
Nothing out there is ordinary.
~Dr. Wayne Dyer

Traffic on the freeway parted like the Red Sea — my mind left spinning through a gliding sensation of cinematic slow motion. Stillness, soundless. Not a car in sight for the brief span of horror in the blink of my eye.

Ever notice the quietness of a miracle?

The way it infuses the air, aromatizes bitterness against a backdrop of muted gray doubt, then shatters the mental sound barrier of fearful chatter in the aftermath of your private epiphany?

Etched inside my mind, traced inside the chambers of my heart, is a memory I'll never forget — reminding me of life's fragility. Our ancestral spun thread, from which we all dangle on the dawn of each new day, can snap at a moment's notice.

I was six months pregnant with my firstborn — glowing, roly-poly, and happy. When waking, seeing the sunrise was more exciting than the last — when the coolness of night alongside the love of my life enveloped and cuddled me to sleep, and when my imagination felt inadequate to capture the breadth of love I'd feel for another human being I hadn't yet physically met.

Given another day of discovery to be enchanted by the growth of this tiny human and me, our bodies synchronized cells and DNA for future evolution were nothing short of miraculous. Hormones igniting a fire deep inside my soul that will forever burn until the long-wicked fingers of time snuff its flame.

I would like to say it was an ordinary day, but I no longer believe in ordinary days. Time has taught me every day above ground is an extraordinary day.

I was on my way to shop for new maternity garb. My tummy had been begging for at least three more inches around my expanding waistline.

My hubby stayed home to watch a "big game." I kissed him goodbye, waddled out the door, and hopped into my brand-new white Hyundai.

This small, economy people-mover had recently made its U.S. debut. It was perfect for my daily excursions to the grocery store, doctors' offices, and the post office to fulfill orders for our home-based business.

A few miles from home, I entered the freeway in midday weekend traffic. Cars whizzed by all around me. I was in the right lane for less than five minutes when an old, brown Cadillac relic on my left revved his engine to switch into my lane.

I don't think the driver ever saw me. He kept moving in my direction, and I was too stunned to honk.

In the same way a great white shark might sideswipe a tiny fishing boat, the long, wide back half of the brown "battle-lac" seemed destined to swat me off the road, down a small embankment.

Panic-stricken and yelling a few choice words, I overcorrected to the right in order to avoid a horrible crash. It would have been a major pileup. My car whirled around three times like a plastic toy top before stopping.

In an instant, there were no cars in sight, as if the universe had choreographed my guardian angels to stretch their wings across the five-lane highway and hold traffic back long enough for me to emerge from pure shock as my moistened hands gripped the steering wheel like a human vise.

My baby never moved, which frightened me even more.

I sat dazed in a dust cloud, rubbing my belly, with tears welling in my eyes. I was facing oncoming traffic, which I could see in the hazy distance. I had landed a few feet near the next exit.

Realizing I had mere seconds to calculate how fast traffic would catch up to me, I somehow found the nerve to drive in the wrong direction toward traffic on the freeway for half a minute and then make a sharp left turn to get off.

With my hands still quivering on the wheel, I pulled over to a curb on a quiet street to whisper a thankful prayer and beg the gods to spare my baby the slightest harm.

After calming my senses, I stuck to the original plan and continued my journey. My court of guardian angels had already saved my life. There was no other human explanation.

Although the incident played over and over in my mind through a mirage of what-ifs, there was no logical reason to go back home. Gratitude overrode the thoughts of doom shrouded in what could have happened.

I learned never to underestimate the simplicity in a day. The miracle lies tucked inside the in-between enlightened moments when we're taught to examine all the things we have to be thankful for on our planetary journey.

By grace, my life continues. The day I thought started as ordinary turned into one of the most extraordinary days of my life, shifting my perspective, reshaping my internal scope gifting me with a measuring stick to compare all the days to come that would never be ordinary again.

Guardian angels sit watchful on my shoulder.

— Toya Qualls-Barnette —

27

Divine Direction

*Insight is better than eyesight when
it comes to seeing an angel.*
~Eileen Elias Freeman,
The Angels' Little Instruction Book

I t was one of those dusty, turquoise-sky September days in Southern California. Just a hint of pollution in the air. At 10:00 in the morning, it was already seventy-eight degrees, heading to the upper eighties.

My daughter and I thought it was the perfect Sunday to cruise up the 5 and visit relatives who lived an hour and a half away. We had our favorite music blasting and were singing along, as always. The freeway traffic was heavy, but everyone was moving along at a rapid pace.

As we drove, I saw a small, white truck in front of me with a refrigerator bouncing in the truck bed, held in place by ropes. To my left, I saw one of those buses that transports prisoners. Their faces peered bleakly out from their bus windows. When I glanced that way, Marvin Gaye was singing "Got to Give It Up," a power-packed, dancehall favorite. My daughter, Binky, and I were dancing in our seats.

"No more standin' upside the wall..."

"Finally got myself together, baby, now I'm havin' a ball," we sang along.

That's when I heard the voice. It was a male voice, and it clearly said, "Pull over to the right lane now!"

Without reason or explanation, I stopped singing, glanced quickly in my mirrors to make sure I was clear to pull into the right lane, and made the maneuver. My daughter's head jerked a little bit at my unexpected lane change.

"Did you hear that?" I asked her.

"What?" Binky asked.

At exactly that moment, the white truck that was carrying the refrigerator in the middle lane, the lane I had just moved from, spilled the refrigerator onto the freeway. The car that had been behind me in that lane was hit by it, and then the refrigerator continued bouncing into the left lane and causing a two-car pileup, hitting another car, and then rolling onto the gravel earth beneath the highway divider. I witnessed it all in my rearview mirror.

"Hear what?" my daughter asked again.

"The voice that told me to move us over to the right lane," I answered as I sped away from the multi-car pileup. "That voice saved us." I exhaled in awe of what I had just experienced.

"I didn't hear anything except Marvin Gaye," she said, staring at me with a puzzled look on her pretty face.

"We should pray," I told her.

I turned off Marvin's dance song. In the quiet car with the sound of wheels on asphalt and sirens in the background, we thanked God Almighty for saving us.

To this day, I wonder whose voice that was, but I have accepted that when "spirit" speaks to me, I should listen and obey. It saved us from calamity that day on the freeway.

My mother and my Aunt Maude believed that sometimes a spirit is sent to protect or enlighten us. If we are listening, its voice can give us divine direction. After that experience, I believe them.

— Dee Dee McNeil —

28

Double Protection

We all have a guardian angel, sent down from above.
To keep us safe from harm and
surround us with their love.
~Author Unknown

One weekend, I was pet-sitting for my brother-in-law. I was looking forward to some quiet time with one of the best dogs ever, Nella. No one would have guessed that Nella was a re-homed dog. She seemed like she had been a part of the household forever. She was sweet, playful, protective and very loved.

Nella had a routine, and I tried to follow it as closely as possible, so we always went outside to do her "business" through the downstairs back door. There was also a light that always stayed on above that door so I could see into the large yard when I took her out. The door was always locked, but the screen door on the outside was not.

It was getting late, and I decided we should do one more yard run before heading to bed. I unlocked and opened the inside door. Suddenly, the light above the door went out. I flipped the switch a few times and figured the light bulb must have blown. I told Nella that we would just have to go out in the dark and hope my klutzy self didn't trip over the hose or something.

So, I grabbed the screen door handle and got ready to head outside, but the screen door would not open. It was like it was cemented shut. The lock was not engaged, but the door was not opening. At the same moment, Nella began growling and her fur prickled, which was very out of character for her. I began to feel a bit uneasy, so I shut the inside door and relocked it. The outdoor light came back on. I opened the inside door again, and the light went off again. Once again, I shut the door.

As a rule of thumb, Nella never went outside via the front door because it faced a highway. It was for her protection. I put a leash on her and walked her out the front door because I couldn't get that screen door to open downstairs.

When we got outside, she ran to the driveway and growled even louder, looking to the backyard. She yanked at her harness and desperately tried to get at whatever was back there. Her growling and fussing grew stronger and stronger. Finally, however, she did her thing, and we hurried back inside.

It was getting late, so we headed to the bedroom, which overlooked the backyard. Within the viewing area of the light, I could see nothing, but there was a vast darkness that the light did not illuminate. So, when Nella lay on the corner of the bed and continued to face the backyard on high alert, I was a bit nervous.

My prayers went up during the evening, and thankfully no further incidents occurred. At dawn, Nella and I headed downstairs. Without thinking, I opened the main door, then the screen door, and we headed out. Then it hit me. The screen door had opened without the slightest effort, and the light burned brightly above the doorway.

I still do not know what was hiding in the darkness that evening. I do know that I had double protection: an angel who kept me from venturing straight into the danger and a pup named Nella who had stood her ground and stayed on watch. I felt doubly blessed.

— Pastor Wanda Christy-Shaner —

29

Love Never Dies

Life doesn't come with a manual.
It comes with a mother.
~Author Unknown

I had just sat down on the white, cushioned glider chair, with my legs resting on the matching ottoman. A week earlier, our son had been born and I was still learning what it meant to be a parent. I had not found the comfort of a routine and never even knew what day it was. I reminded myself that I had endured seventeen hours of labor and ended with a caesarean delivery of a healthy boy.

At 2 a.m., sleep-deprived and practically sleepwalking, I found the chair inviting after breast and bottle-feeding our little one. I was overwhelmed and exhausted, unsure how to care for this beautiful child. I felt alone in the dark and I was filled with self-doubt. He was my responsibility and yet I was unsure how to take care of him. He didn't come with a set of instructions and having lost my mother years earlier, I had no one to ask. Where was she now and what would she say? Tears turned to a quiet sob, as I used my pajamas to wipe them off my face.

What happened next is difficult to describe. Much like sipping from a warm mug of coffee or tea, I felt a calmness slowly flow through my entire body. I looked up from my chair in the corner of the room and while I saw nothing in the darkness, from the foot of the crib I recognized my mother's voice instantly as if she were standing there.

"Karen, you think too much. You need to go to sleep and rest your mind. Stop worrying. Everything is going to be okay. I will watch over him. Your body has been through a lot. It needs to heal. You'll feel better in the morning sweetie, I promise. Now go. Get some rest. I'll be here." I felt my body relax as the room filled with the scent of her apron; a smell I would find as I wept in her lap as a child. I was immersed in comfort only my mother could provide.

I was numb, almost frozen in place, surrounded by the distinct and powerful presence of her spirit. I was not afraid because I had learned from her stories that love never dies, it just changes forms. Once again, she was right. She knew what I needed to hear at that exact moment, and I listened.

The next morning, the encounter seemed like it was just an odd, inexplicable and hazy dream. Yet I knew it was real because it felt real. I still had my doubts, but I was strangely relieved to know that our son had my mother watching over him. I didn't talk about that night with anyone except my husband for fear of being judged. I moved on and healed slowly, wanting to shelve that memory or perhaps forget it entirely.

Eleven months passed and our son learned how to walk. While celebrating Christmas at my father's house, he quietly followed his uncle out from the festivities and away from our attention. Discovering an open door that led to a staircase, our curious toddler decided to attempt his first step down the stairs, on his own. Predictably, he proceeded to fall down the carpeted stairs as his uncle watched in disbelief from below.

Remarkably, there was not a scratch or a bruise on his body. No broken bones or bumps to his head. Just a look of bewilderment and amusement on his face. Later that evening, his uncle described the fall as if "someone caught him mid-air as he cartwheeled downward, landing in slow-motion." Ironically, my father added he had a "feeling" he needed to finish carpeting the stairs the day before. We were thankful on so many levels, but I couldn't stop myself from wondering if my mother had somehow intervened.

Many months later, I was tidying our bedroom when our son

came marching in and stopped at our long, mirrored dresser. Atop the dresser was a small display of picture frames. I watched as he pointed to one of them, a picture I had taken of my mother sitting back on a chair during one of our many family celebrations. She looked like she had been laughing and then smiled at the camera, capturing such a sweet moment of happiness.

"Who is that?" he inquired.

"That's my mommy, your Grandma Janet," I answered.

Grabbing it with his tiny hands, he looked at it closer and said, "She's funny."

"Oh really? I asked amused. "Why do you say that?"

"Because she plays with me in my bed until I fall asleep," he said, and then carefully returned the small frame to the top of the dresser. Distracted with chasing the dog, he ran out of the room. I looked at her picture and wondered. Then I dismissed his words and chalked it up to the innocence and imagination of a toddler and his make-believe world.

Later, while debating a visit to my mother's grave for the upcoming Mother's Day weekend, our now three-year-old son blurted out, "I wanna go and I'm going to bring a special rock to put on her grave. We need to go." It wasn't even a question in his mind. He immediately ran to his bedroom and began scouring his collection of special rocks from our various hikes.

We went to the cemetery, and he proudly placed a rock on her tombstone while saying, "There you go! I picked out a special one just for you."

He turned toward us with a smile and said, "It makes her happy." He innocently patted the tombstone and came back to stand with us as we finished with prayer before leaving.

The following year, we talked about going to the cemetery again. We asked if he wanted to take a special rock with him and place it on Grandma Janet's tombstone.

As he worked on his wooden puzzle at the dinner table, he replied matter-of-factly, "Oh no, I don't need to do that anymore. Grandma said that I was a big boy now and very smart. She told me that it was time for her to go and that I had lots of people who love me and will watch over me."

That was it. He said it so fervently and wasn't sad about it at all. There was no need to visit the cemetery anymore. She was happy, he was happy and so were we. It was time to let go.

I still feel her presence daily, reflected in my memories and her words of wisdom that are still applicable to this day. But now I know and understand better than ever, that love never dies, it just changes forms.

— Karen Blair —

Answered Prayers

30

Even the Small Prayers

Miracles are instantaneous, they cannot be summoned,
but come of themselves, usually at unlikely moments
and to those who least expect them.
~Katherine Porter

The first thing I noticed, as I stepped off the airplane in Sacramento, was the heat. The sign outside read ninety-eight degrees. Very different from the humid seventy-five of the upstate New York summers I was used to, but not surprising; if you're going to California in the middle of summer, you have to expect heat.

It was my first visit to California. It was also my first time on a plane and my first vacation without my family. Far from being intimidated by these firsts, I was excited about this visit to my friend's house.

From day one, we were a whirlwind of activity. I only had two weeks, and we were determined to squeeze in everything. We drove down to Disneyland, swam in the Pacific Ocean, visited a ghost town, and took walks through downtown Sacramento. We stopped at the state fair and we went panning for gold. We visited a few of the missions and heard Mass at my friend's beautiful church.

The only problem was, I was getting homesick, and the more time went by, the worse it got.

I missed my family, playing games and talking and even fighting with my siblings. I missed my house, and my own bed, and food that didn't include things like avocado and hot sauce.

Most of all, I missed the weather.

I have always loved rain. I sit on the porch during thunderstorms and watch the lightning slice through the air, listen to the fall of rain so heavy and constant it sounds like a great bucket of water being poured out of the sky. I slide on a raincoat to venture into a spring rain. I go outside after a downpour and breathe in the heavy, earthy smell of a world washed clean.

The trouble was, it was summer in California, and they were having a drought to boot. Every day was bright and sunny.

So as the end of my vacation was looming, so was my frustration. As we toured the state capitol, I could barely muster up any interest, even after the tour ended and my friend and I went outside to stroll the grounds. I had expressed interest in seeing a Ponderosa pine tree, and as the capitol grounds sported every tree native to California, we were sure to find one. We broke off in different directions, looking.

Or in my case, pretending to look. I was on a path of my own — sullen, tired, and homesick, sweltering in the afternoon heat. In my mind, I was carrying on a rather fraught conservation with The Man Upstairs.

"God," I prayed silently, "I am tired, and I miss being home. I want to enjoy the rest of my time here with my friend, but I don't know how. I miss my family, my house, my books, my pillow. And I am so tired of the heat." Finally, in desperation, I added, "I know it's summer in California, but some rain would be really nice."

At that moment, a wet drop hit my arm. I blinked, stared at it, looked around. No sprinklers running, no squirt guns. Then another drop hit me, and another. In a small circle around me, little more than three feet in diameter, the sand-colored sidewalk was being stained dark brown by small drops of water.

I looked up; nothing there but blue sky and one small, white cloud, hovering high above. But sure enough, it was raining.

I laughed out loud. Obviously, the rain had come from Someone a little higher than that cloud, Someone who had heard and answered a tired, desperate prayer.

My vacation ended joyfully, homesickness forgotten, and by the time I returned to New York, I had wonderful memories of a fun trip. I treasured the time I was able to spend with my friend and the adventure of exploring California, but most of all, I treasured that rain, and the message I received that day: God hears all our prayers, and He answers them. Even the small ones.

— C. Durand —

31

Unlocking a Blessing

If the only prayer you said was thank you,
that would be enough.
~Meister Eckhart

After six months of searching, I hadn't found a used car for my sixteen-year-old son. I wanted one that was safe and reliable, along with low mileage and little, if any, damage.

Marcus just wanted a black car. Everything I'd seen required mechanical repairs, was a different color, or blew our $7,000 budget.

My commute to work was almost an hour each way and I often stayed late. Marcus's dad, Robert, battled a serious illness and rarely drove. Marcus needed to attend daily football practice, weekly team meetings and dinners, plus other after-school activities, forcing him to snag rides with friends.

One evening, Marcus arrived home in a teammate's new black car. When DaVaris rolled down the window to greet me, that new-car aroma wafted into the air. I peeked inside, admiring the tan, buttery-soft leather seats.

"Very nice," I said.

His face glowed with pride. "Thanks. Marcus said you guys were looking."

"I'm sure we'll find something soon." I spoke with a confidence I didn't feel. It wouldn't be a new car, for sure.

I turned to Marcus. A wistful look crossed his face as DaVaris waved and backed out of the driveway. That look tugged at my heart.

My desperation fueled my search. Since Robert couldn't help, I spent most of my weekends traipsing through car lots, scouring online sites, or examining vehicles parked on the side of the road displaying "FOR SALE" signs. Nothing. One week, I drove two cars home for Marcus and Robert to consider, but they both turned out to have mechanical issues.

A few weeks later, while combing through online ads, I spotted a dealer's listing for a five-year-old sedan with 60,000 miles. It wasn't one of the models I preferred or the black color my son wanted. Still, at $6,000, our budget could handle it.

At dinner, I shared the ad with Marcus. "Want to check it out?"

He twirled spaghetti on his fork. "I was going to eat, then do homework."

Had he given up? I gave him a hug. "I have a good feeling about this one."

At the dealer's lot, Marcus spotted a sporty black turbo-charged car. His eyes sparkled as he ran his hand over the metallic finish. I could feel his desire but thought a car built for speed wouldn't be a safe choice.

"Let's check out the car in the ad." I guided him to the maroon sedan that I'd seen online. "What do you think?"

The spark disappeared from his eyes. He shrugged. "I could get used to maroon."

A salesman approached and offered us a test drive. But then, he couldn't find the keys.

How could they lose the keys? This was so irritating. I began praying. "Lord, I'm so tired. Please help them find the keys." But we remained locked out.

After a half-hour, Marcus asked, "Can we go home? I have homework."

I felt like I'd gotten his hopes up and then smashed them.

We got in our car to drive home. When praise music played on the radio, I felt more hopeful. Was God interested in anything as material as a car? No. He wanted my trust. And He wanted my son to see it.

Buckling my seat belt, I smiled. "God is going to bring us a car," I said.

When we got home, I told Robert that I was handing the car search over to God.

The next day, I ran into the mother of one of Marcus's classmates — a physical therapist. The family had been trying to find a car for their son. "One of my patients wants to sell his car, but we can't afford it."

I asked what model car, and it turned out to be at the top of my wish list. "Can you arrange for me to see it?"

The next day, Robert and I went to the home of the elderly man who was selling the car. It was shiny black, with hardly a scratch. It only had 12,000 miles despite being six years old!

With so many previous disappointments, I was almost afraid to test-drive it. But the engine hummed and the acceleration was smooth. This car had been well maintained. There remained one hurdle — a big one.

Back at the owner's house, we climbed out of the car. "How much are you asking?" I steeled myself for his answer.

He studied his car as if reluctant to part with it. "I'm ninety-three, and my family wants me to quit driving." He placed a hand on the hood to steady himself. His gaze met mine. "This car is worth more than what I'm asking. But I'll let you have it for $7,000."

The exact amount we'd saved! A lump formed in my throat as I extended my hand. "Deal." I went to the bank and withdrew the money to pay him. Robert drove our car home while I took the "new to us" car to the DMV to have it titled and tagged.

With less than an hour until Marcus arrived, I hid his car in the garage and parked mine in the driveway. When he arrived, I tossed my keys to him. "I'm a little tired. Would you pull my car into the garage?"

I stayed close behind with my camera ready. When he opened the garage door, sunlight spilled into the dark interior. Just as I brought the camera to my eye, Marcus turned to me with a wide grin and a double thumbs-up. *Click!* I captured that moment of joy.

I think God grinned, too. While I thought we were locked out of the market, He showed me that there are doors only He can open. All I needed was a little faith.

— Joanna McGee Bradford —

32

Case of the Missing Glasses

I believe that prayer is our powerful contact
with the greatest force in the universe.
~Loretta Young

"Where are your glasses?" I asked as Collin walked casually into the living room. The glasses were new, and based on the cost, one would think they had been made of solid gold.

"I took them off while I was playing, and I can't find them," he explained in a quiet voice.

"Can't find" is a phrase that most moms hear on a regular basis. It isn't generally a cause for alarm, except when the item is expensive and may have been left in harm's way.

"Well, where did you leave them?" I asked, my voice escalating with concern.

"I was playing and set them down by the driveway," he answered softly.

"The driveway? Really? Is that a good place to leave glasses?"

I wondered how many times my younger son could possibly misplace glasses. The last time this happened, he'd set them on top of a seeding implement that was attached to the back of a tractor. My older son, unaware of the random cargo, moved the tractor to the barn, and somewhere along the way, the glasses fell off the implement into a field of uncut hay. Surprisingly, we found them intact and undamaged but not without first experiencing a significant amount of aggravation.

Glancing out the living room window, I could see that the sun would be setting soon, and my husband would be heading back from cutting hay in another field. If Collin's glasses were anywhere near the driveway when his dad returned home, a tractor with hay mower attached would instantly turn the new glasses into a pile of rubble. I picked up a flashlight and headed out the door while Collin followed close behind.

We looked from side to side as we slowly walked down the long gravel driveway. Approaching the gate near the driveway's entrance, I felt a distinctive urge to hurry. "Okay, where were you playing?" I asked quickly. Collin pointed to an area near the driveway's entrance.

"Be careful not to step on them," I barked impatiently. Combing the driveway for over half an hour brought nothing but frustration. After we'd meticulously covered the area by the gate, we began a thorough search of the surrounding vicinity. Carefully, we searched in a grid formation, crouching low as we hunted through clumps of grass, rocks, gravel and dust until our knees throbbed and our backs ached. Back and forth over the same grid we crawled as we inspected every square inch of earth. There were no glasses.

Complete darkness now enveloped the landscape. We heard the owls hooting, and then, the unmistakable sound of an approaching tractor. It was too dark to signal my husband to stop and too loud to shout over the running motor. Collin and I stepped out of the way and watched in silence as the large machine rolled down the driveway on its way to the barn. The tires reached from one end of the gate to the other as a dense cloud of chalky gray dust billowed up into the night air. The hay mower rattled, and its tires made a crunching sound as they moved across the gravel.

We stood quietly for a moment and then slowly, as if surrendering to an adversary, we walked somberly back to the house. I could tell that Collin felt bad about the glasses. Normally a talkative kid, he was completely silent. His chin lowered, and his dark hair, now covered with gravel dust, hung haphazardly in front of his face. A feeling of defeat welled up inside me as I considered the grim situation.

As I opened the front door, Collin and I stepped into the foyer. He turned toward me with an unexpected expression of confidence. "It's okay, Mom," he announced assuredly. "I prayed about it, and I'll find them in the morning." I was pretty sure that all he would find was the pieces.

That night, I wasn't able to sleep as I worried about how much the next pair of glasses would cost. In the morning, I headed to the kitchen to make coffee and I wondered if we could salvage something from the pieces we would inevitably find. Maybe the metal frames would still be salvageable and we would only have to replace the lenses.

Then, I was startled by the sound of the front door closing. Around the corner came Collin, walking briskly, with glasses firmly affixed to his face.

"What's for breakfast?" he asked as if nothing had happened. A moment of silence ensued as I studied my child's face. Staring at the unblemished glasses, I experienced an overwhelming feeling of relief followed by euphoria.

"Where in the world did you find them?"

"They were on the driveway, right where we looked last night," he answered calmly.

"No way!" I said. "We walked back and forth for over an hour! There is absolutely no way they could have been there."

"I told you I prayed about it," he proclaimed, as though I must not have heard him the first time. "I walked back to the end of the driveway, and they were lying in the gravel, right where I said they'd be."

I thought carefully about what had happened. How could the glasses have been on the driveway? How did the tractor, with tires that spanned the whole width, not crush them? How could we have searched so diligently without finding them?

The mystery remained unsolved, but through the experience, I learned that the faith of a child is like no other. It's overwhelmingly sincere, humble, and honest. It's that kind of unwavering faith that moves mountains — and, apparently, eyeglasses.

— Melinda Pritzel —

33

How God and My Angels Saved Me

True healing involves body, mind and Spirit.
~Alison Stormwolf

"**A**re you sure you still need an ambulance?" I gazed at the hotel manager in disbelief, holding my immobile left hand with my right. How could he be asking?

I was sure it was a stroke. I'd thought that from the moment I saw my arm dangling.

Guided by the kind lady who had assisted me down from the fourth floor, I was led to a chair. This remarkable woman had discovered me in a state of panic, alone with two suitcases and two bags, my arm hanging limp. She shouldered the weight of all my belongings down to the lobby, meticulously wrote down my medication list, and remained by my side until the arrival of the paramedics.

Within seconds of their arrival, the paramedics whisked me away on a stretcher. That's when the tears came. I answered the paramedic's questions in a daze. At his request, I relived the moment when I was walking to my room. I saw rather than felt my heavy bag slide down my arm. I was shocked but assumed it was numb. Then I saw it dangling lifelessly, like it wasn't attached to me anymore. I didn't tell him about the one dreaded word my mind had been whispering: stroke.

Evidently, I gave him all the details of my medications and medical history, but I barely remember doing so. Just like I barely have any recollection of being wheeled into the emergency ward. Somehow, my clothes were changed, an IV needle was inserted, my hair was pulled into a bun, and my jewelry was removed. It felt as if I was being prepared for death.

When the doctor performed a scratch test on the left and right sides of my body, I realized that they suspected a stroke too. Four aspirins and two CT scans later, I was admitted to the ward on the third floor. Any confirmation depended on an MRI in the morning.

Now, I was scared. And my husband was on a fifteen-hour flight.

I considered my new reality. Being admitted meant a stroke was the most likely explanation. An MRI meant it could be confirmed, and my life would be changed permanently. I would not be flying to London tomorrow as planned.

I don't do well when I'm not in control, so I turned to the only thing I could control at that moment: prayer. I prayed hard, and I prayed with everything I felt. I prayed all that night, for a miracle, for my faith to return, for a spark of courage even as small as the Biblical mustard seed.

The next day dawned, and it was time for my MRI. I started shaking. I was claustrophobic, and they would need to cover my face with an immobility mask. I couldn't bear the idea. This wasn't a negotiation, though. I had to do it. Again, I turned to prayer.

I entered the machine knowing I had no choice. I lay down on the table and let them start the machine. I was shaking from fear, not the November chill. They slid me far into the tube, and only my lower legs stuck out.

"God and my angels, please give me some mustard seed faith. Please let courage overtake my fear."

Then, it happened. A strange calm came over me, and my breathing relaxed. I saw six angels line up on both sides of my legs. Their soothing energy rose through my body.

"Help comes in ways we can accept" rang out in my mind.

From that moment on, I responded to every instruction from the operator. I didn't even react when she placed the immobilization mask on my face. She was amazed at this drastic transformation. I simply smiled and thanked her for being patient.

From the minute I returned to my room, things changed. My appetite returned. I slept well. My sense of humor returned. I made friends with my nurses and even comforted the one who had a run-in with a nasty patient. My arm began to get better. I didn't have full control over the muscles, but I was using it and was grateful for every movement. My faith came back. I was not scared anymore.

I reassured my husband and told him I'd see him at home in two days. No one believed me, but that was okay. I knew it would happen.

Two days later, I left that hospital with my mother-in-law. I walked out with a fully functional and strong arm. I held my purse on it, to remind myself of my miracle. The doctors struggled to find the impacted part of my brain. When I was diagnosed, I was told to expect memory, balance, and concentration issues.

None of that came to pass. I went back to running my business, learned a new language, sketched some beautiful pieces, and published 100 articles in the next two years.

Every time I hold my puppy or hug my husband with my two working arms, I send gratitude to that stranger who helped me, to God, and to my angels. And I keep a jar of tiny mustard seeds in my kitchen as a small reminder.

— Sarina Byron —

34

An Unexplained Happening

*A miracle is when the whole is greater than the sum
of its parts. A miracle is when one plus one
equals a thousand.*
~Frederick Buechner, The Alphabet of Grace

Christmas was fast approaching, and I was beginning to wonder if everything on my to-do list would ever get done. Our out-of-town guests would be arriving shortly, and my children would soon be off for Christmas break. My list of things that needed to be bought, baked, cooked, decorated, or wrapped was a mile long, and I was running out of time.

I grabbed a pencil and paper and began to devise a plan of attack. With a little luck and some careful planning, I might be able to get it all done before December 25th.

While sitting at the kitchen table writing out the last of my Christmas cards, a sad thought crossed my mind. I don't know why I thought of it or where it came from, but it wouldn't go away and was making my heart heavy. I had heard through the grapevine that the husband of one of our school moms had walked out on his family, leaving them financially struggling and emotionally devastated.

The mom's name was Becky. Her daughter rode on the school bus with my three children. Several of us moms dropped our kids off at the school bus every morning and collected them after school at the same place. We would chat with each other while we waited for the bus to arrive before and after school.

Becky had a kind and gentle way about her, but she seemed shy. She never joined the rest of us while we chatted. I don't know what made me think of it, but I couldn't get Becky out of my mind. My heart broke for her and her daughter, and I wondered what Christmas would be like for them this year. I prayed for Becky's family and asked God to comfort, encourage, and help them feel loved this Christmas.

I believe God heard my prayer because, the very next morning, I felt led to do something that I did not feel at all comfortable doing. I honestly don't know where the idea came from, but I knew that I was going to have to do it. I would ask the moms at the bus stop to contribute some money toward Christmas gifts for Becky and her daughter. This horrified me because asking people for money was not something I ever did.

The next morning, the usual group of ladies was at the bus stop waiting in their cars. My heart pounded as I got out of my car and approached the first mom. She rolled down her window and listened as I shared my idea with her. When I asked if she would like to contribute a small amount toward some gifts for Becky and her daughter, she said she would love to and handed me twenty dollars.

That was encouraging and made it easier to approach the next car. This mom also thought it was a fantastic idea and gave me fifty dollars. I moved on to the next car, and then the next one, and the next, each time being met with smiles, words of encouragement, and very generous donations. Tears ran down the cheeks of one mom as she wrote me a cheque for one hundred dollars!

My good friend Sharon was in the last car I approached. Sharon loved the idea and asked if she could be a part of it by helping me shop for Christmas gifts and food items for the hamper. I was so grateful for her help and glad we could do it together.

The moment I arrived home, I checked my wall calendar to choose a date for the shopping trip with Sharon. With Christmas just around the corner, it was an especially busy time, and every square on my calendar had something written on it. Commitments, promises, a million things to do… When would I be able to fit in a shopping trip with Sharon?

The next morning, I was on my way to an appointment when my car started to make a horrible, grinding noise. I was about to pull over to the side of the busy road when I noticed I was almost at the shopping center. This seemed like a safer place to stop, so I drove slowly into the parking lot and pulled over.

As luck would have it, I was very close to an auto-repair shop. I went inside for help. The mechanic moved my car into the garage and informed me that there was trouble with the bearings in the rear wheel. It would be unsafe to continue driving, but he could fix it right away. He told me he would need the car for at least two hours, so I headed over to the shopping mall to wait.

As I opened the door to the mall, I bumped into my good friend Sharon, who had also just arrived. I told her about my car troubles and having to wait two hours for the shop to repair it. Sharon looked at me and smiled. "Why don't we go shopping for Becky and her daughter while you wait for your car to be fixed?"

That seemed like a perfect idea. When we arrived at the department store, we noticed a huge sign in the window, "ONE DAY SALE 40% OFF." It was the perfect day to shop, and the money we had collected was going to go even further than we had anticipated. We had so much fun shopping together and found some beautiful Christmas gifts for Becky and her daughter.

A few days later, Sharon and I went shopping for food and goodies to fill the Christmas hampers. Despite another full day of commitments and appointments, we somehow managed to squeeze in an hour of shopping at a superstore. With both of us doing the shopping, we were done in less than an hour and were so pleased with all the items we had found.

After filling two huge baskets with healthy groceries and tasty Christmas treats, we still hadn't used up all of the money! We were able to purchase a few gift cards for some fun activities that Becky and her daughter could enjoy together over the Christmas holidays, and there was still money left. We inserted the money that remained into a Christmas card and signed it, "From the ladies at the bus stop."

Becky was so touched by the hampers and gifts that she cried tears of gratitude and appreciation when we dropped them off at her home.

I don't understand how God works, but I do believe He heard my prayer for Becky that evening, and He used me and the "bus stop moms" to help Him carry out His plan to bless Becky and her daughter. Did He go before me and prepare the hearts of each lady who gave so generously? Was my car breaking down when it did, and my bumping into Sharon as I entered the mall, just a coincidence? Was the forty percent off sale just a twist of fate?

I don't know the answers, but I am so grateful that I got to be a part of making Becky and her daughter's Christmas just a bit brighter. I will always wonder how that money stretched so far.

— Maureen Slater —

The Convoy

A mother has to think twice, once for herself
and once for her child.
~Sophia Loren

An instant message popped up from my mother in the early hours of the morning. She asked what I had been doing the night before at exactly 5:30. I assumed she meant 5:30 my time. She said she had felt an overwhelming urge to pray for me and asked God to send me an angel. Several members of her church called her shortly afterward to say they also felt the need to send prayers and that God's angels would keep me safe.

That night, I'd been eating dinner with my team while we waited to move back to our operating base in Baghdad. We started our drive across the city in our three armored Suburbans just after midnight. Shortly into our route, we lost sight of our third truck, and the frequency jammers we used to defeat radio-controlled explosive devices interfered with our communications equipment.

We circled back to figure out what had happened to the missing Suburban and found its occupants sitting along the side of the road in front of an apartment complex in the most dangerous area on our route. They had rolled as far as they could until their truck came to a dead stop.

I set up a security perimeter while some members of the team assessed the situation. The truck had been destroyed from the front bumper to the driver's door. We never discovered what caused the damage, but one of the tires was shredded, and the wheel was warped. A crew started working on getting the wheel off so we could replace it and tow the truck back with us. The lug nuts had tightened to the point that they pressed into the solid metal wheel. The crew couldn't get them to budge.

I was called away from the security perimeter to give it a try. I tried over and over again. I got angry and sat on the ground next to the tire iron with my foot pushing on the bottom and both hands pulling from the top. I screamed and shook, putting every bit of strength into it.

It finally moved! Everyone around me cheered as I forced it off the truck. One down, four to go. I injured my biceps and my back, but I managed to get three of the lug nuts off. When I reached a point of complete muscle failure, a couple of crew members worked on the last two. They were working as fast as they could because we needed to get out of there quickly.

Voices were coming from the apartment complex. We heard thuds, bangs, and clicks. It felt like something bad was coming. I heard a yell from the rooftop: a saying that was commonly used as a declaration of an attack. *This is it,* I thought. *This is where I die.*

As I prepared for a fight and accepted my fate, a supply convoy protected by large-caliber gun trucks approached us. They slowed down to provide a few minutes of protection while we continued to work. They had a lot more firepower than we did, and their mere presence thwarted the imminent attack on us.

Within a minute of the supply convoy clearing our location, we had the truck ready to tow. We were moving faster than those supply convoys usually traveled, and we should have caught up with them within a couple of minutes, but we never saw them again. Weird.

It was unusual for supply convoys to move at night because of the high attack risk. There would be one on occasion, but we passed the staging area for them on our way out, and it was empty. When we arrived at our destination, they weren't at the unloading area. I went through the activity logs, and there was no mention of this mysterious convoy. I never found out who they were or where they came from, but they saved us.

I sat up on the roof of our building, watching the sunrise and thinking about everything that had transpired. I remembered looking at my watch when that convoy showed up and came to a sudden realization. If you account for the time difference between Baghdad and home, it had been exactly 5:30 back home where my mother was.

— Elton A. Dean —

36

The Miracle of Tanka

Don't believe in miracles — depend on them.
~Laurence J. Peter

I f I told you we had three dogs already, you would say we didn't need one more dog. I would wholeheartedly agree with you.

I was a single parent raising five children, four boys and one girl. I didn't need one more being to feed. We certainly did not need another dog. When my oldest son came to me about giving his brother a puppy for Christmas, I was not only against the idea, I was adamant that we were not taking in another dog. My son tried to persuade me by naming the puppy Tanka after his brother's baseball nickname, Tank. The added "a" was to indicate that the puppy was a girl.

That is how we ended up with Tanka. She was no more than ten inches tall and barely weaned. Tanka's mother was a huge Collie mix who belonged to my son's girlfriend. Tanka's father was the neighbor's Rottweiler. Tanka would grow to live up to her name.

Taking in Tanka meant we had two puppies in the house. The other one, Spunk, was our "Safeway dog." Spunk was acquired thanks to my mother via a puppy box in front of Safeway. She was a Pit-Lab mix. Although she would never be Tanka's size, she was still a big dog.

They say "the more, the merrier." I think "the more, the more chaotic" is probably more accurate. Life with four dogs was out of control. In the first year, Tanka grew to her full height, which is to say that she was tall and skinny. We discovered early on that she was a sock eater. Trying to get five kids to pick up their socks was a lot like herding cats.

My high level of exhaustion during this time of my life was the culmination of busy schedules and the constant messes. I should mention that both these dogs decided that they should sleep with me at night instead of with one of the many children. That meant that, at the end of a long day, I was fighting for space in a queen bed with these two big dogs. Obviously, their companionship grew on me. Even though they were supposed to be my son's dogs, they became a comfort to me as I always felt safer knowing they were in our home.

One evening, one of the older boys was coming in the front door, and Spunk seized the opportunity to escape out the door with Tanka chasing after her. I grabbed leashes. The four boys took off with me to wrangle the dogs. We were so close behind that we saw them reach the end of the property. They were only visible as two dark shadows. Spunk darted across the road with Tanka about twenty steps behind her. That is when the car hit Tanka, knocking her to the ground.

As I ran toward her, I called her. She tried to get up and walk toward me, but fell down on the edge of the road. One of the boys yelled that they had caught Spunk. As I reached Tanka, I knew we were in trouble. She was alive and breathing, but her left front leg was bent back unnaturally toward her back. When I picked her up, that leg flopped forward. I knew it was shattered.

The next day, the vet gave me horrible news that I had to convey to my children. I brought Tanka home and placed her on the floor in the living room. The boys all gathered around, and I told them that the vet in our town couldn't set her shattered leg. It was what he considered "bad medicine." The options were to remove the leg or have her put down. The vet did not recommend the amputation because she was such a big dog. We sat there silently for a minute.

My oldest son said, "Can you set it, Mom?"

My medical training consisted of a high-school CPR class, a few books on holistic medicine, and brain mapping for psychology. None of that was going to be helpful. The veterinarian showed me Tanka's X-ray when we were in the office, so I knew the extent of the damage. There were fragments of her shoulder separated at the top of the bone. The idea of setting it seemed like a bad idea even as I was mulling it over.

"We can try," I heard myself say out loud. To this day, I'm not sure where that came from. The logic was that we would always still have the option to remove the leg.

My kids sprang into action, helping me collect surgical tape, two tree branches, and an old bed sheet. This had no hope of working. I splinted her leg on the inside and outside. On the inside, I wrapped part of the sheet around the top of the branch to cushion it when it pressed against her chest, basically making her another leg. We then taped it and secured it around her and her leg. Then we secured the other branch to the other side of her leg and taped it all together.

Tanka looked like the kids had been playing Frankenstein with her. Both the branches were a quarter of an inch longer than her leg, so she wasn't putting pressure on her leg when she walked. She was perfectly still through this entire process. I almost feel like she had a faith in us that wasn't based on any reality I knew.

We all got on the floor around Tanka, and together we said a prayer asking God to heal our dog. It was a prayer said through tears, a heartfelt plea to save a member of our family. In my soul, I was just hoping I wouldn't have to put her down. Prayer has a way of calming us in our times of need. This prayer made me feel very calm but I also knew this makeshift splint didn't have a chance. We needed a miracle.

Then, as my kids often do, one of them said something hilarious. Tristan (Tank) said, "Mom, don't worry if this doesn't work. Having a three-legged dog is the coolest thing ever." This statement was confirmed by the other children, who instantly decided that they would call Tanka "Tripod" if her leg had to be removed.

Over the next few weeks, we had the added chore of helping Tanka get up every time she wanted to go somewhere. In general, she seemed unbothered by the splint, and it helped her walk. Eventually, we took off the splint after she started trying to pull on the tape with her teeth. Although I don't remember the timing, it seemed like she quickly stood and ran on that leg. I don't want to give the wrong impression that her leg was perfect. The leg was turned slightly. However, it healed straight enough to be usable.

The leg never bothered her after the splint came off. When we returned to the vet, Tanka did so walking. The vet said while he wouldn't have ever recommended it, but she appeared fine with her healed leg and he no longer saw a need to remove it. I watched her for a long time, and her leg never bothered her, even in the snow. She played and rolled around like nothing had ever happened. Looking back, it was amazing that she never even had arthritis in that leg.

Over the years, Tanka played with Spunk, chased things, got into the trash, ate socks, and protected our family. The kids eventually moved out, leaving behind three of the four dogs, including Tanka. Tanka outlived Spunk by over a year.

Do I believe in miracles? Yes, I do.

— Michelle Jackson —

37

Vanished

I believe in prayer. It's the best way we have
to draw strength from heaven.
~Josephine Baker

P ray. Wait. Trust. These words are inscribed on a small sign that sits in my home office. They are not just words of encouragement. They are words to live by.

Growing up Catholic, I was taught from an early age about the power of prayer. My prayers as a child resembled a grocery list. Every night, snuggled beneath the blankets, I would recite the names of my family members, friends, and all my deceased relatives. Great-aunts and -uncles (even those I had never met) were given their place of honor in my prayers, and, truth be told, the slow, methodical listing of each ancestor helped me fall asleep.

As a teenager, prayer became more of an accessory. It felt like something to clasp in times of need — like a necklace that I could reach up and twist between my fingers when I needed comfort. I breathed silent whispers into the universe when I needed help, usually before a big test or an uncomfortable breakup. These prayers were usually last-minute and quickly crafted, more like urgent pleas than conversations with God.

Fast forward to adulthood, marriage, and motherhood. These life events changed my relationship with prayer forever.

Navigating through life with young children and trying to guide them physically, emotionally, and spiritually prompted long discussions with God everywhere — in the shower, in the car, on the way to the pediatrician's office, returning home from a play date. The quantity of my prayers increased even if the quality remained slightly adolescent. And yet these prayers served as important precursors to what lay ahead.

At the age of thirty-five and seven years into (what I thought to be) a normal, happy-enough marriage, my husband was unfaithful. My life, as I knew it, ended.

I shook my fist at heaven and demanded a do-over.

The next fifteen years proved to be a jagged story of hope, brokenness, resilience, desperation, and despondency. For both of us. We did all the "right" things (sought counseling, honest dialoguing, joined a marital support group). We did all the "wrong" things (harbored blame, distanced ourselves, hated each other).

He turned into himself. I turned to alcohol.

As the years progressed, my emotional pain morphed into a beast with an ugly face. My reliance upon wine went from being an end-of-day method of relaxation to an everyday dependency.

Time passed, and wine became my new spouse. I looked forward to sitting with her after work, crying with her as my marriage fell deeper into a black hole, soothing my wounds with her balm of inebriation.

Predictably, my use (overuse) made the days darker and the nights more fretful. My husband called me out on my behavior, but that made me angrier. And it made me more insistent on its use. Anything that bothered him made me feel better.

As time wore on (and by "time," I mean years), I came to worry about my relationship with wine. I knew it wasn't healthy. I knew it had passed the point of "normal." I knew the only way out was going to be a bad exit. I hated the way I felt, physically and emotionally. Each day, I apologized to God for my behavior, my habit.

I started to pray. I mean, really pray. I prayed while I drove, while I ran, while I shopped. I asked God to take away this cross. To give me the power to resist its temptation.

I tried to stop. I became an expert self-negotiator. "I'll have two glasses tonight but none tomorrow." "Today was a particularly stressful day, so I deserve a quick glass." "It's the weekend." "It's Monday." "It's a holiday." "Tonight only." "My New Year's resolution will be to stop." "I'll give it up for Lent."

It didn't work. Every morning's promise was broken by evening's five o'clock shadow.

And it's always five somewhere.

Years went on, and so did my prayers. I never gave up, but I felt more and more desperate. I prayed, and I prayed, and I prayed.

It would be sensible to ask why I didn't seek help. Why not join AA or talk to my doctor? Why not reach out to a friend or speak to my siblings? There are no satisfactory answers to that question other than I was caught in a web of denial, shame, stubbornness, and fear. Yes, fear.

The truth was that I didn't want to give up my wine. I didn't want to relinquish my one pleasurable indulgence. Some people like dessert or potato chips or cigarettes. Wine was my vice of choice. And I clung to it with the ferocity of a drowning woman to a buoy.

I spent many moments of many days feeling deeply ashamed. I was also angry. I was mad at myself, mad at my life, and mad at the world. I felt lost, out-of-control, and hopeless. I prayed some more.

And then, one day, it vanished.

Vanished.

I woke up, and as I did every day, thanked God for a fresh start. I went through my workday, but when I arrived home and headed toward the refrigerator, I found I didn't want a glass of wine. So deeply embedded was my habit that I poured one anyway. But when I took the first sip, it didn't taste good. In fact, it tasted bad.

I chocked it up to a fluke and went to bed.

The next day, it was the same. Even the smell of an open bottle made me slightly nauseous. A sip made me grimace.

Day three, day four, day five… all the same. I started to wonder, to question. What was going on?

Days turned into weeks. At a routine doctor appointment, I asked the physician to check my tongue, stating that I was experiencing some "changes" in taste. This, of course, wasn't exactly true. The one and only change was my sudden distaste for wine.

She checked for thrush. None. She asked if I had had Covid. I hadn't. With no professional explanation, I left her office, again filled with bewilderment.

I began to believe. Really believe.

The weeks have turned into months that soon will turn into a year. I don't try to explain the inexplicable. But I believe in my heart that God answered my prayer. After years of struggle and pleading and honest attempts, He lifted this cross from me.

When I think of all the people in the world who struggle with debilitating illnesses and issues, I know my condition doesn't compare. But I do know that it was destroying me from the inside out. It was leading me down a tunnel that would end only in death. It was robbing me of the very last remnants of my dignity and self-respect, my personhood.

God restored me. He answered my prayer. He brought me back to life.

Pray. Wait. Trust.

Words to live by.

— Molly Mulrooney Wade —

38

Divine Deer

*There are far, far better things ahead
than any we leave behind.*
~C. S. Lewis

"I can't sleep. I don't have an appetite. I've been crying at the most inopportune times. I think we've made a terrible mistake."

My friend Laura listened patiently as I cried to her on the phone — she in her century-old farmhouse and I in my car, parked at Whole Foods in the Indiana city where we'd relocated. Our closing had been fourteen days ago, and every time I stopped over at the residence we now owned, I fought a bad feeling in the pit of my stomach.

It all felt wrong. We didn't fit in. I missed my friends. I didn't think it would ever feel right.

We'd moved to be near our children and grandchildren, two cherished girls born three months apart. Living close to all of them was truly amazing, beyond anything we could've dreamed. Nonetheless, we'd left the place where we had the same zip code for decades, where we knew everyone, and everyone knew us. In Indiana, no one knew us and no one cared.

"I felt that way when we moved from Oregon to Wisconsin," Laura said. "I really understand."

"What did you do?" I asked.

"Well, you might think I'm crazy," she said, hedging, "but I asked

God for a sign."

"No, I don't think you're crazy. What happened?"

"The first night we opened the front door and walked into what was, at the time, a cold, drafty, decrepit place. I thought we'd lost our minds. I was despondent and asked God to make it clear that He had us here for a reason. I thought we'd made a horrible mistake, too. We spent time inside, but the minute we stepped outside to the car, I saw a deer just feet away. It was majestic and it seemed to appear from nowhere and was staring at us. An immediate peace surrounded me. It completely changed my attitude about being here."

It was the first time I had heard this part of her Wisconsin story, and I loved it. I met her after they'd settled there, when I soon learned what fruitful things God had done, and still does, through her family and their renovated homestead.

We talked a bit longer, and before hanging up, I thanked my friend for her steady voice of reason and her promise to pray for me.

I drove, returning to the rental we'd been sharing with our son and daughter-in-law during the time we were looking for a house and they were building theirs. My husband and I would be moving to our new neighborhood the following weekend.

As I reflected on my conversation with Laura, I asked God to give me a sign, as well as serenity in my soul that this town would begin to feel like home.

I pulled into the driveway and took the groceries I'd bought from the trunk. My heart filled with the anticipation of seeing our granddaughter when I got inside. I was going to miss living in the same house as her. And adding to my depressed outlook was the fact that I was grieving the loss of my mom, who had passed away only a few weeks earlier.

When I entered the kitchen, the baby was napping, but her mama was walking in from the backyard. She had an astonished look on her face.

"What is it?" I asked.

"You're not going to believe it!"

"What happened?"

"I was on the deck when I saw a huge deer in the neighbor's yard! His antlers were like this," she said, gesturing with her hands.

"Are you kidding?" The rental house, in a crowded suburb, bordered a bustling high school. Fences separated neighboring properties, and we'd never seen a deer in the vicinity.

"No!" she said, turning to the window and pointing. "As I watched, he jumped over that neighbor's fence into the yard next to us. Then he jumped their fence into our yard. He circled around and finally jumped over the back fence. He looked like he was flying!"

My jaw dropped. The back fence was taller than my six-foot son.

"What?" she said, looking at my expression and smiling. "You don't believe me?"

"Oh, no… That's not it at all," I said, shaking my head as I felt goose bumps. "I absolutely, most certainly, do."

— Debbie Prather —

God Cares for Piano Players

Cast your cares on God; the anchor holds.
~Frank Moore Colby

"I s Anna really thinking of music school?" I glanced up from my seat in the studio waiting room to see Anna's music teacher standing in the doorway.

"Of course, Carol! She's been talking about it for a while now." I paused, then frowned. "Don't you think she's able?"

"Oh, yes." She moved aside to let a student pass. "But you only have an upright piano."

I waited, watching her face. What did our piano have to do with it?

"To prepare for auditions, she needs to practice on a grand piano." She held up a hand. "I know, she prepped the Schumann piece beautifully without a sostenuto pedal."

I smiled, remembering Anna's flawless performance at the recital.

Carol raised her eyebrows. "But how did it sound when she practiced?"

I thought back. Unlike a sostenuto pedal that holds only the notes played at the precise time the pedal is depressed, our piano's middle pedal sustained all sound from the lower half of the piano. Every time Anna had depressed the pedal, the notes had clashed and blurred. We had asked her to practice the piece when few of us were home.

Carol broke in on my thoughts. "You see? That's the issue. She needs to be able to hear the effect she's aiming for. She has to practice on a grand."

My heart sank. Buying a grand was impossible. We'd spent more than we could afford to buy our studio upright.

Anna appeared at the door, music bag in hand, and I rose to leave. "Thanks for explaining, Carol. We'll have to think about it."

On the drive home, my thoughts churned.

The year before, we'd gone to see a five-foot Steinway baby grand recommended by our piano tuner.

"You have to see it," he'd said. "They only want $5,000. That's a deal!"

Anna and her brother had played it. Back in the car, they shook their heads. "There's something wrong with the bass section. The action isn't quite right."

Not long afterward, a friend who'd bought a baby grand for her musical daughter told us the girl still practiced on the family's old upright. Asking around, we learned a studio upright is often a better instrument than a grand under five feet, six inches.

Yet an adequate grand would run at least $10,000, well out of our price range.

To keep our four children in Carol's studio after our income plummeted, we had devised trades to contribute toward the fees. We painted her studio entrance and stairs and cooked high-end meals for her every week. I found it hard to scrape together additional money for the competition fees, clothes for the performances, and even the gas for driving to lessons.

Could Anna practice somewhere else? Her time on the piano would increase to several hours a day as she prepared for auditions, and practicing at that level wasn't pleasant listening. I couldn't imagine anyone else wanting the hours of repetition in their home. Nor could I think of a church with a suitable situation.

Another friend's words came back to me. A month earlier, she had leaned over her cup of tea to give me some advice. "Don't automatically say no to your children's impossible requests. Pray first."

When her fourteen-year-old had pleaded to take riding lessons, she'd scoffed to herself. Their family of seven lived on a bus driver's income. Nonetheless, she and her son had prayed about it together. To her amazement, doors had opened. He'd been hired to muck out stables, then offered the chance to ride, take lessons and, finally, train horses. The family had never paid a cent.

"God knows what each child needs," she told me. "If God wants something for them, he can provide a way even when it seems impossible to you. But you have to ask."

Her words had pierced deep. For the past six years, I'd made most decisions based on money. I hadn't thought to include God in the decision-making. That night, I confessed to God my lack of confidence in him and asked him to remind me to turn to him about each need.

It seemed ridiculous for a grand piano to be a genuine need, but Anna had her sights on a piano performance degree. God would know if this were a true necessity. Night after night, Anna and I asked God to sort out the problem for her.

A few weeks later, our piano tuner called. "I've had an odd request from a woman moving here from Texas. Her new home isn't ready yet, and she doesn't want to put her grand piano into storage. She's looking for a temporary home for it. Would your family be interested? It's five feet, six inches, I think, and you might have it as long as six months."

Disbelief and joy coursed through me. I told him we were interested and hung up the phone to dance around the kitchen. "Look what you've done, Lord!"

Soon, piano movers set a shiny black Baldwin grand in the space we'd cleared in the living room, and Anna began practicing in earnest.

After a full year — and hundreds of hours of practicing — our benefactor reclaimed her piano. Concerned but not despairing this time, I prayed for God's help.

Not long after, the piano teacher called, triumph in her voice. "My sister is moving back to the area and is sending her nearly six-foot grand piano ahead. I thought you could house it for her!" We rejoiced together.

That winter, Anna auditioned for music school and was accepted. Her freshman year, she commuted to the university and continued to give the piano hours of use. Her sophomore year, however, she moved to a house close to campus and began practicing on music school pianos. Within a few weeks, the owner sent movers to cart off this second grand.

How perfectly God arranged those pianos for Anna's needs!

— Betts Baker —

Chapter
5

Miraculous
Coincidences

40

A Blue Wall Beneath the Ocean

*Angels love to create synchronicities because each
synchronicity produces an illumination point for
a soul to connect the dots on life experiences.*
~Molly Friedenfeld

Sophie's tiny hand gripped mine as we stood outside St Paul's Cathedral. How could I get inside that church? Around us, hundreds of people thronged the pavement. Some were in tears as they stepped toward the thick rope separating us from the empty cathedral steps.

It was September 2001. England had been my home for eighteen years. Yet here I stood with my three-year-old daughter's hand in mine, more homesick than ever.

The day before, when I spoke with a woman at the American Embassy, I asked how I could attend the service.

"Just get there early," she said.

With a three-year-old to look after, my naïve idea of early was an hour before the service began. Standing now amongst the crowd, I realised my mistake.

I should take us both home. My throat tightened as I glanced back at the empty cathedral steps.

Friends here in the UK had been supportive, shocked along with the rest of the world by the carnage of 9/11. I couldn't explain to them how I longed to be with people who, like me, grew up in New York. People who watched from their backyards while cranes erected the Twin Towers along the skyline. I wanted to weep with people who had celebrated birthdays, graduations, and anniversaries at the Windows on the World restaurant or met with friends in the Twin Towers' underground shopping mall. I wanted to stand with people who, whether they believed in prayer or not, stood praying for their New York school friends, for former work pals.

I wanted to pray for my brother, a cop whose precinct was directly opposite the World Trade Center. For forty-eight hours, my family and I didn't know if he'd survived.

He had, but now he was toiling in concrete hell, searching for his colleagues who ran into that second tower.

I checked my watch. It was 10:30 AM. The service started at 11:00.

I marched up to a policeman on the other side of the rope. "Excuse me," I said. "How do I get in?"

"You don't," he said, barely looking at me.

"But I'm an American."

He scanned the crowds. "There are hundreds of your compatriots here. No one is getting in. Not unless you have special dispensation."

"My brother is a New York cop," I said. "He's been working twenty-hour shifts searching for his buddies in the rubble. Is that special enough for you?"

I waited for him to shrug, to ask me to leave.

Instead, his eyes softened. "Yes, ma'am," he said, lifting the rope. "That's special enough."

"Thank you," I said, gratefully leading my daughter through.

We found space in a pew near the middle of the church. Glancing around, I realised Sophie was the only child present. I heard muffled weeping behind us.

My daughter tugged at my jacket sleeve. The organ music began, and I whispered to her, "You must behave. The Queen is coming."

Sophie climbed onto the pew, eager to see the Queen. As she turned to look at the entrance, the Archbishop of Canterbury appeared. He walked towards us in his robes, the tall mitre on his head. As he neared, Sophie shouted out, "Mummy, is that the Queen?"

People around us tittered as heat rushed to my cheeks. "Shhh…," I told her. "She's coming soon."

About a minute later, the Queen arrived, her expression sombre. She was dressed in a simple black dress and hat, escorted by her son Charles. I whispered to Sophie, "The Queen is the lady in the black hat."

Sophie watched in awe as Queen Elizabeth walked past us. During the American national anthem, Sophie, now on her best behaviour, imitated me. With her hand on her heart, she pretended to sing. At the end of the service, when Prince Charles escorted his mother back down the aisle, Sophie couldn't help herself. As the Queen walked past again, Sophie called out, "Bye-bye lady in the black hat."

The people behind us giggled.

"Are you going to stop crying now, Mummy?" Sophie asked as we left St Paul's. I had assumed she hadn't seen me wiping the tears as I cooked her supper or sat at the table in our garden sobbing when I thought she was asleep.

"Yes. No more crying."

Wearily, we caught the Tube and stumbled home. Sophie's father stood on the doorstep waiting.

"You've been on the news," he said. "The clip has been shown over and over. The camera zoomed in on you both during the American national anthem."

I looked at Sophie, with her golden curls beneath the black velvet beret she'd been wearing. Of course, she must have made an angelic picture standing on the pew, hand on her heart, pretending to sing the American anthem.

As we stepped inside, my answering machine flashed messages. Most likely, they were from friends who wanted to say they'd seen Sophie and me on the news.

I slumped onto the sofa, too numb to speak with anyone. I'd listen to the messages later. With the tragic events of the week, a TV news clip didn't mean anything.

Later that evening, I discovered it did.

My house phone rang around 11:00 PM. When I lifted the receiver,

I heard my brother's exhausted voice. "I had to phone you," he said.

"Oh, my God, how are you?" The receiver in my hand shook as I tried to keep the tears from my voice.

"Look, I only have a minute," he said, "but I need to tell you that I've just been on a break inside our team's shelter." He went silent for a moment before adding, "A horrible shift. Uncovering body parts."

"I'm so sorry," I mumbled.

"Yeah. It's really bad. I came in here for a rest. Wasn't sure I could go on. But then something happened." His voice strengthened. "We have a television here. Someone had the world news on. A BBC clip came onto the screen, and I saw you and Sophie."

My breath halted as he went on. "You don't know what it meant to see my sister and niece on the other side of the world, singing the anthem, praying for us. It lifted me, knowing you were there with me. Enough to get me back out there. To search for someone, something to help families desperate for news."

I thought of this morning. The London policeman, his eyes softening when I mentioned my brother, the lifting of the rope as he allowed us through.

I went back the next day to tell him about my brother, about the news clip. He wasn't there.

If this story finds him, may he know that his compassion for a colleague on the other side of the Atlantic gave that fellow cop strength to carry on during his toughest hours. May he know how, on that September day, the police blue wall of solidarity ran beneath the ocean.

— Karen Storey —

41

Finding Fred

There is always another layer of awareness,
understanding, and delight to be discovered
through synchronistic and serendipitous events.
~Hannelie Venucia

"Traffic is beginning to build on 101 North heading into the city," the traffic announcer declared. That was the last thing I wanted to hear. I was in a rush to get home, back to the East Coast, and I was headed for the non-stop flight from San Francisco to Newark, New Jersey. Looking in the bathroom mirror, I gave each eye one last swipe of mascara and threw the unused blush brush into my travel bag.

Out of nowhere, I heard that familiar still, small voice deep inside me. "You're going to see Fred today."

"Wait, what?" I said aloud. "I haven't seen Fred in over twenty-five years. What are the chances I'm going to meet someone I haven't seen in twenty-five years, especially clear across the country?"

Fred and I had been best friends in high school. We did everything together. But time and jobs had separated us, so I shrugged it off as a random thought. I finished packing and rushed out the door. Within minutes, I was heading north trying to make the 10:00 AM flight.

Within a few minutes, my GPS announced, "Heavy traffic ahead. Do you want to re-route?"

I pressed "yes" on the phone's screen and, subsequently, was directed to the next exit. Eventually, the traffic came to a slow crawl on that route too.

"C'mon, c'mon," I shouted as I banged on the steering wheel. "I have a flight to catch. Move it!" Nobody listened, and our slow, steady crawl got me to the airport with only thirty minutes remaining to drop off the rental car and get to the gate.

I made it slowly through security and ran to the end of the terminal to the assigned gate only to see that the flight had already boarded, and the plane was pulling away. I glanced at my watch: 10:10 AM.

I secured a seat on the noon flight and purchased a bottle of water and a magazine. It was time to relax.

At long last, the announcement came to board. I had a seat near the back of the plane, the last place I wanted to be, but it meant that I was among the first to board. When I stepped into the plane, I heard a familiar voice.

"Don't forget to put your carry-on in the overhead compartment before you take your seat, please."

I looked up and there, assisting passengers, was the flight attendant, my high-school friend, Fred! He looked at me, and his eyes opened wide.

"Elisa?" he said with a big smile.

"Fred?" I responded. "Oh, my goodness, how are you?" I gave him a big hug. That still, small voice deep inside of me said, "See, I told you that you'd see Fred today."

"Hey, everybody, this is an old friend from high school whom I haven't seen in almost twenty-five years," Fred announced to the passengers who had already boarded. A cheer from the small group of passengers turned my smile into laughter.

"Where are you seated today?" he asked.

I whispered, "I'm in seat 23C, but if you have an empty seat closer to the front of the plane, I would love to have it." I wasn't optimistic.

"Okay. Get seated, and if there's an available seat, I'll let you know," he said in a quiet voice.

I stored my carry-on in the overhead compartment and settled myself into seat 23C. If I had to remain in the back of the plane, at least, I reasoned, I had an aisle seat, which made the five-hour flight bearable.

Fred announced the final boarding call and asked passengers to prepare for takeoff—seatbelts buckled, lap trays stored in the seat back in front of you and all electronic devices off. He walked down the aisle ensuring compliance. He stopped next to me and said, "Miss, I have a seat available in 8D. Would you like to move up?" he asked professionally.

I bolted out of 23C and moved into 8D immediately. Once settled, the flight took off smoothly, and I was heading east, home to my children. After the plane reached its cruising altitude, Fred stopped by and motioned that I should go with him. He led me back into the galley.

For the next four hours, we caught up when he wasn't busy. We talked about our families, children, parents, hobbies, mutual friends we had in high school and their whereabouts, politics, music and God. I shared with him the voice I had heard earlier in the day and the events leading up to my seeing him. He was awestruck at such a story.

We laughed at the chances of our meeting up: thousands of passengers every day and hundreds of flights, traffic and missing the 10:00 AM flight, and the like. We chatted about our careers and how they took us places, literally and figuratively, that we never expected as teenagers. After what seemed to be a brief flight, the captain announced that we should prepare to land, so I made my way back to 8D, still marveling at the sequence of events that led me to this divine appointment.

Later that evening, as I drove home from the airport, I thanked God for what had occurred that day. I thought about the delays, all orchestrated so I could enjoy a renewed friendship. Still, I questioned God, "What are the chances that I would meet up with him?"

Once again, I heard that still, small voice.

"Chances mean nothing to me."

"Right. So noted," I replied. "I'll remember for the next time."

— Elisa Yager —

42

A Celestial Wrong Number

When you live your life with an appreciation of
coincidences and their meanings, you connect with the
underlying field of infinite possibilities.
~Deepak Chopra

It took a moment to recognize the muffled voice on my answering machine. The only clue was a tearful "Saffi-Girl." My mom calls me that. Only two other understandable words surfaced in her garbled message: Stepdad. Stroke.

Standing frozen in my kitchen in Upstate New York, I tried to make sense of those words. *My stepdad swims every day. He chops down trees and hauls them around. He grows his own vegetables and actually eats them. How could he have a stroke?*

My stepdad took Mom, my sister Missy, and me on our first camping trip, first canoe ride, and first hike. Growing up in a house full of women, Missy and I never quite knew what to make of our outdoorsy stepdad. He made us do fun things, despite our initial lack of enthusiasm. An ex-Marine, he ran on military time and believed that little princesses could be tough, too.

My stepdad taught my hardworking mother how to swim, love the ocean, and laugh.

He'd been part of our lives so long that it was now hard to remember what it was like before him.

Nobody answered when I called Mom back. I tried calling Roo, my stepsister who lives near them. No answer. I called my sister who lives closer to me. Missy had received a similar incoherent message on her machine. "Should we go?" she said.

"I don't know." I looked at my kids. How could I jump in the car and drive all the way to South Carolina?

"We have to go," Missy said.

I stood in the kitchen freaking out, talking to my sister on the landline and calling South Carolina on my cell. No one answered.

My husband said, "Don't worry about the kids. Go."

After a flurry of blind packing, hugging the kids, and repeated phone calls to South Carolina trying to reach someone, anyone, I hit the road. One state away, I picked up Missy, and we were off.

We drove through heavy traffic all day. We still couldn't reach anyone. We didn't even know what hospital to go to once we got there. Should we go straight to Mom's house? What then? Neither of us had a key, and no one was there anyway.

The stress brought on my migraines. I'd forgotten my meds. Missy had to drive through city after city while my head screamed with pain, and flashing lights sparkled in my vision. We stopped at an emergency room somewhere. It was the lone doctor's last day, and there was cake. He leaned across me to talk to Missy, my cute little sister. He accidentally elbowed me in the head while offering her a slice of cake. It was nothing compared to migraine pain, but it ticked me off.

It reminded me so much of high school.

Back in the car with migraine meds that didn't help, I kept giving Missy the "stink eye."

"What? I didn't do anything!" she said.

It was true, but still...

I squinted at my phone and plugged the adapter into the car cigarette lighter — this was an early cell phone with no speed dial or redial capacity. I again entered my stepsister's number into it despite the sparkling lights in my vision. I knew everyone would be at some hospital together. They all live on the border of North and South

Carolina. If I couldn't reach someone, we'd have to search hospitals in both states.

We were both tired and scared, and I knew Missy was mad at me for being mad at her about the flirty doctor.

With my phone pressed to my ear, I listened to it ringing and ringing, refusing to give up because we were almost to the border of both states. To my surprise, someone finally picked up.

"Hello?" I didn't recognize the female voice.

"I'm sorry. I think I have the wrong number." I don't know why I kept right on talking. Maybe it was the friendly Southern accent. Maybe it was because someone finally answered the phone. "I'm trying to find my stepsister. My stepdad had a stroke, and I can't reach anyone."

"Who's your stepsister?" the friendly voice asked.

"Uh, Roo. Roo O'Leary."

"Who's your stepdad?"

I didn't even pause to wonder why she was asking. Someone with a South Carolina accent had answered. Someone who helped. "Ed. Ed O'Leary. I don't even know what hospital he's in."

"What's your name?"

"Saffi. My name's Saffi. My mom has been married to Ed since I was a kid. He took us camping." I was really babbling. "He's... he's like a dad to me." I couldn't go on without sobbing, so I stopped.

"Saffi, I'm a nurse at Health South. I work in the stroke unit. I'm standing in your stepdad's room right now. Roo and your mom are here, too. You called my cell phone."

I tried to process this information. *I misdialed Roo's number and got a nurse at the very hospital where my stepdad is? She's standing in his room right now? With my mom and Roo? How is that possible?* The throbbing in my head dimmed.

"We don't allow visitors to have their cell phones on in here, but would you like to talk to Roo on mine?"

"Yes! Yes, please!"

Roo came on the line.

"Saffi?" She had the accent, too. I started to cry. "How did you know the nurse's phone number?"

— S.R. Karfelt —

43

Laurie and the Yellow Curtains

Life is magical, and the synchronicities continue
to fill me with wonder every day!
~Anita Moorjani

My greatest fear as a child was going to the dentist. Dr. Watkins was a stickler for cleanliness. He kept an office that was painted white and furnished with stiff furniture and smelled of antiseptic. To say that it was devoid of warmth and character would be an understatement, and there were certainly no toys or a play area for children like there are nowadays. This may have contributed to my complete dread of my annual dental visit.

But every summer, without fail, my grandmother had the task of escorting me onto the bus in Ottawa so we could head down to Metcalfe Street to see my dentist. If I was lucky, I escaped without a cavity and a dreaded second visit.

The only consolation was that if I survived the dentist appointment my grandmother would take me to Zellers department store to buy a treat. Sometimes, it was a new Barbie outfit. Sometimes, it was a new box of Crayola crayons and a colouring book. But, on this day in 1965, it would be a new Easy Reader book by Sara Asheron called *Laurie and the Yellow Curtains*.

I had just started learning how to read, and this book with a young girl on the cover smiling through a window adorned with yellow curtains fascinated me.

I grew up an only child with both my parents and my paternal grandparents in the home. This arrangement helped us pay the rent in a small, three-bedroom duplex in a humble neighborhood called Hintonburg.

To refer to my room as a bedroom is a bit misleading. The room was the size of a closet. I had a bunkbed so I could reach the window by climbing onto the top bunk. There was also a small dresser, but there was no closet and no door. I had a curtain that pulled across for what little privacy I needed.

We weren't unlike our neighbours, all of whom were working-class people with a modest lifestyle. Some homes housed twelve kids or more, and most people were lucky to own one family vehicle. This was a place where children played in the streets until the streetlights turned on and where few people felt the need to lock their doors. We didn't consider ourselves poor, for we had food on the table and decent clothing to wear, but lavish vacations were for those who lived uptown.

As I settled myself onto the back porch to open my new book, the first image was of a beautiful treehouse with a yellow door and yellow curtains. I read about Laurie who lived not in the city, not in the country, but in between where it's just right.

Laurie lived in a very pretty house on River Road, and her good friend and neighbour, Mr. Bill, was a fix-it man. Laurie often accompanied Mr. Bill on his local jobs, which might seem rather odd to us nowadays. His first stop was to make a doghouse for Mrs. Brown's new dog. Laurie asked that he make a pretty doghouse with a yellow door and yellow curtains. However, much to Laurie's disappointment, he just made a cozy doghouse. Next was a henhouse and, as you can guess, Laurie requested a yellow door and yellow curtains. Then came the same refrain for a birdhouse. Clearly, Laurie thought a yellow door and yellow curtains were the epitome of prettiness, but she never got what she wanted from Mr. Bill.

One day, after Laurie had been away on a trip to the big city with her mother, she returned, and Mr. Bill revealed the project he'd been working on during her absence. He walked her into her own backyard and asked her to look up. There in the apple tree was a house with a little ladder. Mr. Bill had built her a beautiful treehouse with a yellow door and yellow curtains. The story ends with the line, "Everyone knows that a little girl needs a pretty house to play in!"

Boy, was I jealous of Laurie! I couldn't imagine having a little playhouse of my own.

Eventually, that book disappeared with the Barbie dolls and colouring books, but I never forgot it.

I loved reading, so much so that eventually I became an English teacher. After sharing my love for literature for three decades, I decided to retire. One of my many goals was to write. I started a novel and wrote a blog for a while, but one day I thought to myself, *Perhaps I should try my hand at writing a children's book.*

I thought back to *Laurie and the Yellow Curtains* and wondered what it was about that book that had captured my imagination so much that I would remember it more than fifty years later. I tried searching for it, but it was no longer in print, and its author had died in 2004. I contacted a couple of book collectors to no avail. Finally, I tried some online searches and landed on eBay. To my utter amazement, someone in Michigan was selling a used copy for a whopping $20 U.S. Regardless of the inflated price, I decided to order it.

Weeks went by before my purchase finally arrived. It was definitely old and used, and the 59 cents that it cost in 1965 was printed on the right upper corner. As I opened the cover, my stomach flipped. I stood there, stunned. Suddenly, tears welled up in my eyes. There on the inside cover, in a young girl's uncertain printing, was the name "Deborah." Even the corner that I had accidentally torn because of so much use was missing.

It was *my* book.

I have no idea how this book that journeyed from Canada to the U.S. found its way back to me, but I was so grateful for its return. The more I pondered this moment of serendipity, the more I came to believe that there was meaning in this, and I needed to determine just what it was.

Like Laurie, I'd always longed for a place of retreat, a small, cozy space where I could be alone with my thoughts, delve into my creative impulses, and pursue my dreams.

And so, this past summer, I fulfilled my young girl's dream of a space to call my own. My "treehouse," a shed that's been spruced up with paint and a comfy chair, sits next to my vegetable garden. It contains memorabilia, music and books, and a beautiful teal-coloured desk. It's where I am now as I write this story. And every time I pause, I look out the window, which is framed by the yellow curtains that move gently in the September breeze.

— Deborah Guilbeault —

Ten Long Weeks

The probability of a certain set of circumstances
coming together in a meaningful (or tragic)
way is so low that it simply cannot
be considered mere coincidence.

~V.C. King

en weeks might seem like an eternity when one is making a life-altering decision, but that's how long it would take for my students to be officially certified as foster parents. Many of the participants were already parents or grandparents, or community professionals of some sort. What could they possibly learn that they didn't already know?

It should be noted that the course is not for the faint of heart. Foster parenting can be extremely rewarding, but my students need to consider all the ramifications before they undertake such an emotional and difficult commitment.

As the weeks pass, the strangers in my classes become friends, and then allies, as they learn about the good, the bad and the ugly of what they can expect as foster parents. While some may already have children placed in their care under emergency circumstances, most do not.

During my time with one particular group, an unlikely alliance formed. Patty, a middle-aged and seemingly gruff woman, seemed to hit it off with a thirty-something, mild-mannered man named David and his significant other. They partnered up during many of the dreaded role-play exercises and team activities.

Finally, it was time for the last group exercise before the much-anticipated graduation ceremony and celebration. During this activity, students would go one by one around the room and talk about what they liked about the class, what surprised them about the class, and what they would change if they could.

As we worked our way around the table, all eyes were eventually on Patty. Not only did she not answer any of the questions, but she started out her message by telling a seemingly unrelated story about how events earlier in her life shaped her.

As a twenty-something living on a farm, Patty's life was difficult and often painful. During this trying period, Patty befriended a teenage boy who had undoubtedly been through some very rough times. His family situation was anything but ideal, and he was often sad, lonely and confused. The pair quickly formed a tight bond as she helped the young man navigate through his turbulent childhood and life in general. He looked up to her, and she greatly valued the bond they shared.

One day, however, the boy and his family abruptly moved away. Neither Patty nor David had any kind of say in the matter, and both were deeply hurt by it. They tried to maintain contact, but, as often happens, time and distance got in the way. They lost touch, and as Patty explained, she never heard from the boy again but thought about him often. She had often wondered what became of him.

At this point, Patty started to tear up as she got up from her seat. She reached into her purse and said, "It wasn't until tonight that I realized." She opened her wallet and took out a photo of the boy she had known so many years before. Staring intently at David, she handed him the photo. Everyone, including David, was confused at what was happening. Suddenly, David burst into tears.

"Oh, my God, it's *you*!" The two were now sobbing and embracing each other, stunned at the miraculous realization that fate had brought them back together all these years later.

By now, everyone else in the room figured out what was happening, and there wasn't a dry eye in the place. A miracle had just occurred, and we were all witness to it. Patty, David and their families vowed to never lose touch again.

I am a firm believer that when you do something for the good, you will be rewarded in ways unimagined. I went on to teach many more classes after that, but going forward, I always shared that story with my students as a testament to how extraordinary things can come out of difficult situations. Sometimes, ten long weeks is just the right amount of time to make a miracle happen.

— Kristen Schad —

The Power of a Wish

When you live with an open heart,
unexpected, joyful things happen.
~Oprah Winfrey

I t was autumn again in one of Pennsylvania's designated "Tree City USA" zip codes. From my front porch, I gazed with mixed feelings at the shafts of golden afternoon sunlight between the clusters of red, orange, and brown leaves still on the trees. There were already plenty in mounds on my lawn.

The beauty of the light and the earthy smells and colors warmed my soul. But it was time to move those piles of leaves off the lawn, which meant hours of hard labor for this seventy-four-year-old body.

Fortunately, our local taxes cover vacuuming our leaves from the curb so we didn't have to stuff them into bags. Unfortunately, it means we must get the leaves to the edge of our properties somehow, and my leaf blower had just died.

I tried to fix it myself. "Mom," my older son counseled when I asked him if he knew a repair person, "things aren't made like they used to be. Just buy a new one." *Easy for you to say, son. I'm the product of Depression-era parents who rarely threw anything away.* However, I found a similar model and ordered it from Walmart.

A week later, as I was raking leaves onto a tarp, I noticed a large box on the front porch. *Aha!* I thought with relief, assuming it was my new leaf blower. *This job will now be quickly finished!*

Much to my surprise, the box was not my new leaf blower but a

PAW Patrol Big Truck Pups Truck Stop playset for kids ages 3 and up.

I called Walmart and spoke to an agent. He promised to get back to me at a precise time two days later after he contacted the third-party seller that was supposed to send me the leaf blower but sent me the toy instead. That time came and went with no contact, but when I logged into my Walmart account the next day, I discovered that a credit had been issued for the full amount of the purchase, with no further explanation.

I went back on the Internet and discovered that a nearby True Value Hardware store had the same Toro leaf blower I wanted, for just a little more than what Walmart charged. I picked it up the next day and easily finished clearing the leaves off my lawn before the last scheduled leaf collection. Another problem solved.

But what to do with the PAW Patrol playset? One small blessing was that the agent also had said I didn't have to return the playset but could keep it or donate it. My nine-year-old grandson had long ago moved on to hand-held video games, and my four-year-old grand-daughter was into Disney princesses, not trucks. According to Amazon, the retail price was $99.99, which made it a very generous gift. What I needed was a suggestion and I prayed that one would be forthcoming.

As that big box continued taking up space in my bedroom, our church bulletin announced the annual Christmas giving programs. Each year, the holiday trees are decorated with specific "wish tags" from various organizations for parishioners to purchase gifts for those less fortunate. I always scanned the tags for something I could afford — often a gift card to a local retail or grocery store — and felt grateful to be able to share my blessings with others. As a single mother for many years, I know how hard Christmas can be for families.

At the end of Sunday's church service, I joined a small group of people studying the tags on the Christmas tree. There were requests for grocery-store cards, gas cards, dolls, games, and even clothing ("Philadelphia Eagles sweatshirt, size large"). As I searched for a gift wish that I could afford, I heard the man next to me say to his young son, "Let's put that PAW Patrol tag back and take this one instead." Maybe he'd already started his own Christmas shopping and knew those toys could be expensive.

Before his young son could argue, I overcame my shock and quickly said, "Did you say PAW Patrol? I'd be glad to take that one!" And, just like that, my dilemma of what to do with that big box was solved.

Now, I've always believed there are powers beyond what we mortals can understand. It wasn't the first time my prayers were answered in a way that appeared to be an unexplained coincidence. Even so, replacing the leaf blower I ordered with a truck playset was a rather complicated way to answer a child's wish for a PAW Patrol toy that Christmas. How did the angels manage to guide a little boy to pick the PAW Patrol tag off the tree? Or to direct his dad, standing next to me, to announce aloud his preference to trade that tag for a different one?

I hope the child who received my gift shared with siblings and friends both the playset and a belief that prayers are indeed answered. For me, it's just one more reason to believe in, and pray for, divine intervention.

— Judy Bailey Sennett —

46

The Rich Uncle in Orlando

And, when you want something, all the universe
conspires in helping you to achieve it.
~Paulo Coelho, The Alchemist

W e lived about thirty miles north of Jacksonville, Florida on an acre of land. One day, we made the difficult decision to move back to our hometown. My husband wanted to switch from his full-time Air National Guard position to a part-time weekend warrior until retirement in five years. He had a job already waiting for him in Orlando as an assistant manager of a steakhouse. So, we planned to move at the beginning of March.

I hated leaving and going back to a now-unfamiliar place. What would we find there? Would we be happy with our decision?

One day, as I mulled over these fears, I looked up at the eaves and saw the gutters clogged with pine needles and leaves from the tall pine trees around our home. Climbing a wobbly ladder to get to work, I viewed someone steering his busted-up banana bike down our long, dirt driveway.

"Hi!" yelled Terry, flashing a semi-toothless grin as he pulled up and stopped.

"Well, hello, Terry! It's great to see you," I replied. "I'd invite you in, but I'm too busy right now." I continued to pull out the pine needles and toss them to the ground.

Terry parked his bike and got even closer to where I worked. When he got closer, he smiled. "Miss Laura, I have a question for you."

"You do? What is it?" I rubbed my hands together to get off the dirt.

"Aren't y'all moving to Orlando?"

"Yes. In a few more days, we are. It's a town just outside Orlando called Oviedo."

"Wow! That's where my rich uncle lives! And it's in a real big house!"

"Your uncle? I didn't know you had an uncle."

"Yeah, I do. In Winter Springs."

"That's not where we are going. It's the next town over."

"But he's near it."

"Right. So what?"

"So, when you see him, I want you to do me a favor."

"A favor?"

"Yes. Say 'hello' to him for me."

"What? I don't even know where your uncle lives, and I doubt I will ever meet him. Central Florida is a huge place. Millions of people."

"Yeah, but you'll see him. I know you will."

"Okay, okay, I promise to say 'hello' to him when I do. Does that make you happy?"

He smiled and said, "Thanks, ma'am! I knew you would."

"Of course."

And with that last comment, he climbed back on his bike and left.

At the dinner table that night, I told Bob, and he just shook his head.

"Those Jernigans are always cooking up something goofy! I wouldn't believe a word he said."

"I agree," I replied, and I forgot the whole incident.

A week later, we arrived in Oviedo and moved into a tiny, rented house. One of the first things we did the next day, after we had semi-unpacked, was to look up a church in the phone book.

The closest one we thought we would like was in Winter Park, which was on the opposite side of Oviedo from Winter Springs where Terry said his "rich uncle" lived. We decided to go to a midweek service to try out the church.

Our first day there, we entered the front door of the small auditorium and found a small group of about fifty people. We sat through the service, and the pastor introduced us as a family who had just moved from northeast Florida.

After church, an older man came up to us and smiled. "Glad to have you folks visiting our church. Where did you say you were from?"

"A place between Yulee and Fernandina Beach called Nassauville."

His ears perked up. "Well, you know, that's funny."

"Why?" I asked.

"I'm from there, and I have three nephews who still live there."

Suddenly, I remembered my encounter with Terry.

"Are you 'the rich uncle that lives in the big house in Orlando'?"

He laughed. "Well, they call me that, but I'm not really that rich. We have a nice house, but we worked very hard for it and are still working hard. By the way, my name is Stan Walker." He put out his hand, and we both shook it.

I stood there in shock. "You must be kidding! You're the uncle of Terry Jernigan?"

"Yes, in fact, I am. It's a pleasure to meet both of you. And I see you have two sons. I have two sons also. Maybe they can come over sometime."

And they did and became close friends with his two. What a strange coincidence. It made our return trip so much more bearable and fortified us for the challenges that lay ahead.

— Laura Bentz —

47

Christmas "Myrakle"

A moment spent with a cat is a moment
immersed in pure bliss.
~Author Unknown

It was Christmastime, and my husband and I drove twenty-five miles to Eugene, Oregon to find a new brand of kitty litter for our two cats. We had twelve pet stores to choose from and randomly headed to one of them.

The kitty-litter aisle was forty feet long, making any choice complicated. We did not want pine litter, as it is hard on the cats' and my breathing. We had tried the newspaper brands, and crushed walnuts were not to our liking. We were not sold on the clumping brands because if they attached to our Persians' long fur, when they groomed we wondered if the litter would clump in their digestive tracts.

We read bag after bag of clay and crystal litters trying to find the right fit.

When people pushed their grocery carts up to the litter section, I approached them and interviewed them about their choice. "Have you used this brand long? Does it hold odor? How often do you change it? Do you have long- or short-haired cats?" Everyone smiled and graciously answered our questions.

Then, a beautiful, blue-eyed woman with shoulder-length white hair, reminiscent of a white Persian cat, tossed a bag of litter into her cart. She told me she had two short-haired cats and I said, "Oh, you look like someone who would have Persians."

She stopped, caught her breath and quietly said, "We did have two. We loved them. But Myrakle died a year ago."

I intuitively knew the answer to my next questions before asking them and started crying.

Tearfully, I choked out, "Was she a rescue cat? Was she orange and black? Was her full name Ms. Myrakle?"

"Yes," she said.

I was stunned! What were the odds?

"Four years earlier, we had fostered an abused, elderly cat for the Humane Society," I said. "We named her Ms. Myrakle."

It had taken us three days to gently clip off all her tangled fur, which was so bad that she couldn't even move her back left leg to its full extension until we removed the last bit of balled up fur. She was the sweetest cat and seemed genuinely grateful for our care. She never fought with our cats and accepted my daughter's two dogs, too.

Sadly, we had to give her back to the shelter when I had surgery. It was a tearful goodbye. We often wondered what happened to her, even after all these years. Just that morning, I had been reminiscing about her.

The woman, Linda, started crying. She recounted her life with Ms. Myrakle. "Four years ago, I told my husband, Gene, that I wanted a cat for my birthday. We saw Ms. Myrakle on the shelter's website. Persians have lovely personalities and we liked how her name was spelled, so we went right over and adopted her. She was elderly and had only a few teeth, so we knew she would be a challenge. Gene would get down on the floor and hand-feed her soft foods like you wrote about in her introductory letter. We both loved her.

"We live close to this store. I never come in on a busy weekend. I have no idea why I came in today. While driving here, I was feeling sad because it has been a year this week since Myrakle's passing from old age. I miss her and our other cat. They both died the same week but a year apart."

Linda and I felt that Ms. Myrakle's love brought us together to assuage our grief and thank us for the gift of loving her. We discussed how she had come from a toss-away breeder after "no longer being of use" and that she was thanking us for her last years of love, comfort and grace.

As soon as Linda arrived home, she told her husband, "I had the most amazing thing happen at the pet store."

He said, "Oh, no!" He began looking around for a newly adopted pet. She laughed and told him that it was "someone" she had miraculously met.

Linda and I are now good friends, united by a cat in heaven.

— Mary Ellen Angelscribe —

48

The Book

Remember there's no such thing as a small act
of kindness. Every act creates a ripple
with no logical end.
~Scott Adams

On an ordinary Saturday, we were driving home after a picnic in the mountains. Our oldest boy was going through a phase of wanting to spend all his money. We had tried multiple ways to teach him financial responsibility, but they had all failed. So, we had decided the night before to let him spend everything he had.

We were about five minutes from home when we saw signs for an estate sale. Our son begged us to stop so he could buy something. My husband and I gave each other "the look." We didn't want to stop, but we had agreed to let him burn through all his money to teach him a lesson.

Normally, I hate going to estate sales. It always breaks my heart seeing strangers pick through the fragments and memories of someone's life. But in this case the house was amazing. Someone had spent a lifetime utilizing their building talents to make such a special place.

The owner had loved to read, too. There were floor-to-ceiling books everywhere. I glanced at a few, but given that they were not my genre, I did not spend a great deal of time looking at them.

Following our son around, I entered another room that was also filled with books. There were books behind a door, ceiling to floor.

When I moved the door, I spotted a small book. There was nothing flashy about it. It was just a small, thin, dark-blue book. I have no idea why I pulled it out from the pile.

The front of the book struck me. It said it was about how God made the mountains and the rivers, and he took the time to make us. It moved me, so I opened the book. On the inside was a long and very personal inscription. Seeing how personal it was, I didn't read it, but I looked at the signature on the bottom. I thought I recognized it.

Ten years earlier, I had worked with a wonderful woman who was also my doula. Since then, she'd gone through a horrible family tragedy, and I believed she moved several states away. I couldn't believe that it was her signature after all those years, but I bought the book just in case.

Once I got home, I reached out to her through Facebook. I figured it was a long shot, but I just had a feeling. It turned out it was her signature! And the woman who had passed, the woman whose memorial was occurring at the same time as I was finding the book at the estate sale, was one of her closest friends. It also happened to be a memorial that my friend was unable to attend, and her heart was broken because she couldn't go to say goodbye.

She had given the book to her friend as a thank-you for keeping her on track with God. The book had meant so much to her that she had even taken a picture of it to remember it.

She was overwhelmed that the book had found its way back to her. She came by when she was in the area and picked it up. Through tears and stories of her friend, we reconnected, and she was able to spend time with us. She is going through her own story of tragedy right now, and, although I can't speak for her, I would like to think her late friend got this book back to her because she wanted to say goodbye and remind her to stay on track.

— Karleen Forwell —

49

Flight Home

Where there is great love, there are always miracles.
~Willa Cather

When I met my husband, it was his aviation-loving grandfather who first captured a place in my heart. Soon after Travis and I began dating, we'd visited the quiet street in the central Pennsylvania town where James "CWO Jim" Shilling spent most of his life. Nestled in the Kishacoquillas Valley, Reedsville was abundant in cornfields, churches and Amish markets. As we drove through long, winding roads surrounded by rolling mountains, we passed horse-drawn buggies that were evidence of a simpler life.

I was immediately drawn to the gentle soul behind the soft grin and hearty laugh. He had the same deep-rooted family values that my own grandfather possessed, whose passing five years earlier had left a deep void. The striking similarities between the two didn't end there. They had in common beautiful love stories tragically cut short by cancer.

When I entered his charming house, I could see expressions of that love covering every wall. I remembered the sorrow my own grandfather had experienced when my grandmother passed away, the deep sadness of losing precious retirement years together.

Travis's "Pap" spoke of his beloved Mae as I gazed at her photos. They grew up in the same small town and attended the same school. He played the baritone horn, and she was a majorette. A band trip took them to an amusement park where they rode rides together and were inseparable from that point on.

"She's gone home," he told me with a quiet sadness. "When the time is right, I'll join her up there above the clouds."

Walking around his cozy house, it was clear there was a second love in his life. Airplane photography graced almost as many walls as Mae. Pap had a love of piloting and a deep admiration for the impressive flying machines that allowed it.

He recalled in detail the specifications of each and every aircraft. His face took on a radiant glow when he spoke of a memorable flight he piloted from Florida to Cuba in 1949. He was engaged to Mae and working his dream job flying a brand-new, state-of-the-art Ercoupe. The model, designed to be the safest fixed-wing aircraft that aerospace engineering allowed at the time, had just recently debuted.

He flew this cherished plane to an air show in Miami where he and several other young pilots were invited to Havana. Pap lit up as he described how the Coast Guard formed a pathway with ships to create a flight path for them into Cuban airspace.

A few years later, he was called up for the Korean War, and he and Mae moved from Pennsylvania to Grenier Air Force Base in New Hampshire and later to Dow Air Force Base in Maine. The Ercoupe was gone by the time they returned to Reedsville years later to raise their family. He was disappointed to learn it had been sold and moved to another airport across the country. Pap had an impressive military career serving in the Army Air Corps, but he recalled that first job at Mifflin County airport flying the magnificent Ercoupe with a distinct fondness.

Over the years, I treasured our friendship and chats on his porch. My job required frequent travel, and Pap was always interested in not only the kinds of planes I took but my adventures in each city.

I made a habit of calling his cellphone from each airport as I waited for my flight. Most days, he answered from the Mifflin County airport where he gathered each morning with fellow retired pilots to share coffee and aviation memories.

As Travis and I started our own family, my travels slowed, but my phone calls with Pap continued and often centered on his great-grandsons, Kyle James (named for him) and Tyler. We incorporated airplane decor into their bedrooms in his honor.

As Pap entered his nineties, he was in congestive heart failure, and his health and ability to live an independent life quickly dwindled. When driving and walking became more difficult, his daily airport breakfasts became few and far between. At one of those breakfasts, though, something extraordinary happened.

A well-dressed man weaved his way through the crowd, clutching a piece of paper and asked each retiree an urgent question. Finally, one pointed toward Pap with a look of shock. "That's who piloted that plane, that's who you're looking for: James Shilling, CWO Jim."

Pap's friend said, "Jim! You're not going to believe this." He shook his head in astonishment. "This man just flew here… with your old plane."

The man was a college professor from across the country when he purchased and restored an Ercoupe from the 1940s. After relocating to nearby Penn State University, he was disappointed to learn his new collegiate airport didn't have an open hangar, and he was temporarily redirected to Mifflin County. When he registered the plane at Mifflin that morning, he was stunned to learn that his aircraft had originated there.

James Shilling's favorite plane from a nostalgic time in his life had returned to him nearly seventy years later. Travis and I had a hectic schedule with our busy boys in suburban Philadelphia that weekend, but we both knew there was no question we'd make the four-hour drive to central Pennsylvania. I soaked in every detail of Pap's story that day.

As we loaded the car to return home, I ran back to give him one more hug. "Jenny, when are you going to write my story?" he said with his hearty laugh. "It'll be a bestseller."

Pap's death a few weeks later was a long-awaited homecoming with his beloved Mae. Each time we hear the distant roar of a plane in the sky, I imagine them flying together high above the clouds just as he said they would be.

One of his treasured airplane pictures hangs in our family room to remind us of a beautiful love story and an Ercoupe's miraculous flight home.

—Jennifer Kennedy—

50

Heaven's High Five in a Hotrod

*Blessed are they who see beautiful things in humble
places where other people see nothing.*
~Camille Pissarro

I have a quirky habit that I never told anyone about; I read license plates hoping to see signs from the universe. Whenever I spot a license plate with "my" numbers, or my initials, or any other meaningful wording, I imagine it's a sign from heaven supporting me. Sending me love.

I never told anyone about my highway habit. One reason is superstition of the same sort that keeps us from telling our birthday wishes out loud before blowing out birthday candles; if we do, they may not come true. But the main reason I never told anyone is because I'm a lawyer, and lawyers are supposed to be super rational. Like Sgt. Joe Friday's famous phrase on the vintage TV show *Dragnet*, we're supposed to think on the straight and narrow: "Just the facts, ma'am. Just the facts."

Heck, even I thought it was a bit woo-woo to think that a car could be my personal heavenly message service. I don't need a lawyer's mind to know that mere coincidence, and not the synchronicity I long for, might be afoot.

But just as there are no atheists in foxholes, my recent traumatic diagnosis of breast cancer and the long series of treatments that followed left me grappling with the fear that the surgery, chemo, and radiation hadn't gotten it all. This fear keeps me on high alert for any kind of sign from above that I'm going to be okay. If it comes from a dancing spoon, a flying pony, or a talking tree, I'll entertain the idea that it's a "high five" from heaven, my longed-for sign. That, or a sign that I need serious meds.

The sign came on one of those spectacular, sparkling days in early June where the green on trees is still tender, the flowers are fully feathered, and nothing on the edges of things has turned brown. One of those gift days, the kind I often joked about wanting to bottle and sell.

My husband and I were driving to an evening wedding a few hours away from our home. We were making such good time on the way to our hotel that we decided to take a detour to a mall that was famous for unique boutiques in addition to several high-end department stores.

When we veered off the main highway, we both spontaneously rolled down our windows and breathed in the clear, crisp air. I reached up, opened the sunroof, and unveiled a high, light blue arc of universe. What a joy to be alive!

Having a life-threatening diagnosis had its perks. I learned to savor, cherish, and be more fully present in the moments of my life. Even the little ones like driving down a road on a gorgeous summer day. But even though I was learning to be more fully present, more skilled at savoring, I could never quite shake the gnawing fear I carried that clawed at me. Did they get it all? Was I going to be okay?

As we continued down the highway, I saw in the distance the massive mall on a hill on the righthand side of the road. As we were about to veer off to the right toward it, a beautiful, elegant, silver hotrod convertible with the top down zipped by us to our left. The license plate read, in capital letters, "BLESSED."

My first reaction was astonishment and something akin to bliss. *That's my sign! My sign that I'm going to be okay!*

But Sgt. Joe Friday quickly got a chokehold on me, as did my inner cynic, and the two of them boxed that thought right out of the ring. *Come on! Enough of this signs and symbols from the universe nonsense. This license plate has nothing to do with you. Some guy in an orange jumpsuit sent it.*

All this mean-spirited inner chatter burst my happy bubble. I comforted myself by thinking that even if the license plate weren't a sign meant for me, the owner was sending out good vibes in the world with thoughts of gratitude. And that was a good, positive thing.

My husband turned off to the right toward the mall, and the beautiful, elegant, silver hotrod convertible with the top down zoomed off in the opposite direction to the left, down the highway and out of sight.

We drove up the ramp and entered the mall parking lot, which was huge. It must have been a very popular mall because the macadam practically disappeared under the sea of cars. Acres and acres of cars. We drove around looking for a place to park and luckily, after a short search, we found a spot.

We walked around window-shopping for about an hour or so, then decided to hijack a little more time for a quick latte in an elegant coffee shop. We grabbed seats by a big picture window that opened out onto the mall. A few feet away was a fancy, antique, Viennese carousel. Sipping our frothy lattes, we watched gleeful children riding the colorful, hand-painted horses. Round and round. Lots of ups and downs. One couldn't find a better metaphor for life. I thought of my roomie from college, how her son was getting married, and how unbelievable it was that time had passed to get us all to this point in our lives.

We gave ourselves a five-minute warning to gather our things and get going to our hotel. We still had plenty of time before the wedding, but the way the parking lot had been crammed so full we were nervous it might take a while to find our car.

We retraced our steps on the polished marble floors until we arrived at our exit point to the parking lot. Funny enough, when our eyes panned over the lot to look for our car we had no problem finding it. The blacktop was practically empty, save for a handful of cars randomly parked here and there. Where our car was parked, though, was virtually abandoned, except for one other car that was parked nose-to-nose with ours. I smiled to myself, for I had the impression that the cars were kissing.

And then I had a shocking realization. On that summer afternoon in June, before the wedding of my college roomie's son, I finally received the proof I needed. Lawyer-like proof. Proof beyond a reasonable doubt. The car kissing ours was a beautiful, elegant, silver hotrod convertible with the top down. Its license plate? "BLESSED."

— Diane Young Uniman —

51

The Miracle Gift from Heaven

Never. We never lose our loved ones. They accompany
us; they don't disappear from our lives.
We are merely in different rooms.
~Paulo Coelho

It was September 2023, and I was on the sideline watching my daughter's high-school soccer game in Madison, Connecticut when I saw a mom whom I had met before but whose name I had forgotten. I went over to reintroduce myself, and we started chatting. She reminded me that her name was Maureen (Mo). She mentioned that she was getting ready to bring her other daughter to college for her freshman year. I remarked how late it was for a college drop-off and asked where she would be attending. Maureen said she was going to Cal Poly and that they used to live in California until moving to Connecticut in 2014 to be near her mom.

I said, "Oh, my cousin Julianne's son is going there as a freshman, too. They live in Santa Cruz."

Maureen said that's where they used to live. I thought, *Small world.* I told her that my cousin had been a single mom of two sons since her husband Tim died suddenly sixteen years before from a brain aneurysm. It happened just two weeks after she had given birth to their second son, Thomas, and while their elder son, Harrison, was two years old.

At that, Maureen said, "I think I know your cousin. That story is familiar. I think we were in a playgroup together with the kids. If it's the same person, my husband did some work on her house after her husband died, and she gave him her husband's surfboard. In fact, I was just asking my husband two weeks ago to remind me where we had gotten that surfboard from, and he reminded me it had been from a lady I had known in California."

It was a warm September morning, but Maureen and I had chills all over.

I immediately texted my cousin Julianne but it was just 7:45 AM her time on a Saturday, so I wasn't sure how long I would have to wait to hear back. Fifteen minutes later, she texted back that she did remember Mo and that she had given her Tim's surfboard. She said she wasn't thinking in those early days after he passed because they were dark days for her. She wished she had hung onto his surfboard because now her younger son was surfing.

I immediately went back to Maureen to tell her it was indeed my cousin whom she had known all those years ago in those mommy-and-me playgroups on the other side of the country in California. With tears in my eyes, I said, "Maureen, I think I'm supposed to return that surfboard to my cousin. I think that's the reason for this conversation."

She said, "Yes, I think you are."

And, just like that, a seemingly random conversation in a small town in Connecticut turned out to be a divine intervention. There were so many things that had to happen for this to come together. If I hadn't forgotten Maureen's name, if it hadn't been the weekend before she was bringing her daughter to college, if neither of us had moved to Madison (us from New York State in 2017), if she hadn't just talked to her husband about the surfboard, and countless other events, this discovery would never have happened. Then, of course, there is the fact that she still had this surfboard sixteen years later!

It was beyond "small world." This was just too much to be random. I believe Tim was letting his family know, as his son was preparing to go off to college, that he's very much still with them and part of their journey in surfing life's waves.

As if the story wasn't amazing enough, when my husband went to ship the surfboard, he found out it was going to cost $360. But when the UPS franchise owner heard the story, he loved it so much that he offered to ship it all the way to California for free, even ordering a special box for it. The surfboard traveled again across the country and arrived safely back home in Santa Cruz on October 6, 2023, to its original family in California, where it was greeted with tears and amazement.

— Erin Pfeifer-Andrin —

Chapter
6

Messages from Heaven

52

Dad and Beyond

No one in this world can love a girl
more than her father.
~Michael Ratnadeepak

M y father and I were always close. Almost all the photos of me as a young child are with my father. When I was growing up, my dad always had time to talk, go for a coffee, or take a walk. He took me to college every year, helped me move into my first apartment, and was always available to talk on the phone when I felt low.

Family members always said that we had similar personalities. But there was one area where we diverged. My father was a chemistry professor who was highly skeptical of anything "supernatural." He didn't believe in ghosts or life after death, whereas I was uncertain.

Several years ago, physicians diagnosed my father with stage 4 lung cancer. Terminal. Although he had never smoked, he was dying from a terrible disease. He lived for four more years. One night, he called and requested that I come as soon as possible. I got on the next flight. He lived one week longer, and I sat by his bed talking to him every day.

"Dad, do you believe there's something after this life?" I asked gently.

"No, sweetie, I don't. You know that," he said.

"Dad, I think you're wrong. I think you'll see that."

"I suppose," he said with tears in his eyes.

The day he died, I went to the top of a bluff and looked out over the ocean. Although I was alone, I had the uncanny feeling he was present.

A few days later, I went for a run. I ran a route that ended with a steep hill, which I always disliked. As I approached it, I clearly heard my father's voice say, "Annie, let's go!"

Surprised, I bounded up the hill.

When I thought about it later, I reasoned it was just my imagination. I missed my dad, and the little girl in me wanted to hear his voice.

Many months later, the dining room lights in my home began going on and off repeatedly during a family meal. I turned them off completely, but they continued to flash. It was unsettling, and I had the strange feeling my father was involved.

I shouted, "Dad, please stop!"

The lights stopped.

Several months later, I was traveling for business, and I ended up near a New Age bookstore. I had a couple of hours to kill, so I entered the store. In the entryway, there was a sign, "Psychic Readings in Back." I was skeptical but intrigued. The "psychic" sported a mustache and a ratty sweater.

Well, twenty dollars isn't so bad. I guess it's just entertainment, I thought.

When I sat down, he paused and said, "You have a male energy around you. It's your father."

"Really?"

"Yeah, he's gone to the other side."

"That's true," I said.

"But he's with you."

There was a brief silence.

He looked at me directly and then he said something that left me completely dumbfounded: "He'd like to apologize for the lights."

— Anne E. Beall —

53

The Puzzle Piece of Love

Once a brother, always a brother,
no matter the distance, no matter
the difference and no matter the issue.
~Byron Pulsifer

My brother died suddenly and peacefully in his sleep at age seventy-one on a cold December morning. He was five years older than me and always my big brother. My tears washed away the candlelight of our menorah.

The first memory I have of Jon was when I hurt my finger and he washed it with soap and water, circled a bandage around my tiny thumb, and held my hand in his. Over six more decades, he would always watch out for me even from too far away for bandages and tenderness.

The day after he passed away I had already scheduled a massage for self-care. I was going to cancel it but knew I needed it, then more than ever. There were no words, but touch might soothe my soul.

I did share with the massage therapist that the loss was like a puzzle piece had been taken away. And that space left me feeling that I was walking with my slippers on the wrong feet. She was gentle and reassuring and I was comforted by her touch. I was glad I hadn't canceled.

The next day I awoke to her text. She had a small gift for me and wondered if I could stop by. When I did, she invited me into her warm office that always smelled of lavender. She said, "I have a story to tell."

After our massage she had felt the sadness of my new loss, imagining the pain we all feel when we lose a "puzzle piece" of pure love. She wondered where she could find a tiny puzzle piece to remind me a brother's love never dies. That evening was cold and windy and she decided to stop at an old friend's home for warmth. Her friend welcomed her with a hug, and shared how proud she was that after many weeks she had completed a large, complicated wooden jigsaw puzzle!

When my massage therapist looked at her friend's puzzle she noticed one small piece resting near an open space in the center.

"Why don't you put that last piece in?" she asked.

"Oh, it doesn't fit," said her friend. "It actually doesn't belong to this puzzle; it was in the box but it isn't mine."

"I know whom it belongs to," said my therapist with a smile.

She knew that puzzle piece would become mine. It was Jon's final gift from wherever he has traveled. It rests deep in the pocket of my heavy winter coat that wraps me like a blanket, like my brother's love.

— Priscilla Dann-Courtney —

54

I Don't Believe in Signs

Hope is faith holding out its hand in the dark.
~George Iles

Fifteen months after my husband Dan died, I was just starting to get my feet under me. Maybe my eight-year-old daughter and I would survive this, I told myself.

My landlord called me while I was in the middle of the grocery store. I wish I hadn't answered that call, but I did. She informed me that they would be selling my house, and I had ninety days to move out.

I had just lost my husband and now, without any choice or control, I was losing my house. The house I loved. The house where our best memories were. The house where our daughter had said goodnight to her daddy for the last time.

"I'll buy it!" I said. "I'll buy it right now!" I couldn't fathom leaving.

She told me the selling price. How I didn't fall on the floor right then is beyond me. Maybe it was because I was holding onto the cart. Housing prices in my area were skyrocketing, and there was no way I could afford it.

I had to get out. I had no choice. I had to pack up all our things, including Dan's things. I had to decide which of his things I was going to keep. It was something I wasn't ready to do but I wasn't on my schedule anymore.

We moved in with Dan's parents while I looked for a new home. I was determined to buy in the same area so that our daughter wouldn't have to switch schools. With the housing market as it was and my meager budget, this seemed an impossible task.

I connected with a real estate agent who told me it couldn't be done, that a house in that area at that price didn't exist. Nevertheless, she understood my circumstances and said she would help. My friends and family said that finding that real estate agent was a sign from Dan that it would be alright. I told them I didn't believe in signs.

We looked at houses. They were all too much or in the wrong area. We explored ideas. Maybe I could get a roommate. Maybe I could convince the school to let her stay, even though we didn't live there anymore. Neither of those were good options. Maybe we would just live with my in-laws forever. That probably wasn't feasible either.

One day, my real estate agent sent me an e-mail with a house listing. It was the ugliest house I had ever seen in my life. I didn't want to live there. "You can afford it," she said. "Just drive by it and peek in the windows." I told her I would, just to humor her. I drove to the house. I peeked in the windows. I looked at the yard. It confirmed my suspicions: It was the ugliest house I had ever seen, and I didn't want to live there.

A few days later, she had me meet her there so I could see the inside. She insisted, but I had already made up my mind that I didn't want to buy this house. We walked through it, and I was unimpressed. She tried to make it appealing. "You can put in new carpet. This is all just paint! It just needs a little elbow grease. Well, okay, there are some major things that need fixing, but it can all be fixed."

I wasn't convinced, although it was in the perfect location, and it looked like a nice neighborhood. She said, "This is the only house you can possibly afford in this area. Besides, it's a sign." She pointed up at something. I groaned.

"I don't believe in signs," I said. Then, I proceeded to buy the ugliest house I had ever seen.

We continued to live with my in-laws as I fixed up our ugly new house. I did everything I could by myself or with the help of friends and family. I ripped up the nasty, stained carpet and found hardwood floors underneath. My dad and I tore down the old, rotting deck. My sister-in-law helped me tear down the wood paneling from the 1970s. Underneath it was another layer of wood paneling. We painted and cleaned everything. I hired people to put on a new roof, install a new septic tank, and fix the broken plumbing.

One year later, it is no longer an ugly house. It has turned into a lovely home, one where a young widow and her daughter can try to rebuild their lives. It is a life without Dan, but it can still be good. It is a home where all the neighbors look out for us. Almost every day, when my daughter gets home from school, she drops off her backpack and runs across the street to her best friend's house — a friend we didn't know existed until we moved into this house.

Every time I open my front door or look out my living room window, I see the sign the real estate agent was pointing to. It's literally a street sign. We live on the corner of Dans Avenue.

— Jennifer Stults —

55

Ciao Bella

*While we are sleeping, angels have
conversations with our souls.*
~Author Unknown

s a Life Enrichment Director, my job was to introduce residents to their new assisted living home and
engage them in activities to improve their quality of
life. Understandably, adjusting to unfamiliar surroundings and new faces is difficult for most of them… but it was easy for
Theresa.

When I first met Theresa, she pointed out her uncontrollable
tremors and apologized beforehand for her messy table manners. "God's
been good to me," she added with a smile.

Often, I heard Theresa fill conversations with stories of her long-lost
loves: a devoted husband of fifty years and a young son who passed
away too soon. Though no one appeared interested, she would go on
as if she were telling a fairytale.

"Oh, I'm not so much," Theresa said. "I wish you could have
known my husband, Renzo." I thought I had heard all I could about
her husband, but she talked as I polished her fingernails a warm pink,
and I listened.

Theresa's cheeks blushed as she recalled the "firsts" that most
couples share, like a first walkabout under the stars, a movie, a dance,
and their first kiss. "He proposed marriage on my twentieth birthday."

For the next year, I made sure Theresa attended every possible outing and activity. One Thursday morning, Theresa, a devout Catholic, was absent from Mass. I went to her room and found her still lying in bed. "Are you going to Mass today?"

Theresa gave me an engaging grin and begged me to come closer. Patting my cheek with her hand, she said softly, "I'm sorry, Bella, but I can't go. I'll be leaving soon."

"Where to?"

"Heaven," she answered. "Last night, my Renzo came to me in a dream and promised to come back for me."

I found this hard to believe because she had been to exercise and Bunco the day before and she seemed fine. "Maybe you're a bit tired," I said, leaving her to rest.

The following day, Theresa remained in bed, lighthearted and carefree, clinging to the notion that her beloved Renzo would be returning soon. Somewhat alarmed, I requested that the visiting priest come by and give the anointing for the sick. Afterward, I pulled her covers just below her chin to say goodnight. Theresa patted my face again and whispered, "Ciao, Bella. I must go now."

I smiled, believing I would see her the next morning. "Tomorrow will be a new day. You'll see!" I told her.

Theresa died that night. I had truly not expected that. But she had been so certain. There had been no doubt in her mind that her devoted Renzo, who vowed never to leave her behind, would come back for her as promised.

— Cindy Horgash —

56

The Pigeon

A man's daughter is his heart. Just with feet,
walking out in the world.
~Mat Johnson

I walked numbly outside into the warm August air. The construction was underway across the street from us for the Marshall County Blueberry Festival, held every Labor Day Weekend. It was a reminder that the rest of the world was going on, even though time had seemed to stop for my family when my father took his last breath.

"Please, God," I prayed silently, "give me the peace to know that he made it up there okay and is finally free of the pain he has endured. Can he see everything that's going on with us down here? We would sure be disappointed if he had to miss it."

The wounds I had sustained from the loss of my father remained as fresh as the soil that had been placed atop his recently created gravesite. Just under two weeks had passed since the afternoon that his stage 4 small-cell non-Hodgkin's lymphoma had robbed him of his ability to breathe. He received a formal diagnosis from the emergency-room staff at our local hospital in May of that year, although a summer of appointments with his oncologist and chemotherapy treatments did little to rid his body of the disease.

To anyone living within 50 to 100 miles of Marshall County, Indiana, Labor Day Weekend is known as Blueberry Weekend. We always joked that Blueberry Weekend slowly outranked Christmas as

Dad's favorite time of the year. The thousands of people in attendance would awaken the social butterfly within him. (However, if I'm being honest, it hardly ever had a chance to sleep. The man could carry on a conversation for hours.)

T-minus two days until festival weekend, my mother, who continues to serve as my pillar of strength and grace, looked broken. She had lost the love of her life, her high-school sweetheart with whom she had shared dreams of retiring, traveling and enjoying grandchildren throughout their golden years.

There sat the empty chair at the dining room table, the open section of the living room sofa on which he'd spent lazy Sunday afternoons napping and watching marathons of *Gold Rush* or *Street Outlaws*, the unoccupied side of my parents' bed, and the knowledge that my then twenty-three-year-old self would have to spend the rest of her life without one of the two people who had the largest impact on her.

I felt robbed, as though his cancer had simply snuffed out his presence, which I had taken for granted. Now, his seat would remain empty at holidays, weddings, vacations, or even just lazy summer afternoons on the lake. He wouldn't get to share in any of my future milestones.

Later that evening, as I was pulling weeds from our front yard, I saw a glint of something silver. There, at the edge of our property, perched a charcoal-colored homing pigeon. Its feathers were dotted with spots of brilliant silver. Figuring that we were merely serving as a pit stop for the bird on the way to its destination, I finished my yard work and went on about my evening.

"Shell," my mom whispered the next morning while looking out the front door. "I saw that same pigeon right there yesterday afternoon, and I'm pretty sure that it hasn't left." As if on cue, our little visitor focused his gaze on me with intense interest and began to walk in our direction.

I braced myself for an interaction that I was sure would result in feathers flying when Simon and Jackson, our Goldendoodle and Golden Retriever, bounded over. But the pigeon seemed to welcome the dogs' sniffing noses. Who ever heard of a bird not flying off in a panic when confronted with big, slobbery dogs?

My mother and I were sure this pigeon was the earthly embodiment of my father's heavenly spirit. And sure enough, it continued to stare at me in a knowing way. Gobsmacked, I was eventually able to stammer out one word: "Dad?" The pigeon seemed to look back at me as if to say, "Well duh, who'd you expect?"

Growing up, we had always been a churchgoing family. My mother and grandmother instilled in me the importance of paying attention to God's signals and messages. For example, in the seventeen years or so since his passing, my mom continues to receive pennies from my grandfather. She once told me that she considers them his "tokens of approval."

A little while later that same afternoon, my dad's two close friends, Terry and Dave, pulled in with a smoker in tow. They filled the driveway with laughter and the heavenly aroma of smoked ribs. Given that the combination of great friends and great food was one of Dad's greatest joys in life, I wasn't at all surprised to see the pigeon meander over to where they stood and join the inner circle.

That's when I realized that I had the answer to my prayer, begging and pleading with God for peace and reassurance of my dad's liberation from his earthly pain and his blissful existence up in heaven. More than that, God granted me reassurance that our father, in spirit form, would continue to celebrate all the phases of life with us. And for granting me this peace, I continue to thank God.

The next day, I checked to see that the pigeon had indeed stayed a fourth night. In the past few days, it had made a habit of venturing down the sidewalk and greeting the vendors and craftspeople whose campers were parked next door for the Blueberry Weekend. That had been exactly what my father did every year.

That whole weekend was a gift from God. The bird remained with us for a few days, until it left as suddenly as it had come. I never was able to identify the tracking number around its ankle, although it wouldn't make a difference to me. I already knew who he was.

— Shelby Harrell —

57

Messenger in My Driveway

Remember that although bodies may pass away,
the energy that connects you to a loved one is
everlasting and can always be felt when
you're open to receiving it.
~Doreen Virtue, Signs from Above

When my fourteen-year-old son was killed by a drunk driver on the street in front of our house, I felt as if I had no reason to be on Earth. My heart was shattered, our lives were wrecked, and I knew I would never recover. I would never see him or hear his voice again. I was his mother, but as sudden as a crash on the street, my identity was gone. I wasn't his mother anymore because he wasn't alive anymore.

During those first weeks, I was someone I didn't recognize, questioning my own existence, questioning my faith. Was there a heaven? Did God even exist? Was my baby just gone, closed into a grave, never to live again in any form? During the funeral, I sat numbly in the front row of the church, next to the coffin that held my beautiful boy, wearing my black dress and staring straight ahead, unseeing.

At some point, I lifted my eyes to the crucifix that hung high above the altar, fixing my gaze on Jesus's sorrowful face. Looking into his sculpted eyes, I asked, "Why did you do this to me?"

I was sad, confused, bereft, empty and inconsolable. I was also restless. I couldn't sit still. I moved from room to room constantly, chafing at visits from friends or neighbors who came to show kindness and support, even friends of Andy who wanted to tell me what he meant to them. I felt the need to thank them but to tell them I was busy. I had to go. Where? I did not know.

My wonderful father-in-law, who lived down the road, spent hours sitting on our porch in the swing, filling in for me by greeting visitors and performing the simple courtesies that I couldn't get myself together enough to do. He was a busy farmer and certainly didn't have the time for these tasks, but he did them because I couldn't.

I took long walks around the neighborhood. I roamed our fields, through woods and back to the creek that ran along the edge of our property. At some point, I realized what I was doing. I was looking for Andy. I was checking every corner, every space, every street and pathway in the futile hope that I might find him or something of him, that he might speak to me and let me know that he was okay, happy and still the child I missed so much. I needed, more than anything at that point, to hear from him, in whatever way I could, if I could. If his spirit thrived, rising above the broken body that had lain on the street, I needed to know that, for certain, for sure, without a doubt.

The day came when, while my father-in-law sat sentry on the porch and my husband worked out his own pain and heartache by working in our back garden, I found myself standing under the grape arbor talking out loud to my son, not knowing if he could hear me.

"Please, Andy," I begged. "Please, I have to know that you are okay and that I'm still your mom. Please let me know, please." As always, Andy didn't respond. He couldn't. He was gone forever, and I would never hear from him again.

I made my way to the front porch and dropped wearily onto the swing next to Dad, sighing with resignation and despair. We talked about the weather, the crops, who had come to express their condolences that afternoon, and what we would have for dinner that evening.

Cars drove back and forth on the road, drivers making their way to wherever they were going. These people were living their lives, going home from work, going to pick up their kids from school, going shopping. They had no idea they were driving over the very spot where my son was hit, minutes after he had spoken his last words in a voice we would never hear again.

One of the cars passed slowly, turned around, drove back and pulled into our driveway. I looked at my father-in-law, puzzled, and he shrugged. "Who is that?" he asked. A woman got out and began to tentatively walk up the driveway to the porch where we sat. She looked somewhat familiar.

"I don't know who it is," I replied. "She looks familiar, but I can't think where I've seen her." We waited as she mounted our front steps.

"Hello, I hope I'm not disturbing you. I just saw you sitting here," she said. At that moment, I remembered who she was. She was a teacher at Andy's school, and she had attended his wake. I didn't really know her well, but she had shared some sweet memories of my son at school. I was still trying to work out her name.

"I hope you don't think I'm crazy. And, honestly, I think I might be crazy, but…" she hesitated. "Well, when I was passing the house, I saw you sitting here, and something very strong told me to turn around and come back because there was a message I needed to deliver." She turned to me and said, "Your son wants you to know that he is okay, and you are still his mom."

I gasped, speechless and stunned. Dad looked at the ready to leap between us and order her off the porch from whence she came. I put my hand on his arm and faced her. "Thank you," I said. My voice broke, and her face relaxed. I knew she had taken a risk driving into my driveway to give me this message.

It was the message I so badly wanted. It was a message from my son, and it was the inspiration I needed to begin to build my life again — not the same life I had lived when Andy was on Earth but a life I could enjoy, knowing that his spirit lived and he waited for me to join him someday.

That message was the most precious I had ever received. I gave the nervous messenger a hug and a smile, and she made a quick exit. Oddly, although I would never forget her, I haven't seen her since that day. Our paths just haven't crossed. However, even if we never meet again, I will always be grateful that she ignored her well-founded misgivings and came into my driveway to deliver a miraculous message from a precious son to his grieving mother.

— Luanne Tovey Zuccari —

58

Goodbye from Beyond

You may be gone from my sight, but you
will never be gone from my heart.
~Henry van Dyke, Jr.

My father-in-law was the only male role model I had ever known. He was kind and strong. He was never one for traveling, but when we decided to move to Virginia from our hometown of New York City, he became enamored with the idea of traveling the country. He talked about buying his favorite car, a 1983 Cadillac Seville, and running away to the West Coast. I would tell him, "You sound so excited that I wouldn't be hurt if you ran away without saying goodbye."

His dreams of a life on the road were not to be. Two weeks after our move, doctors found a tumor the size of a cantaloupe in his lung. The day of his diagnosis, I hugged him like I never had before. I didn't want to ever let go. I wanted to thank him for teaching me how to fix a lawnmower, and for being such a good father to my wife and grandfather to my kids.

Growing up without a dad can make you calloused to simple things like telling someone you love them. Now I realized I was running out of time.

The doctors gave my father-in-law just months to live. He was not in good health anyway. With COPD and overall poor lung health, he already had two strikes against him. So, you might imagine our surprise when he made it a full year. Unfortunately, he ended up dying in a hospital room away from his daughter and grandkids. He never had the chance to say goodbye.

I was sleeping in the living room when I was awakened, not by a phone call but by our computer. It was the same computer he would spend hours playing on. I had shut off the computer for the night hours earlier. The fact that it cranked open with blue light and a humming CPU startled me out of my sleep. I walked up the stairs to my bedroom when my wife's phone rang and we got the news that he was gone. My wife rushed with my mother-in-law to the hospital.

Telling my children their beloved grandfather had passed was one of the hardest things I've ever had to do. The next few days were like a fog. We tried to find solace in recounting stories and remembering his bad jokes. But we could not shake the pain and loss of not having him around. I thought of his final wish, to travel the world, but now he was gone.

Three weeks passed. Every day when I came home from work, I would look at the chair where he sat to watch his favorite TV shows. I felt the emptiness in the house, and I was crestfallen knowing that we never got to say goodbye.

One night, I was visited in a dream by my father-in-law. He wore his favorite outfit: a red tank top and oversized basketball shorts. He walked up to me and gave me a hug. He said, "It's okay. Tell them I am okay. I am fine." I could not speak. I felt like my vocal cords were frozen. He said, "Tell them I am fine. I am happy." As he turned and walked away, I could see him fade into darkness.

The next morning, I told my wife about the dream. To my surprise, she told me she had had a similar dream.

Her dream had us all eating at a picnic table, all seven of us, even the dog. We walked away from the table, except for my father-in-law. He sat with a melancholic smile. She said to him, "Come on, Dad. Let's go!" But he did not move from the table.

Then he turned to her, smiling, and simply said, "Go on. I love you." My wife and I could not explain how we could have similar dreams on the same night. There was only one explanation. Her father had reached out to us from beyond to bring us closure. He came to us to say goodbye and give us one last chance to say goodbye, too.

— Freddy B. Nunez —

59

Birthday Greetings

To live in hearts we leave behind
Is not to die.
~Thomas Campbell, "Hallowed Ground"

I woke up to a bright, blue spring morning, excited for this next chapter in my life. I had been divorced for six years and had just bought my first home. It was moving day. Little did I know that our lives were about to be turned upside-down.

My ex-husband Mike would be picking up Ryan from school and bringing him to the new house at 7:00 PM. At 3:30, Ryan ran into our rental.

"Dad didn't show up! I need to call him right now!"

"He's probably just running late," I said.

My mind was concentrating on the Tetris game of packing the moving truck. Ryan came out of the kitchen after trying to call his dad with an angry look on his face.

"He's not there," he whined.

"He will be here. Just be patient," I assured him.

Every thirty minutes or so, Ryan tried calling his dad again, and he became angrier and angrier at being stood up by his father.

"Please, just take me over there," he pleaded.

"Ryan, it's moving day! I can't take you over to your dad's today."

After the whirlwind day of getting everything moved out of the rental, we were all exhausted. I tried to call Mike one last time and, again, had to leave a message.

"He must be really sick," I mused. "I'll call him in the morning and see if he needs anything."

The next morning, my first thought upon waking was of Mike. I called him again, but there was still no answer. Fearing that something might have happened to him, I called the police and asked them to perform a wellness check. The officer said they would send over someone and call me as soon as they had an answer.

I went to work unpacking and organizing the new house. It had been over an hour since I called the police, and I was getting impatient. I grabbed my phone and called them again. An officer answered the phone and put me on hold. Coming back on the line, he informed me, "Ma'am, the officers are still at the scene and will call you back shortly."

Hanging up, I felt a lump in my stomach. "At the scene?" What did he mean? It sounded ominous, and I did my best to remain positive, but I felt the panic rising within me.

Putting a load of bedding into the washing machine, I was interrupted by the ringing of my cell phone.

"Ms. Green, this is Officer Stratton. I'm sorry to tell you that we're at your ex-husband's home, and he is dead. It appears it was a self-inflicted gunshot. Is there someone we can call for you?"

The next days and weeks were a nightmare. Mike's funeral would take place in California, but the boys and I decided not to go. We chose to have our own private memorial in Idaho. It was a loving tribute to him and a healing experience for us.

In the blink of an eye, it was the end of July and my birthday. I wanted to celebrate by taking the boys to our county fair. We indulged in hot, greasy funnel cakes as we walked through the animal exhibits. As always, the night ended with a free concert. It was perfect.

When we got home, RJ went into the house. "Mom, there's a message for you on the answering machine," he announced.

"Well, of course there is. It's my birthday. Who is it?"

"You need to listen to the message yourself."

I walked into the kitchen with RJ close on my heels. I pushed the button on the answering machine and was met with loud, scratchy static. Then, I recognized a soft voice below the static. It was Mike!

"What is this?" I demanded.

"I don't know, Mom. Listen, I turned the volume up and down, and the static gets louder and softer, but the voice doesn't change." I could see the fear in my son's eyes, and I became furious.

Who would play this horrible joke on us? Mike's voice was very distinct, with a slight New England accent. We couldn't make out what he was saying, but it was definitely his voice. As I continued to play with the volume, fear overtook RJ, and he slammed the delete button. The machine went quiet.

A few weeks later, I decided to make an appointment with my friend Jane who does energy work. I told her about our experience with the answering machine and my message from Mike.

"It really freaked me out. I couldn't imagine who could be so cruel as to play this prank on us, but the voice was Mike's. I want this stress to go away."

"Let's get you on the table and get your energy balanced. If you don't mind, I'll try a little channeling."

Lying under the comfy blanket, listening to soft music, Jane began to perform Reiki, and I relaxed. Softly, Jane began to speak to me, and my skeptical mind listened.

"Mike is here with us, and he wants you to know how very sorry he is, not only for the way he ended his life, but for the way he treated you during your marriage. He loves you and the boys. He's in a better place now. He's learning lessons that he should have paid attention to in life. He's not hurting anymore. He's found peace."

My little voice was telling me that Jane was just saying the words that any good friend would say.

"Mike wants you to know that your grandma is always with you," she continued. "He wants you to know that he is and will always be watching over the boys. He says that your grandma wants you to know that whenever you go into your bathroom cabinet and take out her perfume and sniff it, that's her reminding you how much she loves you."

My eyes flew open as I gasped. No one, not even Mike, knew that I kept my grandma's last bottle of Emeraude eau de cologne in my cabinet and that, occasionally, I had the strong urge to take it out and relish the scent that was my grandma. As I'd draw in the scent, I'd always smile and say, "Hi, Grandma... I love you."

As the tears ran down my cheeks, I knew deep within my heart that Mike had connected with me. Messages from heaven are possible. Our loved ones who have passed on can connect with us if we take the time to listen.

I was comforted that Mike had found the peace that he had so desired in life. Never again would I doubt our ability to connect with those who have gone before us.

—Erin Kani—

60

My Two-Year-Old Delivered a Message

Just a thin veil between this world and that world of
beauty and love. Just a thin veil that hides the
view of our Spirit loved ones above.
~Gertrude Tooley Buckingham

I'd been grieving the loss of a very important person in my life — my mother-in-law Maryjo — since her unexpected passing nine months earlier. I never knew how to address Maryjo's death with my toddler, Natalie, so I didn't broach the subject.

Natalie was a month shy of turning two when her grandma died, so I assumed she didn't remember her. I was shocked when she was two and a half and she asked, "Where's Geema?" out of nowhere.

I'm not even sure how she knew the word "grandma." My mother was referred to as "Nana," and I hate to admit it but I hadn't talked much about Grandma Maryjo, despite my fierce promises to keep her memory alive for my girls. I'd been too busy trying to keep my composure.

Natalie could only say a few words when Maryjo was alive, and "grandma" was not in her limited vocabulary back then. What made her think to ask where her grandma was after all this time?

The question knocked me off-kilter. How do you describe the finality of death to a child? She was just an innocent being who wrapped herself in the magic of Santa Claus and the enchantment of flying rainbow unicorns named Donut.

I attempted to distract Natalie with the shiny, new school bus she insisted on snuggling that night. But I knew Natalie deserved an answer as to where her grandma went.

After I got over the shock of her asking, I told Natalie that her grandma lives in heaven with God now.

That was the end of it: a short answer riddled with complexities that most adults can't fully process.

Until three weeks later on my wedding anniversary.

My wedding was Maryjo's wedding, if I'm being honest. When Mike announced to his mom that we were going to elope, she told us we were wrong to do so. She planned our entire wedding. Every part of it.

The giant ballroom with magnificent chandeliers and gold fountain statues. So much gold. (We're Italian-Americans.)

The four-course dinner followed by pizza, spaghetti, and tiramisu. (Yup, still Italian-Americans.)

People still talk about how stunning our wedding was. I am so glad we didn't elope. I imagine a lot of brides would have gone Bridezilla on their mothers-in-law for taking over their special day, but I was no such bride.

I wanted the big day for Maryjo because it meant so much to her to celebrate her only son getting married. I came to realize that eloping would have disappointed a lot of people, and a wedding is really for everyone else.

It was our first wedding anniversary without my mother-in-law and it was made more poignant because we were packing to move to my husband's hometown — the place Maryjo had desperately wanted us to be. We had tried for years to relocate there without success, and then six months after Maryjo's death, my husband's transfer request at work was approved.

When I went to get Natalie up from her nap on the day of our anniversary, my daughter's eyes did not meet mine. She was looking at the ceiling with a big smile on her face.

"Geema's house," she said matter-of-factly, pointing her little finger up toward heaven.

I nodded and smiled, surprised she remembered a conversation we had weeks ago.

A lump formed in my throat, as often does when I think of Maryjo. I lost my words as my wide-eyed toddler absorbed the pain radiating from me. As I went to lift Natalie out of bed, she said something that almost brought me to my knees.

Natalie placed her little hands on my cheeks, looked directly into my eyes (soul), and said, "Geema with God. Geema happy."

Those two short sentences had the strength to lift the weight of the world off my chest.

And with that, I exhaled.

I wasn't even aware that my lungs could expand and contract so freely again until that moment. I became dizzy with the new rush of oxygen flooding through me.

Natalie then proceeded to tickle the air and laugh. She tickles everything — apparently, even the spirit of her deceased grandmother.

Maybe my daughter just chose that day to remember what I told her about her grandma. Or, perhaps, it really was a message from beyond. Perhaps, on our first wedding anniversary since her passing, the week we packed to move to her hometown, Maryjo wanted us to know she is happy, and it's time we should be, too.

Grieving this loss has taken more than I knew I had. I can't explain the feeling of relief that washed over me when I heard my daughter's sweet voice speak words I desperately needed to hear.

Now I can tell myself confidently, *Maryjo is with God. Maryjo is happy.*

Someway, somehow, it's time my husband and I pick up the pieces and find happiness again.

It only took a message from my two-year-old to give us permission to do so.

— Kendra Phillips —

A Missed FaceTime Call

Those whom we have loved never really leave us.
They live on forever in our hearts and cast their
radiant light onto our every shadow.
~Sylvana Rossetti

"Woof, woof," Dad barked at my Shih Tzu, Daisy, as I held her close to my iPad screen. Daisy echoed him, wagging her tail and pushing her nose toward my father's image.

"Good dog," Dad said.

Dad's way of exciting my dog used to annoy me, but now it was something I missed. Due to the pandemic, it had been four months since I'd seen my eighty-eight-year-old father, who suffered from dementia and lived a short drive from my house. His ritual of barking at Daisy when he entered my home hadn't happened in a long time.

I lowered my fluffy, black-and-gray dog onto my lap. Daisy rested her head on my arm like she knew I needed extra love.

"I'm sorry I can't see you," I said to my father.

"I see you right now." He grinned, his blue eyes sparkling. "Do you have anything for me today?"

I opened my astrology app to Scorpio and gave him his reading, twice. He told me what he ate for dinner and who had called. I didn't know if he made everything up but it didn't matter. He inquired about what I did, and I gave him a full report about my online writing workshop and yoga class.

"Want to say hi to Steve?" I asked and turned my iPad to face my husband, who was cooking dinner.

"Hi, Buddy," Dad shouted and reminded me how lucky I was to have Steve. I loved that my father loved my husband, whom I'd unexpectedly met while taking an extended leave of absence from my Wall Street lawyer life to help Dad in Missouri, just three years prior.

Each day when I FaceTimed with my father, we had the same ritual. He barked at Daisy. He asked for his astrology reading, twice. He shouted, "Hi, Buddy," at my husband. But as the months rolled on, he couldn't tell me what he ate for lunch or dinner, although he assured me it was good. He told me no one called, although I knew my brother had spoken with him minutes before me. Then, in November, Dad got sick. He bounced back and forth from the hospital to the nursing home to the hospital again. The day before he passed in December, I was allowed to visit him to say goodbye.

Three days later, my father-in-law died. I prayed for our fathers and for Daisy, who had significantly declined. I knew my husband and I couldn't cope if Daisy died in December, too.

At nearly sixteen, Daisy's twice-daily insulin shots didn't seem like they were enough. Her accidents had increased, and her doggy diapers required frequent washes. On occasion, she got confused and walked into a wall. Steve and I discussed whether we needed to put her to sleep. Daisy's vet said she wasn't in pain and to give her extra love. We gave it to her in spades.

But then in mid-February, Daisy's eating abruptly changed. One day, she ate only chicken, the next only beef. She shook her nose and barked to demand a different option. For four days, she wanted only pizza. But on day five, she refused a slice. She then walked through the kitchen and collapsed. Steve and I took shifts holding her wrapped in a blanket.

"Should I take her to the vet?" he asked.

"No. She's not in pain. Let's keep her home," I said.

Steve wiped the tears running down my cheeks.

The next morning, I had a conference call about a writing project. I went to my home office with a cup of coffee while Steve sat on the floor in our bedroom in front of the fireplace with Daisy. After my meeting, I walked into the kitchen. As I washed my mug, I said in my head, "Dad, help Daisy cross over."

I heard my father's voice say loudly, "Woof."

I couldn't help smiling as I walked back to my desk, needing to write some notes from my call before I forgot anything. A few moments later, I looked up. Steve was beside me wrapping his arms around me. Daisy had passed.

I returned to my room and sat next to where my dog lay and stroked her fluffy fur for the final time.

When Steve took Daisy to the vet, I cleaned up her spot in front of the fireplace. Later, we had a memorial brunch, swapping our favorite Daisy moments and photos. Afterward, I went back to my office to work.

Sitting at my desk, I opened my computer and gasped. A notice for a missed FaceTime call from my father appeared on my screen. It had been months since his last call, and I didn't have a calendar entry to call him. Our calls were at random times, when convenient.

"Thank you, Dad," I whispered through tears, knowing the notice on my screen confirmed that my father had indeed helped Daisy.

— Tess Clarkson —

Angels Among Us

Garden Center Angel

Hear blessings dropping their blossoms around you.
~Rumi, as interpreted by Coleman Barks

I stepped out of the elevator, practically sprinting through the building's lobby. I nodded to the security guard and smiled as I said, "Have a great weekend. See you Monday."

It was 3:54 PM. Admittedly, I had left my office a bit early, but heck, it was a Friday. In an earnest attempt to meet a pending deadline, I had worked late all week and was physically and mentally exhausted. I was so looking forward to the weekend.

As I hurried toward my car, I felt the lingering warmth of the late-afternoon May sun, so welcome after a harsh winter. I was planning to spend the weekend working in my yard and planting seeds for my garden.

My weekend plans also included a personal favorite: my initial springtime trip to the local garden center. I would find myself visiting the garden center throughout the spring and summer months, but that first trip was always extra special.

Just as I pulled out of the office parking lot, I remembered that I needed milk. I decided to stop at a convenience store a few miles down the road. However, when I reached the next major intersection and impatiently waited for a red light to turn green, a much better idea occurred to me. Why wait until tomorrow to visit the garden center? There was a market in the same parking lot so I could preview the garden center and pick up the milk at the same time.

I drove straight to the garden center, parked my car, and began to stroll its outdoor displays. I took a deep breath and inhaled the pleasant aromas wafting through the center: lilac, hyacinth and gardenia. I was admiring a hanging basket, bursting with deep purple and white petunias, when I looked to my left and noticed a woman pushing a shopping cart packed with flats of the most beautiful flowers I had ever seen. The flower's petals were dainty ruffles in a striking shade of blue. I was curious about what kind of flowers they were.

The woman looked directly at me, nodded, and offered a warm smile. She was wearing a beautiful pantsuit, which was remarkably the exact color of the flowers in her cart. I figured it was probably her favorite color.

There was something about her. She did not look familiar, yet I felt like I knew her. Had I met her before? I began to wonder but became quickly distracted by an announcement informing customers that the garden center would be closing shortly. I had certainly lost track of time.

I dashed over to the market, bought my milk, and walked to my car. The lot appeared empty, except for my car and one other. As I walked by the other car, I noticed a man lying on the ground. He was on his side, facing the front wheel on the driver's side. I initially thought he was reaching for something underneath his car, perhaps a loose grocery item. I continued to my car but suddenly felt compelled to turn back and see if the man needed assistance. I walked over and said, "Sir, are you okay?" No response. I repeated it louder, "Sir, are you okay?"

The man slowly turned his head, groaned, and mumbled, "I fell. I cannot move my leg. It's very painful… must be broken; my hip, too."

I scanned the parking lot. It was just us. Where was everyone? There wasn't even an employee locking up.

The man's voice weakened as he added, "Please… call 911."

Panic-stricken, I answered, "Yes, sir. I will. I am looking for my cell phone."

I tossed the carton of milk on the ground and began to frantically fumble through my pocketbook. My heart was pounding. I suddenly heard another voice; it was the woman in the blue pantsuit! Where had she come from?

She spoke in a gentle, soothing tone. "Your cell phone is in the right pocket of your coat."

I dialed 911, and I froze…. I was speechless. I heard her voice once more. She calmly said, "Repeat after me." In a succinct and clear manner, she stated our location, the apparent condition of the man, his leg and possibly his hip being broken. I repeated her words verbatim to the dispatcher.

The man groaned again. He sounded completely out of breath as he attempted to utter a string of words. "I cannot breathe, need inhaler."

I responded, "Where is it? Where is it, sir?"

Once more, I heard the woman's sweet voice. "It is on his car's front passenger seat beneath the red sweatshirt."

I opened the passenger door, and there it was, tucked under the sweatshirt. I squatted next to the man and said, "Do not move. Here is your inhaler."

Just then, an ambulance came barreling into the parking lot. Within seconds, the man was on a stretcher. He turned to me and said, "Thank you."

I answered, "Oh, please do not thank me. Thank this truly kind woman right here. She is the one who deserves the credit."

I turned… and she was gone. Vanished. Where did she go?

The man responded, "What woman?"

I was completely baffled. I scanned the lot; it was empty except for the man's car and mine. Suddenly, I noticed something in the far corner of the lot. It was the woman's shopping cart, still packed with those blue flowers! I walked over to it, hoping to see her. After standing alone and bewildered, I decided to finally head home.

I looked down at the cart one last time, touched the flowers' delicate petals, and noticed a sticker on the side of the flat. It indicated the proper care and instructions for planting and growing the flowers. More importantly, in bold black lettering, it stated the flower's name: Blue Angel.

— Patricia Rossi —

63

Double Play

*We should not assume; however, that just because something
is unexplainable by us, it is unexplainable.*
~Neal A. Maxwell

ama's health had been gradually deteriorating. It
had become routine for her to be transported by
ambulance to the local emergency room each week.
However, on this occasion, she required an extended
stay at the hospital for observation. While we all dearly wished for
her to be back home, it was a relief to know she was receiving round-
the-clock care.

The day after her admittance, we had tickets for a Yankees night-
game. My husband John and I decided that our two daughters needed
a distraction from worrying about their great-grandmother, who played
a large role in our family. She had been the pillar of our family, raising me due to my mother's illness after my birth and caring for my
daughters during their childhood.

Despite our heavy hearts, we decided to head to New York, catching the five o'clock train after we visited Mama in the hospital. We
had found her to be weak but comfortable. She mentioned the kind
and patient EMT who had responded to her call the previous night, a
Yankees fan who had put her at ease.

We opted to take the train to Yankee Stadium from the West Haven,
Connecticut station, known for its quiet and secure environment, with
ample parking. None of us knew how to take the train to New York

and then make the right connection to another train to the stadium in the Bronx. But we met a friendly young man wearing a Yankees jersey and baseball hat, who seemed well-versed in traveling to the stadium. We decided to do whatever he did.

When we had to change trains in Harlem, and our new train wasn't on the correct track, we clung to our new friend. When he briefly disappeared from view, we felt a surge of anxiety, only to be relieved when he reappeared just as swiftly. Once aboard the connecting train, we stood close behind him, secure in the knowledge that we were on a direct route to the stadium.

During the journey, I shared with my daughters the visit I had had with Mama earlier in the day. I explained that I would need to call her when we reached the stadium, as she was fretting about our safe arrival in New York. I relayed Mama's words about the kind and patient EMT, mentioning that she had said, "That young man stayed with me. He was so patient and reassured me that everything would be alright."

Suddenly, the friendly young man we had been trailing turned to me with an incredulous look and said, "I was the EMT who took care of your grandmother last night."

It was as though that young man had been an angel in disguise, sent to care for Mama and, later, to guide us.

— Jacqueline Ford —

64

An Angel in Uniform

Angels can fly directly into the heart of the matter.
~Author Unknown

I hated going down that dark, shadowy street, especially late at night with all the office buildings and warehouses locked up tight, but there was no other route to go home from my friend's house. Not only was that nerve-wracking, but I was also wondering how I could sneak into my house without waking my parents.

I sensed the driver in the car to my right looking at me. A quick glance confirmed it. The young man sat staring straight at me. At twenty-one years old, I found this uncomfortable but not unusual. *Fortunately,* I thought, *I'm turning left, and he's headed straight ahead.* The light turned green, and I turned left into the inky blackness, eager to get through the darkness to the highway and civilization.

About a quarter mile down the road, a car pulled up alongside my driver's door. It then moved slightly ahead, swerved right, and forced me off the road. To avoid crashing into the car, I pulled over. Our cars sat parallel, with my front wheels angled on the grass beyond the low curb and my rear wheels still in the street. In the glow from the headlights, I could see the car door swing open. The driver exited his car and stormed toward mine.

At this moment, I had two thoughts: *Maybe he needs directions.* And, *I wish Dad had fixed this broken window of mine,* the one that couldn't roll up all the way.

I quickly realized the guy didn't need directions when I heard him swearing and yelling, "You cut me off!" As he got closer, I saw it was the driver who had been staring at me while we sat at the light.

Where had he come from? I hadn't seen another car on the dark road after I turned.

He kept ranting and stomping toward me. Then he did the unthinkable. He stuck his arms through the opening above my window and wrapped his hands tightly around my throat. I tried to wiggle away, but it was too hard to maneuver out of the bucket seat and seat belt. I thrashed about, and when one of his hands slipped off my neck, I bit it. I chomped on that hand like a dog with a steak and wouldn't let go. He yelled louder, if that was possible.

My heart raced. Even if I got away, he'd sure follow me. And where would I go for help anyway? It didn't matter, because I couldn't figure out how to put my car in reverse, much less drive away. And my teeth were locked onto his hand as his other hand still grasped my throat.

I thought it was my imagination when, from somewhere to my right out on the grass, I heard a strong, masculine voice call out, "Is everything okay over there?"

The growling stopped, replaced by a suddenly calm and respectful voice. "Yes, officer, everything is fine."

Hearing the word "officer," I opened my mouth and started to scream — or weakly tried to. With the grip of my teeth released, the assailant jerked both his hands out of my car.

As the officer's flashlight illuminated us, my attacker started to explain, "She cut me off, officer."

I just tried to breathe. Squinting, I looked toward the beam of light. At first, I could barely make out the shadowed officer standing by my right front bumper, but slowly I could distinguish his short-sleeved khaki uniform and the distinctive shape of his police hat. There was a streetlight behind him that I hadn't noticed before, with its light casting a halo around the officer. How on earth did he get there — standing like a statue, hands on hips, by the right front corner of my car in the grass? How did we not notice the arrival of his patrol car, now parked on the street beyond my attacker's?

"Let's go down to the station, folks."

And, like a parade, the three cars headed to the police station with the officer in front and me in the rear.

When we got to the station, the officer told me to sit in one room and he led my attacker to another. I was too shaky to drive home and unsure what to do. Afraid to press charges because I didn't want him to know where I lived, I called my parents. My fear of waking them up had been replaced by other, more immediate and dangerous concerns.

Up to that point, I sat stoically, holding myself together, but hearing my dad's voice on the other end of the line, all my anxiety rose to the surface and overflowed. My voice failed me as I sobbed.

When my dad arrived, he burst into the station like an outlaw in the Wild West storming through saloon doors. Red-faced, with neck arteries bulging, he bellowed, "Where is he? Where's the son-of-a-#!#!#!"

Now, it was my turn to calm my dad. We discussed my fears, but my dad wanted no part of them. He insisted we press charges.

Up until now, my assailant smugly sat motionless on a bench. When he heard that he was going to be charged, he went berserk, screaming and flailing so much that the officers put him into a straitjacket. Seeing him through the window into his room, tightly bound in white and glaring at me, added to my fears. I couldn't believe I had survived being alone on a dark road with this maniac.

All this time, I looked for the officer who had come to my rescue. He was nowhere to be found. His name wasn't on any of the paperwork. When I asked another officer about him, she shrugged. It was a small police station, so he shouldn't have been hard to find. And he was Black and it seemed like everyone else in the station was white. They said he didn't work there, so all I could figure was that he was an officer of the law, but not part of the local police. Perhaps he was a state trooper who happened to be on the service road by the highway and spotted me.

For six months afterward, until the court appearance, I stayed very close to home, only going out to work or school. Facing my attacker in court was one of the most difficult things I ever had to do. My angel officer didn't participate in the court proceedings. A different officer was there in the courtroom with me and my family. In fact, after our interaction on the street and in the station, I never saw him or heard anything about him again. As mysteriously as he had appeared, he disappeared.

At court, I discovered that my assailant was my age. His first of a long list of criminal driving offenses occurred seven years earlier at age fourteen, three years before it was legal for him to drive. During his testimony and looking for pity, he extended his hand to the judge and displayed an arc-shaped scar, evidence of where I had bit him. Seeing it, the judge roared, "What was your hand doing in her car?"

In the end, the young man proved that he had moved to Florida and was going to stay there. Incredibly, the New Jersey judge thought that was punishment enough!

As for me, I took small comfort that this man no longer lived in my state, but much greater comfort in the fact that a mysterious angel officer intervened at just the right time.

— Susan Allen Panzica —

A Lost Faith Found

Miracles come in moments.
~Wayne Dyer

I was in my early thirties when my first marriage ended. I was on the way home from my lawyer's office after signing the separation papers, and I was so distracted that I drove to the first apartment I had shared with my soon-to-be ex-husband.

As I came to the intersection in front of the building, the light turned red. I sat there waiting for the light to change, and I began to sob. My seemingly perfect life, if you measured it by expensive possessions and extravagant pleasures, was falling apart. I was afraid I would lose everything and I believed that I had earned the right to feel sorry for myself.

I asked God why this was happening to me. All the money and material possessions I stood to lose meant something. I was successful in the eyes of society and everyone around me, so I believed I was experiencing true suffering.

It had been raining all morning, but as I sat in my vehicle crying, something happened. The rain seemed to stop almost instantly, and as the clouds parted, the sun emerged. Beautiful and bright, it shone through my windshield as if it meant to console me.

Then, out of the corner of my eye, I noticed movement and saw a pretty girl no older than twenty in a wheelchair. She began crossing the intersection in front of my car. As she passed, I found my eyes locked on her face. It was glowing in a way I had never seen before. It was peaceful and calming, and her eyes were filled with such warmth and love that it felt as if they were whispering to me as she passed.

The whole thing lasted a mere moment. When she reached the other side of the road, she disappeared from my sight as quickly as she had appeared. I sat in my car with no one behind me or around me for two more changes of the intersection lights before I was able to drive. I drove for a minute, maybe two, before I pulled my car over on the side of the road and wept again, but this time for a different reason. It was no longer out of self-pity but shame.

That moment was an awakening for me. I had become so consumed with attaining all the material things that I felt had worth and value that I had missed it: The true meaning of life was in the simplicity of just being alive. I had become someone who lived with a sense of entitlement, as if life was a right and not a privilege that had been given to me. In that moment, that girl's glowing face had shown me where I had lost my way — that we have it all in every moment in each day, not in money, possessions or privileges, but in the simple gift of being alive.

I drove home that day in a daze, lost in my thoughts. I don't recall if I slept that night or if my mind just wandered as I played the events of my life over and over again. But when the sun finally rose the next morning, I realized that I had to change.

I spent the next five years on a journey of rediscovery, re-teaching myself all that I had forgotten, like how to treat others with patience, compassion and kindness. I learned to appreciate every moment, no longer taking any of them for granted. I realized that true success in life wasn't measured by how much I had, but by how I lived, and what I did with all I had — my time, my words, and what I shared with others who were in need.

Life changes fast and in an instant, so it's important for us to be aware of the everyday miracles we are given. They can change our direction forever if we are paying attention.

The definition of a miracle is an extraordinary event manifesting divine intervention in human affairs. My miracle wasn't an extreme event, but it did help me find something I had lost. It helped me find my faith — a faith that once believed in something bigger than myself.

Can I say for certain that what I experienced that day was angelic? I guess it's all relative to what we believe. But what I can say for certain is that my mysterious helper that day in that moment was divine intervention, a message sent. Her purpose was to redirect me and lead me back to the path from which I had strayed. So maybe all miracles don't have to be extraordinary or grand to be instrumental in our lives. Sometimes, our angels come in simple forms or in small moments, but that doesn't make them any less powerful or meaningful.

— Nanette Norgate —

A Fluffy Little Angel

Your Angels stay with you through each precious day,
loving, protecting, and lighting your way.
~Mary Jac

I was eighteen and home from college for Christmas break. I had lost a lot of weight walking all over campus and wanted to keep walking while I was home. Often, the only chance I got to go was after dinner when it was dark. My parents weren't happy about me walking by myself, so my thirteen-year-old brother Joe would go with me.

We walked for several nights together. Every night when we passed a particular house, I would jump because this family had an old Rottweiler who didn't have a good reputation in the neighborhood. Sadly, he was tied up outside all the time and would bark and snarl at everything and everyone who passed his house. Each night, I would be so happy when I would finally hear his chain catch and knew we were safe.

One night, the chain didn't catch, and the dog kept running toward the road. He stopped not far from us, and I was terrified.

I instinctively stepped in front of my "little brother," who immediately stepped in front of me as he saw himself as a man whose job was to protect me. A few minutes prior to this, he had found a small, broken screwdriver in the road. He knew that was the only defense we had against this dog, so he held it tightly in his hand as we waited to see what would happen next.

It was a standoff: the dog waiting for us to make a move while he snarled and barked, and us waiting for him to charge as he slowly walked closer to us. He was only about ten feet away when I said, "God, please help us."

From out of nowhere, a fluffy white dog, not much bigger than a cat, came barreling into the road and got between us and the Rottweiler. I couldn't believe my eyes when this dog appeared and then began barking and yapping at the bigger dog and chased him away.

They disappeared down the road with the white dog at the Rottweiler's heels. Joe and I turned and made our way home as fast as we could, knowing it was our chance to escape.

We had never seen that little dog before, and we never did see him again. The next night on our walk we saw the Rottweiler secured with a new and better chain. We were also armed with post-office-issued dog repellent that my dad had gotten from work — just in case. But I knew I didn't have to fear that Rottweiler anymore because my guardian angel was a fluffy little dog who wasn't afraid to stand up to him and protect me.

— Patti Alexander —

A Miraculous Healing

Believers, look up — take courage.
The angels are nearer than you think.
~Billy Graham

When my son was a child, he loved to say prayers to his guardian angel each night before bedtime. It was a routine that he continues to this day, and for good reason.

Many years ago, my son was driving to an appointment to clean carpets at a restaurant late at night. He had to be there to clean after closing time, so off he went in his truck to get the job done at midnight. As he drove along the highway, everything seemed normal. There wasn't much traffic on the road at that time of the night, so he cranked up his radio to listen to his favorite music as he drove along the deserted highway.

Suddenly, another truck ran a red light and broadsided Randy's truck on the driver's side. His vehicle spun out of control and came to rest in the middle of the road, now a twisted piece of metal.

While Randy lay dazed, bleeding and in pain, the other driver got out of his truck. He was rip-roaring drunk and mad as could be. Randy recalled the man reaching into the cab of Randy's truck and raising his fist to strike him while cursing him. Out of nowhere, a very large man suddenly appeared and wrestled the drunk to the ground in a headlock. Soon, another passerby saw the accident and called the police.

The drunk was arrested for impaired driving, and Randy was

transported to the hospital. At 1:00 in the morning, our phone rang. It was the hospital telling us our son had been in an accident and was in critical condition. We sped through the night to the hospital. Randy had a punctured lung, and his neck was broken just like Christopher Reeve. It was the worst break one could have. The doctors said he was paralyzed.

Throughout the night, we kept vigil and prayed for our son. The doctors said it did not look good, and Randy might not survive. As dawn broke, I went outside and found a bench to sit on and pray. I prayed every prayer I could remember and ended by praying to the angels, especially Randy's guardian angel. I called my parish priest and asked Father John to pray for Randy and offer the morning mass for him.

About that time, unbeknownst to any of us, Randy had a visitor. It was the stranger who had restrained the drunk at the accident. Randy would later recount waking up and finding the man standing beside his bed. The man gently touched Randy's neck and chest and said, "Don't worry, son. You will be fine."

Randy immediately regained the use of his arms and legs. He rang for the nurse to come and get him out of the halo they had placed him in to protect his neck. When she arrived, she was startled to see Randy fully awake and asking to get out of bed. He had no idea where the stranger had gone, but he remembered him as the man who had restrained the drunk at the scene of the accident.

No one knew where the man came from or where he disappeared to. Later, the police said they did not see anyone at the accident except Randy and the drunk. There was no sign of the man Randy described. No one in the hospital had seen him either. The nurses' station was right across from his room, and the nurses did not see anyone coming or going.

The doctors took Randy back to do an MRI and CT scan. They could not believe their eyes. His neck was no longer broken, and his lungs were fine. He was released that afternoon.

Yes, there are angels among us, and they watch over us day and night.

— Christine Trollinger —

68

Angel in the Desert

I believe we are free, within limits, and yet there is an
unseen hand, a guiding angel, that somehow, like a
submerged propeller, drives us on.
~Rabindranath Tagore

The desert is a beautiful place to explore, but it is also a dangerous place if you lose your way. My mother found this out one day when she was in her late sixties. She was out in the Nevada desert with her local rock club. She was with her boyfriend, searching for gems, crystals, or small stones of particular colors, shapes and sizes.

Her boyfriend said he had to go to the bathroom. He asked if she would be all right by herself. She assured him that she would be fine. She had her jug of water and umbrella for shade and told him not to worry. He pointed to the mountain and then to the red flag on the car and said to use those as reference points and always keep them in sight. He pecked her on the cheek and hurried off while she continued to look for rocks.

Being a farm girl from Wisconsin and having been on these rock-club hikes numerous times, it was surprising that she did indeed get lost. She couldn't see the flag on the car or remember which mountain peak her boyfriend had pointed out. To her, all the mountain peaks looked the same. She walked around fruitlessly.

Suddenly, she heard an awful scream coming from the ground in front of her. Scared, she looked down to see a desert tortoise with a jumping cactus stuck above its eye and another on its front leg. It screamed again while trying to pull its head into its shell.

She said to the tortoise, "What happened to you? Don't you know any better than to walk into a cactus?" She bent down and got onto her knees. "Now, hold still. This will probably hurt."

She used her umbrella handle to pull off the cactus pods. A few needles remained, stuck in the tortoise's skin. She told him, "Let me do your leg first." She pulled out the needles, one by one. With each pull, he would jerk a little. She poured some water on his leg to soothe the pain and then talked to him again. "Okay, now the ones above your eye. I need you to hold very still."

While she pulled, she continued to talk to him, telling him how dumb she was for getting herself lost in the desert. She also asked God for help and guidance. She didn't know if it helped to keep the tortoise from moving, but she thought it did. And it made her feel less nervous.

She removed all the cactus needles and poured her water over the tortoise's head to wash away the blood. To her, the tortoise looked thirsty while she poured the water. She poured more of her water into her cup, and he took a good, long drink. She had never seen a tortoise drink before. Come to think of it, it was the first time in her sixty-eight years of life that she had ever seen a tortoise in the wild.

Once he was better, she stood up to continue her search. She told the tortoise, "Now stay away from those cactuses," and the tortoise disappeared. She walked out into the desert, three knolls over, and saw nothing. Then, she decided to walk back to try a different direction. She passed the wet spot that was left in the dirt from her water and headed off in another direction. As she rounded the bend, the tortoise appeared again by her feet. She stopped suddenly, almost stumbling over the tortoise. "Oh, what are you doing here?" she said while she looked around. "Are you back to say thank you? You're very welcome."

The sun was starting to set behind the mountains while she contemplated her situation. She watched the tortoise as he walked out about ten feet away. He turned around and looked at her, and then walked back. He pulled on her shoestring and then walked out about ten feet, turned and looked at her once again. *How strange,* she thought and asked him, "Do you want me to follow you? Okay, what do I have to lose? This way or that? I guess this way," and she followed the tortoise.

The tortoise walked steadily while she followed along behind. She was just about ready to turn back around when she saw the red flag on the car. Then she heard the group calling out her name. When she crested the knoll, her boyfriend came running up, full of worry. They were just starting to form a search party.

That night around the campfire, she told them about her angel in the desert. When she told me in the weeks to follow, I praised God, thanking Him for sending that tortoise to my mother for guidance.

— Rick Kurtis —

69

The Butterfly People

The bravest are surely those who have the clearest vision
of what is before them, glory and danger alike,
and yet notwithstanding, go out to meet it.
~Thucydides

On May 22, 2011, my hometown of Joplin, Missouri was hit by an EF-5 tornado. With winds exceeding 200 miles per hour, this gigantic twister cut a six-mile-long path of destruction through our city. At times, the slow-moving tornado was three-quarters of a mile wide. Over 8,000 structures were demolished, including schools, businesses, firehouses, churches, homes, and a hospital.

The damage was in the billions of dollars, and the event was later described as one of the most devastating tornados in American history. Worst of all, the tornado injured over 1,100 residents and took 161 lives. More people might have been lost in this disaster if it had not been for the "butterfly people."

The tornado had barely departed when we began to hear stories about butterfly-like people who had protected residents, especially children, during the storm. The stories were numerous and were reported independently by people who didn't know each other. They came from individuals of various ethnicities, economic levels, and social backgrounds, but the accounts always described the same thing: beautiful, human-like beings with brightly colored wings who appeared only briefly but whose presence calmed, protected, and kept people safe until the storm passed. These winged creatures were invariably referred to as butterflies or butterfly people, and their presence was always regarded as comforting.

In one account I heard, a child was strapped in his car seat when the tornado hit. He could not move as the car was struck with flying glass and debris. Remarkably, the boy emerged unscathed from the wreckage. As soon as he was released from his seat, the boy described how a beautiful butterfly had wrapped him in its wings and protected him.

A young girl recounted being lifted high into the air by the storm, but a butterfly person quickly wrapped its wings around her body and brought her back safely to the ground.

A mother, holding her daughter, was running for shelter when the wind knocked them to the ground. Seeing the tornado lift a car in the air and push it toward them, she cradled her daughter in her arms, believing they would be crushed — but the car never hit them. When the woman released her daughter, the child said she saw butterfly people above them, and they had prevented the collision.

When the tornado hit, one father lay over his daughter, grasping at weeds and grass, trying to keep them anchored to the ground. Even though the tornado tore the shoes off his feet, the father and daughter remained unharmed. The daughter reported that a huge butterfly had held them down.

A four-year-old boy was blown miles away into a field, but he remained unharmed. The child told rescuers that butterfly people caught him and set him down safely.

Another girl was in a parked truck when the tornado hit. The tornado picked up the vehicle and tossed it hundreds of feet from its original location. Pinned in the wrecked truck, the girl reported being touched on her shoulder by the calming hand of a butterfly person.

An adult Red Cross volunteer described a butterfly person standing near a grieving family after the tornado passed.

These are just a few examples of the many accounts of the butterfly people. While such stories may seem implausible or even impossible, they were all very believable when you listened to the person telling them. For me, the stories inspired hope and provided a sense of peace in the midst of so much destruction.

Some people theorized that the stories were simply hallucinations. Others felt the stress and trauma of the storm precipitated the stories, and the accounts served to help people cope with the disaster by explaining why some people lived and others did not. But none of the theories or speculations explained how different people independently saw and reported the same thing.

Others believed the butterfly people were angels, but both the children and the adults described the protective beings as insect-like creatures with brightly colored wings, and they always called them butterflies or butterfly people.

I can't explain how the butterfly-people stories came about, but to me they were amazing and miraculous. I believe the presence of the butterfly people was a miracle, and they were here to help those who needed protection and give hope to others. I know the stories inspired many residents and helped our town recover. To us, the butterfly people have become a symbol of being reborn to a new life.

Although it has been twelve years since the tragedy, the stories about the butterfly people endure. So pervasive and lasting are these stories that our city has put up a large plaque describing the protective butterfly people and the stories told about them. Butterflies have even been adopted as a symbol of our city's rebirth and recovery from the disastrous tornado. Today, we have butterfly sculptures, statues, paintings, signs, and murals all over town. It's as if we never want to forget the miracle.

— Billie Holladay Skelley —

70

200 Pounds of Comfort

*Always remember to help people by welcoming them
into your home. Some people have done that and have
helped angels without knowing it.*
~Hebrews 13:2 (ERV)

Christmas has always been my favorite holiday, and Christmas Eve was traditionally the big celebration day in my family. Christmas Eve in 2017, though, was anything but. My husband was gravely ill and getting sicker by the hour. He had finally fallen into a restless sleep on the couch, so I tiptoed out to feed the birds and to have a quiet place and time to pray and have a good cry.

After I filled the feeders, I crept to the back deck, where I could let go and bawl my eyes out without anyone hearing me and hopefully without waking Curt. I was huddled on the deck, burrowing my face into my knees, when I felt a cold, wet nose snuffling the base of my neck. When I looked up and looked behind me, there stood an English Mastiff. I will openly admit that if I could afford to feed and care for one, an English Mastiff would be my top choice of companion dog. About three feet high with an average 200 pounds of love and drool? What's not to like?

I know every dog on our road, and I knew I had never seen this one before. He was well groomed, well fed, had a collar on... obviously somebody's baby. When I said hello to him, he walked around, plopped his big self in my lap, and rested his head against my chest. That's all it took for the floodgate to open. I threw my arms around him and clung to him while I cried, and he just lay there, occasionally whimpering as if in sympathy, and allowed me to blubber all over him. When the storm finally abated some, and I felt like I could get an ever-so-tenuous grip on myself again, he stood up, licked my cheek, and then loped on up the road.

I looked for him every day afterward but did not see him again until the day I came home from the hospital after Curt died. When I pulled up, there my angel sat, like he was waiting for me. I managed to get about two steps away from the truck before falling into a heap on the ground. Like before, he plopped into my lap, snuggled his head into my chest, and let me cling to him until the worst of the storm abated. Like before, he stood up, licked my cheek and trotted on up the road.

I have never seen him again, and no one I have talked to has ever seen him. Maybe they weren't supposed to. God knew I needed a comforting angel, and He sent one in a form that He knew I couldn't resist. If angels can appear as a flaming bush or a blinding light, then who's to say that they can't appear in a form complete with four feet, fur and 200 pounds of love and drool?

— Sarah Criswell Guldenschuh —

71

Visits with Mom

*Watching a peaceful death of a human being reminds
us of a falling star; one of a million lights in a vast sky
that flares up for a brief moment only to disappear
into the endless night forever.*
~Elisabeth Kübler-Ross

I had mixed feelings about leaving Northern California, where I had been born and grew up. We were moving to the land of one million freeways, tourism, smog, and Hollywood. The glamour of Los Angeles seemed exciting. The freeways, frightening.

But my husband's job was taking us there.

I adjusted to life, got a good job, learned the highway system, made friends, and enjoyed exploring the ethnic neighborhoods offering foods, architecture, and entertainment not found in my hometown. Window shopping on Rodeo Drive and visits to Disneyland added to my pleasure.

There were many drives back to northern California for holidays, birthdays, and emergencies. My mother's health was declining. She had experienced a number of strokes and a fall causing a broken hip. Her deterioration became more evident with each visit. Her memory was fading, her body growing frail. Her eyes had lost their luster. Her ability to carry on a conversation had become limited.

She had moved from an apartment to live with my brother and his wife in their home. I realized this was a sacrifice on their part and felt so grateful to them. I knew they had given up much to support our mother's needs.

The hardest visit I had with her lasted about a week. My brother and sister-in-law had gone on a well-deserved vacation. I flew up and rented a car. I planned to settle into my brother's house, play, talk, take walks, go for pie and coffee with Mom, and invite some old friends over as I was back in my hometown.

But Mom had different ideas.

The moment I walked in the door, she asked me to go to the store and get her some sleeping pills. I put down my suitcase and checked the medicine cabinet. There were perhaps four or five different brands of sleeping aids on the shelf.

"Mom, you have lots here. Are you having trouble sleeping?"

"None of those work. There's a new one out. I saw it on TV."

"I'll go tomorrow. The flight and all wore me out. I'll make you some nice tea, and you will sleep fine."

Her look showed me that I had disappointed her.

The days passed, and we talked a little, but conversation was hard. I cooked, and we watched TV. The request for a different sleeping pill continued.

I had peeked in on her several times each night, and she was sleeping soundly. But each morning, I would hear her complaints about sleeplessness. I was wise enough to not contradict her but listened and assured her that I knew she would sleep well tonight. Then, I would change the subject.

When I returned to Southern California, I cried for hours. My mother was no longer the mom I had grown up with. She had been a great cook and exhibited a sense of humor and a love of musical comedies. She enjoyed discussions about Eastern religions. She liked playing canasta and eating out in nice restaurants. But that mom was gone. I knew she would not come back but would continue to decline into her own world and her delusions of sleepless nights.

A few months later, my brother asked if Mom could come and live with my husband and me. They felt they had done all they could for her, and things were not getting better.

My brother flew with her to the Los Angeles airport, and Mom became my responsibility.

While I drove from the airport to my house, I pointed out things to her. Then I realized that she could hardly see as she would nod and say "pretty" but be looking in a totally different direction.

Both my husband and I had to work, so I hired someone to come in each day and be with her. She seemed resentful that I was not there 24/7.

The request for sleeping pills continued. I put red candies in a bottle and told her she could only have one per night as they were very potent. She took the "pill" and drank the calming tea I brewed. She seemed content until the next morning when she again complained about not sleeping.

We did have some fun. We would go out for pie, have company over for dinner, and watch movies I thought she would enjoy, but she'd fall asleep about halfway through the film.

One day, Mom appeared extra weak and quite confused. I took her to the ER. She was hospitalized and never returned to my house.

She went to a convalescent hospital where I visited with her daily after work, staying until she fell asleep. A little over a week later, I received a call at work that she had been moved to an intensive care unit at the hospital and was unconscious. She had had a major stroke.

I called my brothers, and they came, as did her grandchildren, my adult daughter and son. We stood by her bedside, telling her it was okay to go, everything was taken care of, we were fine, and we loved her very much.

The family's vigil at her bedside lasted several days when we sensed it was very near the end. I held her hand and knew it would be my last goodbye.

As her labored breathing became silent, I sensed a very strong male presence in the room. I heard a voice say, "Come with me, Wanda."

"Oh, you want me to come this way?" I heard her words within my being as clear as if she had spoken them out loud.

"Yes, come with me."

With that, I felt her leave.

No one else in the room had heard these voices, but I knew the presence was that of an angel. Not with wings, halo, and glowing light, but a calm, loving presence to take my mother on to the next place she was destined to go. I knew, beyond any doubt, that she was now fine, taken care of, not needing to ask for sleeping aids, no longer declining but ascending.

I did not cry when she died. I had mourned her passing when I had returned home from my week visit with her. All tears had already been shed.

But this time, I had been gifted by participating in a gentle, easeful transition and an angelic visitation.

— Cheryl Potts —

Chapter
8

How Did That Happen?

72

Cancellations I Can Live With

The best luck of all is the luck you make for yourself.
~Douglas MacArthur

I was almost turned away when I first phoned my breast specialist. She was booked solid with no openings for months. But while I waited on the phone, a cancellation came in, and I got in to see her within days.

Inflammatory breast cancer moves fast, and by the time most women are diagnosed, they are at stage three or stage four. According to the doctor, I needed a mammogram, ultrasound, and biopsy before she could know for sure, but I could see the concern in her eyes as she left the room.

When she came back, she carried a pile of papers. "This never happens!" she said, tapping the top of the stack. "I don't know how she did it, but Jennifer managed to get a mammogram and an ultrasound appointment for you next week. This is a miracle!"

A miracle sounded great, and I immediately counted each blessing — first, getting in to see my breast doctor in just days, and now two appointments, compliments of Jennifer and her magic wand.

The following week, I had my mammogram and ultrasound. Afterward, I was led into the special room reserved for women who will hear they have breast cancer. Christmas cacti — my favorite plant and the only green growing houseplant I'd ever been able to keep alive — lined the shelves, and I took it as a comforting sign as I awaited my grim news. Within minutes, the radiologist and her diagnostic specialist, Chris, arrived and gave me their condolences, a hug, and an appointment for a biopsy scheduled weeks away.

"Don't you have anything sooner?" I said. "My doctor said time is of the essence, and this cancer is exploding."

"We're sorry. That's the soonest we can get you in. You're lucky you're waiting weeks instead of months."

"Can you put me on a waiting list?"

Chris smiled. "We can, but no one cancels their biopsies, so please don't get your hopes up."

But I did have my hopes up. Why get into my breast doctor within days, then the ultrasound and mammogram, only to succumb to cancer before I could even get treated?

A few days later, Chris phoned me. My heart skipped a beat as I waited for her to speak. "You're not going to believe this, but I have a cancellation for next week. Do you want it?"

I almost screamed with excitement. "Yes!"

The biopsy confirmed I had stage three triple-positive inflammatory breast cancer that had invaded my lymph nodes. I was given a poor prognosis, but I refused to let that get me down. I felt like I was in a great place. I never felt angry, sad, scared, or alone, only watched over. And, so far, getting my tests done had filled me with hope.

When my breast doctor asked who I wanted for an oncologist, I told her I didn't know anyone and asked her to please pick someone who was extremely good. Later, I learned she had taken my words to heart and chosen the doctor who she would have picked for herself. Knowing my condition, the oncologist got me in immediately.

Although he didn't quote statistics, he made it clear that my only chance was to get started right away on chemo. I had already wasted precious time by waiting to call the doctor. Once again, I faced the challenge of getting tests and lab work done to ensure my body could handle the treatment, since chemo can damage the heart and liver and cause a host of other horrible side effects.

After I'd seen the oncologist, I handed the receptionist my appointment papers. She phoned the scheduling department to schedule my echocardiogram. After what seemed like forever, the receptionist said she had no openings close by and asked if I minded driving far away. It took us an hour to drive to the cancer center. Adding another hour would be worth it if I could get in right away.

"There's an opening at the end of August," the receptionist said. "Do you want it?"

My heart sank. "Tell her thank you for trying, but no. I'll be dead by August." That was the truth.

Suddenly, the receptionist's eyes grew big. "Oh, you're kidding," she said to the person on the other end of the phone. The receptionist beamed. "You're not going to believe this, but while searching for something farther away, someone called and canceled their appointment. It's next week and here at the medical center. Do you want it?"

"Yes!" This was unbelievable! During our drive home, my husband had tears in his eyes upon hearing that once again I'd gotten scheduled immediately. We couldn't wait to get home and share this amazing news with our sons.

After such splendid serendipity, I hadn't expected another hurdle. But days before my first chemotherapy treatment, I learned I had elevated liver numbers and would need a liver ultrasound. My cancer was spreading like wildfire. I didn't have time to waste, but it was my choice: wait until I got tested or go ahead with my chemotherapy treatment. After all the miraculous cancellations, the choice was easy. I would start chemotherapy.

Minutes later, the receptionist and the scheduling department worked to find me an appointment for my liver ultrasound, the earliest being late September. Of course, that wouldn't do. And, like clockwork, another unbelievable cancellation appeared out of the blue, blowing my mind.

After so many blessed cancellations, I felt as if I'd won life's lottery many times in a row. My heart overflows each time I think that I saw my breast doctor for the first time on May 5th, and by June

2nd I was getting my first treatment. I do not know how my story will end, but had it not been for my divine appointments, my story would already be over.

—Jill Burns—

73

A Good Life After All

*Each day offers us the gift of being a special occasion if
we can simply learn that as well as giving, it is blessed
to receive with grace and a grateful heart.*
~Sarah Ban Breathnach

It was the evening before Halloween, and I was up to my elbows in a triple batch of pumpkin cookie dough. I was baking for the first time in the tiny kitchen of my first apartment, a one-bedroom townhouse nearly six hundred miles from my family and friends in Pennsylvania.

I hummed as I sifted dry ingredients together into a floury mountain, finally feeling a tiny bit at home. I smiled as I thought of my mother, who celebrated every occasion by baking. I could picture the plaque hanging above her stove: "Bless my humble kitchen, Lord, and warm it with your love."

My kitchen was humble indeed, and these days God often seemed as far away as my mother did. Though I'd had enough sense to get a teaching job before loading up the U-Haul, following my college boyfriend to Charlotte, North Carolina had been impetuous. Now I was paying the price.

Why hadn't I considered the possibility that he would change his mind about wanting to marry me, leaving me stranded in a city where I knew absolutely no one?

Despite my efforts, I'd made no friends at the nearby church I started going to. My cheerful hellos to neighbors led nowhere. The middle school where I taught was in a small town thirty miles east, which made socializing with the other teachers difficult. Besides, most of them were older and married, full of talk about husbands and children that reminded me of my own woeful love life. And I was too ashamed to address the question I could tell they were bursting to ask: Why in the world are you here?

The past several months had been challenging, and not just because I was heartbroken. It was hard, and sometimes scary, to live alone, to find a doctor and dentist, to figure out how to pay the rent and all my other bills on a first-year teacher's salary. I couldn't even afford a phone. Instead, I trudged to the convenience store across the road from my apartment to use their payphone, dropping in quarters and dimes to keep hearing the voices of people I loved.

Moving here felt like a huge mistake, but I was determined to honor my year-long contract. And it would be humiliating to give up and crawl back home. Could I make a life here? Should I?

I felt as abandoned by God as I had been by my boyfriend. The only thing that kept me going was throwing my heart and soul into my forty-plus students. I taught small groups of them remedial English and math as they taught me how to talk Southern. "Well, dawg, Miz Ryne, this thing on my head is a toboggan, not a ski cap."

They were lively, bright and challenging, the closest thing to family I had. So, a few days before Halloween, I'd had the brilliant idea to treat them like family, Ryan-style, and bake for them. In honor of the holiday, I chose my college friend Nancy's pumpkin cookies with cream-cheese frosting.

It had seemed like such a good idea, baking cookies. Buying cinnamon, nutmeg and allspice had felt so hopeful. But I hadn't counted on how hard it was to make a triple batch of cookies in my poorly equipped kitchen. Three cups of shortening and sugar, three eggs and three cups of canned pumpkin filled up my largest bowl. Where was I going to put the six cups of flour? Even my largest pot wasn't big enough.

I decided to move some of the mixture to a pot and some into another bowl, and then work one-third of the dry ingredients into each. Oh, for my mother's beautiful Sunbeam Mixmaster! It was tiring to stir in all that flour by hand.

Finally, I was finished. I dropped thirty neat spoonfuls of dough onto a greased cookie sheet and slid it into the oven. Then I turned, as I always had in my mother's kitchen, to fill another cookie sheet while that batch baked.

That's when I realized there was no other cookie sheet. I only owned one. I looked at the time: 8:49. Eleven minutes until the stores closed. (This was before twenty-four-hour Walmarts.) Could I make it to the Richway a few miles away? But what about the cookies I'd just put in the oven?

The scent of warm cinnamon made me want to cry. I was flunking adulthood. I was a fool who was going to be up half the night sliding my one cookie sheet in and out of the oven and then frosting all those cookies. And there was no one to help me. God sure wasn't warming my kitchen with His love, I thought, with not a little self-pity. No blessing for me. I wish I could say I prayed, but I was too disheartened, too bitter.

Just then, my doorbell rang.

It took a minute for the sound to register because I'd never heard it before. The only person I knew in Charlotte was my ex-boyfriend, and I was sure this was not him.

"Who is it?" I called through the door.

"We're with Junior Achievement," a young female voice called back.

"Junior Achievement? What's that?" I had never heard of it.

I shrugged and opened the door. Standing there were two teenagers, a boy and a girl.

"We're from East High School," the boy explained. "We're learning how to run a business through a program called Junior Achievement. We decide on a product, and then we sell it."

"That's right," agreed his business partner. "Would you like," she asked, holding out a sample, "to buy a cookie sheet?"

Yes, a cookie sheet, delivered right to my door by two angels in jeans and T-shirts.

For a moment, I was stunned, but I pulled myself together to thank these beautiful kids and tell them that a cookie sheet was exactly what I needed.

I suddenly felt sure that I was right where I should be, that I could and would make a life here in Charlotte — a good life, a life rich with possibility and fulfillment.

Those pumpkin cookies were the best I've ever made, baked with a heart made light by gratitude. My students loved them.

— Maureen Ryan Griffin —

74

Last-Minute Change of Plans

To her, the name of father was another name for love.
~Fanny Fern

Many years ago, when I was nineteen, a friend of mine gave me a ticket to see the Rolling Stones. Their U.S. tour was sold out, but six of us, close friends throughout middle and high school, were going together.

It was back when we didn't all have cell phones. I was still living with my parents while working full time and going to college. As a courtesy I always let them know my plans.

The week before the concert, my friends and I figured out whose car we were taking, who was driving, where we'd stop to eat, and what route we'd take for the three-hour drive. All we had to do was wait for the date.

Concert day finally arrived, and my outfit and makeup were spot-on well before the departure time. Surprisingly, my dad came home from work early. There was something off about his demeanor. He set me down at the kitchen table, furrowed his brows, and looked me in the eyes. I knew what he had to say was serious. His voice was quiet when he said, "I really don't want you to go to the concert tonight."

"Why not?"

"I have a very, very bad feeling. I've been physically sick all day over it. I don't think any of you should go tonight."

"We've had it planned for weeks, Dad."

"I know. You can make your own choice, but I would really prefer you stay home. As a favor to me, I am asking that you please do not go to that concert. Maybe you all could do something else a little bit closer to home. I'll pay for whatever you want to do."

I'm not going to lie. My first instinct was to say, "Thank you, but I'm going anyway." It was the Rolling Stones. I might never have another chance to see them live. There was something about the look in his eyes, though, and the way he spoke so softly that gave me pause.

My reply was curt and bordered on disrespect. I had tears in my eyes as I told him, "Okay, I'll stay home."

"Will you please ask the others not to go?"

I knew there was no way my friends were going to listen to Dad's request. "That's not going to happen, Dad. I'll ask them, but they're going to go anyway."

I made the last-minute call to one of my friends to cancel. Donna wasn't receptive to my dad's request. "Wait. He wants us not to go because of a 'feeling'? That's ridiculous. He just doesn't want you to go. You're nineteen and can do what you want, you know." Part of me agreed with her assessment, but Dad had never made a request like this one before.

I washed my face and changed into my pajamas for the rest of the day. I bitterly kept to myself while five of my best friends went to the concert. I watched a movie, read a little, and finally went to sleep. At 2:15 AM, our house phone started ringing. I heard my dad running to the phone but couldn't hear his part of the conversation. There was a knock on my door, and Dad asked me to get up and come to the living room.

I was still groggy from sleep when my dad said, "That was Donna's dad on the phone. There was a serious accident tonight. The girls were hit head-on by a drunk driver. Jenna and Donna are okay with minor injuries. Emma and Grace will be in the hospital for a few days, but they will recover. But, sweetie, I'm so sorry. Jeannie died on impact."

I visited the hospital the next day where I cried with my friends and their families. We all attended Jeannie's funeral and stood together holding hands as they laid her to rest. Her family's grief was heartbreaking.

I was distinctly aware of how fortunate I was not to have been in the car that night. It was before seatbelts were mandatory and there wouldn't have been enough for all six of us anyway. With six of us squished in the car, the outcome could have been even worse.

I had survivor's guilt. I was lucky I had given in to my dad's heartfelt request, but what if I had pressed harder for my friends not to go to the concert? I played the events in hundreds of different scenarios in my head. Hindsight and a million what-ifs couldn't change what happened, and it was a hard pill to swallow.

I'll never know the answers to my questions, but I'm thankful I was open-minded about Dad's "feelings" and followed his instincts. That would not be the first time that his instincts made a big difference in my life. What was it that day? Intuition? Angels? God? I simply know it was a gift.

— Dawn Smith Gondeck —

A Little Dip of Comfort

Wherever we are, it is friends who make our world.
~Henry Drummund

I had known Donna for eleven years when she passed away after a heart operation. We'd met in an online group of grieving mothers, women who had lost a child. Donna had lost a son, just like me. We would talk and cry together nearly every day in e-mails, comforting each other and finding ways to cope with the deep sorrow we were experiencing. On the birthdays of our children, we would donate to a worthy cause in memory of all our precious ones.

Once a year, our group would try to get together in person in one of our hometowns. I had seen Donna at four of our "retreats" over eleven years, and she was truly our group clown. She had ways of making us laugh by wearing a big, floppy hat or strutting like a model inside one of the clothing stores at a mall where we would shop together. We were really going to miss her.

Just days after her passing, I was recalling several e-mails she'd written, and I remembered that she often mentioned this new "creamy spinach dip" she purchased at her grocery store. Donna went on and on about how much she loved this dip and how she could eat a whole jar. She let the whole group know that she just could not get enough of it, and she earned the nickname we gave her: Dippy Donna.

Days later, I went shopping at my local grocery store. I picked up a few things and headed to the car with my purchases. After I loaded them in the car, I returned the grocery cart and pushed it into the line of carts in the rack. Suddenly, I noticed a jar of something rolling in the cart in front of mine. It must have fallen from someone's grocery bag and was left in the cart.

I could hardly believe it when I reached down and picked up the jar. It was the very dip that Donna had talked about so reverently in her e-mails to us! I don't believe it had been there long because it was still cool from being inside the store. There was no one around to check with to see if it might belong to them, so I figured I had been gifted with my very own jar of Donna's favorite dip. I could hardly wait to tell the other moms about my message from our dear Dippy Donna in heaven!

— Beverly F. Walker —

76

Alan's Heart

Love recognizes no barriers. It jumps hurdles,
leaps fences, penetrates walls to arrive at its
destination full of hope.
~Maya Angelou

Alan screams, his face red, angry that he cannot enjoy breakfast at his mother's breast. The pre-op nurse touches the sedation cocktail to Alan's lips. It is flavored with something Alan likes for it quiets him briefly.

My brother Pearson and his wife wear the look of exhaustion and fear that has carved itself into their faces over the past two weeks. Mai rocks the furious baby, cooing, "I'm sorry, I'm sorry," as she has done so many times since his six-week-old heart failed.

I am the doctor in the family; I am expected to fix all things medical. My younger brother Pearson, Alan's dad, had called me two weeks ago, sobbing. "Alan is sick," he told me. "He might die."

Their baby had a rare congenital heart anomaly. A main artery supplying blood to his heart originated from the pulmonary artery rather than the aorta. This often causes a heart attack in an infant.

All our efforts have been spent arranging for Alan to get from Hawaii to Boston Children's Hospital where the only surgeon in the world to have perfected the surgery that Alan requires does his work. An inordinate number of women named Judy (besides me) have been instrumental in getting us to this point: social worker, nurse, travel agent. The Judys are one way the Universe has been reminding me of its assistance.

Alan calms in Mai's arms as the sedation takes effect.

"I'll take this little guy," says an OR nurse, a young man with a Jamaican accent and infectious smile. Mai kisses Alan on the forehead and hands him over gently. Pearson kisses his son in a slow-motion action that catches my heart. I choke back a sob.

We watch as Alan is carried through the door that sternly states, "Authorized Personnel Only," and we feel time suspended. Alan's outcome is up to Alan, the doctor, and God.

We wait.

As we eat breakfast from the cafeteria, Pearson suddenly stops, a fork of scrambled eggs halfway to his mouth, and winces.

"What's wrong?" I ask.

Puzzled, he says, "Could they just now be making the incision?"

My skin tingles. "Possibly. Why?"

"I felt a sharp pain down the center of my chest." His finger traces a line from the base of his neck to upper belly. "Is that where the incision is?"

Staring at him, I am out of balance and slightly detached from reality. An image appears in my mind of the doctor cutting into Alan's skin. "Exactly there," I tell Pearson. "And right about now. You two must be bonded." I thank the Universe for a sign that a transcendent energy is at work.

Pearson gazes into space, dumbfounded.

We locate the OR waiting room where I introduce Pearson and Mai to the nurse who appears to be in charge. She guides us to a separate room. "Your son's surgery will be a few hours, but you can wait here. It's comfier than that big room."

I thank her and note her name badge says "Judy."

"Your name is Judy," I say stupidly.

"Yes," she says. "What is yours?" She must wonder if I am intellectually challenged.

"Same. There are many Judys taking care of my nephew."

"Ah." She seems to understand. "I'm the OR liaison nurse and will bring frequent updates on Alan's surgery."

Pearson and Mai are still staring at yet another Judy. We cannot believe it.

We settle ourselves in the cozy room. Pearson and Mai look unmoored on the sofa across from me. A large, framed print hangs on the wall above them, a sunlit beach scene from the 1920s. I know the vision of Pearson and Mai sitting below that print will be indelibly etched on my soul forever.

We hover near the edge of sleep, unsure if we are dreaming or awake. At one point, I notice Pearson trying to get my attention without disturbing Mai. He whispers, "I just had a vision of the doctor telling us Alan's heart stopped twice, but he was okay. It gave me shivers. What do you think it means?"

I shrug my weary shoulders.

A little later, Pearson and Mai tell me they are going to the coffee shop for a few minutes. I stay behind, though the possibility that I may be alone when the doctor comes out of surgery fills me with dread.

They are gone for ages. When they return, Pearson appears agitated and anxious. His pupils are dilated, and beads of sweat form on his forehead. I wonder what could have happened between here and the coffee shop. "Is there any word yet?" he demands.

"No," I assure him. "What happened?"

He collapses on the small couch, his figure too big for it to contain, crying with every muscle in his body.

"What is it, Pearson? What happened?" I beg him. I assume the tension of waiting has exceeded his ability to withstand it.

Slowly, his shaking diminishes, and he speaks through his sobs. "Walking back up here, I... I wondered how you were... going to — to find words to tell us that Alan... that he died." I hug him and assure him I have heard nothing.

Just as his sobs are quieting, the doctor enters. He sees Pearson drying his tears. "What is wrong?" he asks. "Has anyone told you something upsetting?"

My level of anxiety suddenly exceeds red alert. I can barely breathe. Convinced he bears bad news, I tell him Pearson is just reacting to the waiting.

The doctor takes off his sweat-soaked OR cap and sits down. He looks very tired. The seconds before he speaks are endless. At last, he says, "Alan is fine."

We exhale a single breath laden with the toxins of our pent-up fears.

He explains that the surgery took so long because when they came off the heart-lung machine the first time, there was bleeding from behind the heart, so they put Alan back on the pump to find and stop the bleeding. It means they had to stop his heart twice. I look at Pearson, wondering if he has caught the significance of this.

The doctor draws a picture of how he moved the coronary artery from its abnormal attachment to its correct location. There is not an ounce of bravado in his telling of the miracle he has just performed.

He reassures us, "The next few hours are critical, but I do not expect any problems."

We thank him with words so inadequate that they are an embarrassment. When he is gone, I turn to Pearson.

"Do you understand what he meant when he said they had to put Alan on the pump twice? It means they stopped his heart TWICE. Your vision was accurate."

He looks at me, mouth open.

And then the floodgates release, and we hug each other and cry tears of exhaustion and elation. Alan's heart is fixed; we can breathe again.

—Judith Jackson Petry, MD—

77

Safely Home

A coincidence is a small miracle in which
God chooses to remain anonymous.
~Irene Hannon

My husband Bill was doing volunteer work the day his brother died, so I was the one who answered the phone and heard the sad news. As I was speaking with my niece, another call came through on my home phone. Of course, I ignored it.

After hanging up, I faced the task of going to see my husband. First, I checked to see who had called and was surprised to see my own name and number on the Caller ID.

That's not possible, I thought, so I pushed *69. Sure enough, the last incoming call was from my own number at 12:39 PM. There was no message.

I arrived at the store where my husband volunteered, and as soon as he saw me, he knew. We hugged and wept. After hearing the details, he went into the back room to call his other two brothers. A little while later, he came back out to the front of the shop and asked me, "Did you get any weird calls today?"

"Yeah," I answered. "I got beeped while I was talking to Jen. The call was from our home phone."

"Were you on your cell with Jen?"

"No. I was on the home phone."

"But that's not possible," he said, then added, "the same thing happened to both of my brothers."

"What?"

"They received calls from their own phone numbers."

With more pressing matters on our minds, we dropped it for the time being. Later, we discovered how odd a "coincidence" it really was.

At 12:39 that afternoon, quite a few of us in the family received phone calls on our landlines from our own numbers, including my brother-in-law's wife and children. We all had different local phone-service providers and lived in different towns.

A couple of nights later, I couldn't sleep. The time of the calls we had all received kept playing in my mind: 12:39. There had to be some significance to it. I crawled out of bed and got my Bible. Starting with the gospels, I looked up every Verse 39 in every Chapter 12 throughout the Bible: Matthew 12:39, Mark 12:39, Luke 12:39... Nothing stood out to me. After scouring the New Testament, I went through the entire Old Testament. An hour later, I climbed back into bed, wondering what it all meant.

As the final viewing was winding down, the parish priest had a time of reflection and prayer by the casket. We gathered around and listened as he read Scripture meant to comfort.

"And this I know, that if the goodman of the house had known what hour the thief would come, he would have watched, and not have suffered his house to be broken through." The priest explained that the thief sneaked up on the homeowner the way that death sneaked up on my brother-in-law.

Shocked, I leaned toward my husband and whispered in his ear, "That's Luke 12:39!"

"It is not."

"Yes, it is. I'm almost positive."

As soon as we dispersed, I went in search of a Bible. I found one and opened to Luke. There it was, the verse that coincided with the time of the mysterious phone calls.

I carried the open Bible and showed my husband, and then my nieces and nephew. Finally, I shared the verse with the new widow, all of us marveling at the gift of the message.

Yes, the thief came, at an hour none of us were prepared to face. But in the midst of our grief and despair, there was hope. Years ago, when long-distance phone calls were costly, my brother-in-law and his wife had a system for the family to let each other know when they arrived safely home after a visit. They'd call and let it ring twice, and then hang up before the call was answered. That simple gesture reassured the parents that all was well.

It appeared that my brother-in-law had orchestrated a repeat of those reassuring phone calls, at 12:39 on the day that he died. Those mysterious phone calls that we all received let us all know, "I made it safely home."

— Hana Haatainen-Caye —

78

Faye Day

Music gives a soul to the universe, wings to the mind,
flight to the imagination and life to everything.
~Plato

The car radio was on the wrong station. That's how it all started. Usually, the kids insist that I put it on the pop station, but for some reason, classic rock blared through the speakers. As I pulled out of the driveway on the way to three different school drop-off lines one morning, the song that was playing was immediately recognizable to me.

"Hey, this is one of your Aunt Faye's favorite songs!" I told the kids. They actually stopped bickering with each other and listened. Their Aunt Faye is my sister, although I never knew her. She died in a car accident when she was eighteen. I was born a year later to my surprised parents.

From every account I've heard about her, she was perfect. Everyone loved her, and she did no wrong. I don't believe any of that, but I understand that no one wants to say anything unbecoming of a dead friend or relative. Luckily, I have my brother, who has always painted her in a more human light. Also, when I was a teenager, I found a bunch of her letters in the trunk of her stuff my parents kept. Reading through those, I was very happy to find out that she was as imperfect as I was. It was good to know that she was indeed human because trying to live up to the memory of a perfect angel was kind of rough.

My brother taught me about her musical likes and dislikes, and I grew up listening to her songs on the records that he had. We had to play them quietly because if Mom heard them, she'd burst into tears. I've passed the stories and songs on to my children, who love to hear about their Aunt Faye.

When I picked up the kids for school at the end of that day, I had a lot of errands to run. To my surprise, the kids wanted to finish what was started that morning.

"What if we had a 'Faye Day'?" said Arielle, my youngest. Her two brothers agreed, and so we spent the rest of the day listening to all of Faye's favorite songs, which I had loaded onto my phone. While driving around, we talked about her, and I told them every story I knew to tell. We had a great day. I would have liked to think that Faye would be smiling up there in Heaven if she knew about "Faye Day." Needless to say, I was very surprised when she answered my thoughts later that night.

We had gotten in from our adventures, and I was sitting at the dinner table reading the mail when my seventeen-year-old son, Eric, came into the room. "Mom, I had a great time listening to Aunt Faye's songs."

"Yeah, we went through every single one except her very favorite," I said. Sadly, my sister's favorite song was "Stuck in the Middle with You" by Stealers Wheel, and it wasn't available on iTunes then.

Eric nodded and left, leaving me thinking that maybe I should check to see if it was on there again. It probably wasn't. I went back to the mail. I was interrupted by a strange sound.

Beep. "Bluetooth connected."

Alexa? I hadn't used Alexa in ages. I didn't even know she was on or plugged in. She had been in the corner gathering dust ever since I got her as a Christmas present the previous year. Plus, my phone wasn't even near me. It was on the kitchen island, and no one was around it. I was pondering what in the world was going on when I heard the first notes of the song — a song that I did not even have on my phone.

"Stuck in the Middle with You" by Stealers Wheel.

I was startled, but I wasn't afraid. In fact, I felt a sense of peace.

I laughed and sat back down at the table. "I'm glad you enjoyed 'Faye Day,' sis," I said to no one visible.

After the song played through, Alexa said, "Bluetooth disconnected," and then she went silent once more.

It was a good day.

— Melinda White —

79

Did You Hear About Paul?

The love game is never called off
on account of darkness.
~Tom Masson

A s I walked out my back door on a cold winter morning, the bright sun reflected off the snow. I looked down to avoid the glare and noticed a small, white Post-it note that was almost hidden in the melting snow. Surprisingly, it was completely dry.

I bent down and picked it up. It was a note from my ex-boyfriend Paul but we had parted on good terms a year before, and he had moved back to his hometown.

The note said, "When you think of me, I'll be thinking of you... Love, Paul."

This brought a smile to my face. I wondered how this little note had ended up outside my door. I thought maybe Paul was in town, but the ink was faded, so I assumed he must have written it the year before. How odd, I thought, that it appeared outside my back door now, in the snow. I put the note in my coat pocket and started off on my walk to the market.

While shopping for my groceries, I noticed a familiar face. It was my friend Dave. He and I had been introduced to each other a few years back by Paul. I couldn't wait to tell him about the note I had found. Before I could get a word out, Dave said in a hushed and somber tone, "Did you hear about Paul?"

I said, "What about Paul?"

Dave said that Paul had passed away the previous night in the hospital. He had been diagnosed with pancreatic cancer a month earlier and had become sick very quickly.

I left my groceries in the cart and hurried out of the market. I was very upset and just wanted to get home. As I walked toward my house, tears ran down my face. I reached into my coat pocket for a tissue. Instead of a Kleenex to wipe away my tears, I felt the Post-it note. I had forgotten about it after receiving the news of Paul's passing.

The little note was my shelter in an emotional storm. It's still a mystery to me how it ended up outside my door or when Paul had written it. I'm absolutely convinced it was Paul's way of saying goodbye.

— Kristine Ziegler —

Bearing the Load

*Deeply, I know this, that love triumphs over death.
My father continues to be loved,
and therefore he remains by my side.*
~Jennifer Williamson

My father was my first crush. He always knew what to say when I was sad or upset. I loved morning hugs when he wore crisp shirts and colorful ties, as well as nighttime hugs after he changed into flannel shirts and worn work pants. His soft evening hugs were scented with the cherry tobacco he smoked in his pipe each night after dinner.

When Mom was preoccupied with my baby sisters, Dad was there for me. He taught my reluctant hands to tie the bows and showed me how to use a key to tighten the roller skates that always slipped off my shoes. He taught me how to fish. Even though we left before dawn, I relished the time alone with him on those trips. He enrolled me in the Lure of the Month Club. I loved opening the box with my name on it. We'd guess the color of the fishing lure and whether it had stripes, feathers, or polka dots. Dad and I would find the perfect place for it in his tackle box. The excitement never wore off.

When I became interested in ice skating, he built and flooded a frame in the backyard. I practiced until I was good enough to skate with Dad at a local pond. The times we glided together across the ice and drank hot chocolate at the bonfire are among my childhood's happiest memories. In my eyes, he was the best dad a girl could have.

Dad was a hard worker who loved to help others. When Mom sent me to call him for dinner, it wasn't unusual to find him on a neighbor's roof blowing leaves from the gutters. When another neighbor's husband suffered from dementia, Dad brought music and sat with him to give his wife a much-needed break. Dad never stopped when he cleared snow from our sidewalk; he shoveled the whole block. He was a volunteer fireman who would drop whatever he was doing to extinguish a blaze.

As I grew, Dad's generosity became part of my personality. I joined Girl Scouts and enjoyed their service projects, volunteered with Special Olympics, and tutored children from the homeless shelter. Dad showed me the joy that comes from helping others.

I admired Dad's industrious spirit. He worked full time and took a part-time job cleaning a dentist's office and other odd jobs to support our family of six and afford a small cabin next to a lake. Once, after Dad came home from work upset, I heard him hammering in his workshop. When he came upstairs, he didn't seem upset. For him, it seemed that work was the cure.

I assimilated his work ethic. It became my way to cope when I was upset, too. In college, I was stood up by a boy I liked. I took the furniture out of my room and scrubbed the floor. The resident assistant said no one had ever done that before.

"Why don't you sweep the floor like everyone else?" she asked.

"This makes me feel better," I said, and it did.

Later, my husband would ask, "What happened at work today?" if he found me washing the kitchen floor when he came home. The year I was assigned a rowdy high-school homeroom, my house sparkled.

When my husband and I purchased a fixer-upper, Dad helped us rehabilitate the house that had stood vacant for over a decade. He helped rewire the kitchen, replace rotten windows, and dismantle a decrepit chicken coop.

My father adored my children. The feeling was mutual. He started making toys for them: wooden cars, rocking horses and cradles.

I was shocked when we learned that my father had bone cancer. He was a strong man. I wanted him to beat the cancer more than I had ever wanted anything. Dad fought to stay with Mom and his three daughters. It was not to be. The treatments stopped working. Pain medicine helped, but not enough. Each day with Dad was precious and agonizing as we watched him fight to be with us in spite of the pain. He didn't want to leave us. My sisters and I promised him we would take care of Mom and each other. He passed soon afterward.

After the funeral, I felt weighed down by Dad's absence, as if I was walking through a dense fog that refused to lift. I funneled my energy into lesson plans that animated my high-school students and turned them into much-needed distractions. At home, I had to face the heartache of life without my father. I needed to keep busy.

I took a tarp to the small, wooded area in the far back of my yard and attacked the soggy leaves smothering the pachysandra. The pile overfilled my large tarp. I hadn't noticed, and I didn't care. I grabbed two corners of the tarp and trudged across my yard toward the curb. The muscles in my arms began to ache as I covered a distance longer than a football field. My leg muscles and back joined in with pains of their own. I walked the length of my backyard. When I reached the front yard and the hill that leads to the street, I dropped the tarp. Tears flowed.

"Dad, I don't know how to go on without you." I stopped and thought how Dad would not approve of self-pity. The can-do attitude I learned from Dad triumphed.

I grabbed the tarp's corners, braced myself for the heavy load, and started up the hill. I pulled and felt no weight. Without any effort from me, the tarp whooshed up the hill and into the street. I stopped to think about what had just happened. Logic told me it wasn't possible. Then I smelled the familiar cherry tobacco scent. I looked around and saw no one. Then I felt a hand squeeze my shoulder and knew Dad was letting me know he was still with me.

— Judy Salcewicz —

81

A Miracle Hello

There are no miracles for those
that have no faith in them.
~French Proverb

Sometimes, people refer to dementia as "the long goodbye." For those of us who have cared for loved ones with the illness, that is often an apt description. What I discovered in my experience of caring for my parents, who both had dementia, is that it can be as much a "blessed hello" as a prolonged farewell. I learned this after several years of living with them both as their daughter and their caregiver.

Mom died on October 30, 2022, not long after celebrating her eighty-second birthday and fifty-seventh wedding anniversary. She had what would be considered moderate dementia and until she went into hospice that October she enjoyed some quality of life.

Dad, whose dementia was a little further along, forgot that Mom had died. For an agonizing eleven weeks, he asked for her daily. He was well enough to see beyond the "therapeutic lying" upon which caregivers must sometimes resort, leaving us with the task of telling him the truth and comforting him in his profound sorrow. He suffered a stroke in mid-February, never regaining consciousness. Mercifully, his death came just a few days later: February 23, 2023. He had just turned eighty-eight.

I am grateful for the unswerving support of my family. All of them rallied around us when we moved from Brownsville, Texas, to San Antonio so that I could have more support in caring for our parents. Losing Mom and Dad was hard on everyone, from the youngest grandchildren to my elder brothers. Mourning them in such quick succession made for an especially unique journey. After they died, it was just me and my dog, Preciosa.

Many people supported me through the grieving process, but nothing could truly prepare me for the first time I went through the holidays without my parents.

When December came, I opted to decorate for Christmas, a holiday my parents loved. I have always enjoyed Christmas music, and one song entitled *"Navidad Sin Ti"* ("Christmas Without You") by the Mexican singer Marco Antonio Solis found its way to the top of my playlist. One line in particular moved me beyond words: *Las lucecitas de mi árbol parece que hablan de ti.* ("The tree lights seem to speak of you.")

Our family believes in God and has a strong devotion to Our Lady of Guadalupe, confident in her veil of protection as we journey ever closer to God. Among my mother's final gifts to me was a gold pendant of Our Lady of Guadalupe, which I treasured. On December 12th, the feast day of Our Lady of Guadalupe, I lost that pendant. Somehow, the gold chain necklace snapped, and I heard the pendant's ping onto the garage's concrete floor.

I frantically searched for the pendant to no avail. I decided I'd look again, especially between the many boxes we still had there. And that is what I did for the next two weeks every time I went into the garage. In all my comings and goings — each one with a heavier heart as Christmas approached — I never found the pendant. I recall times when I looked at our Christmas tree with its colorful lights and asked God, Our Lady, St. Anthony, my father, my mother — any of them — to "speak" to me of the pendant's location.

I participated in the Christmas Eve Midnight Mass with my parish and went to bed exhausted but content. Christmas morning was awful, though, as I awoke alone, with only Preciosa to hug and wish a Merry Christmas. I would be seeing my San Antonio family for dinner, and our entire family would be gathering to celebrate the next day. But, that morning, I was on my own. I found myself aching for another moment of the long goodbye.

I made phone calls and went for a hike with Preciosa. That afternoon, I would head over to my brother's home.

A few hours later, when it was time for us to go, I called the dog and we walked into the garage. Then my heart stopped. There on the floor, right next to the driver's door, was the pendant that Mom had given me. I was stunned. It felt like my parents were hugging me from above. It was the greatest Christmas gift I have ever received, a miraculous, sacred, and blessed hello from heaven.

— Mónica Moran González —

Divine Intervention

82

Listen, You Will Hear a Voice

Whether you turn to the right or to the left,
your ears will hear a voice behind you,
saying, "This is the way; walk in it."
~Isaiah 30:21 (NIV)

"Bobby! Bobby!" Next door, our cousin, Jay, was calling for his youngest brother as we were sitting down for supper. It was a lovely day, no wind, and voices carried through the neighborhood.

Soon, we heard our aunt yelling, "Robert Dean."

Bobby was two, the youngest of five cousins who lived next door. After Bobby had been called several times, Jay was at our door asking if Bobby was at our house. This was a time when doors weren't locked, so now and then kids just roamed through the neighbors' homes, especially in the kitchens by the always filled cookie jars!

We searched upstairs, the porch, the basement, and the garage to no avail. No Bobby.

A feeling of panic was setting in as per the anxious and loud voices of the adults.

My uncle and dad decided to drive around the area; it was a relatively small town where everyone knew each other. Neighbors were checking their garages and porches. My cousins and siblings decided to get on our bikes and go searching. Some were going to head to the neighborhood grocery store just a block and a half away. Some went to the park three blocks away. I decided to go over to the church, which was four blocks away.

I was twelve. My siblings and cousins were eleven, ten, nine, and eight.

As I was about to take off down the alley, I sensed a voice of sorts telling me to cross Mary's yard. I paused and looked around. No one was there. I started to take off again toward the alley, but that voice told me again to cross Mary's lawn.

Mary was an elderly widow with a pristine lawn that we never played on, never walked on, and most certainly never drove on with our bikes.

I stood looking at that wide expanse of lawn right next to my uncle's home, held my breath, and decided to drive quickly across the lawn to the street, totally expecting to hear my mom's voice telling me in no uncertain terms to get off Mary's lawn.

I didn't hear Mom's voice as I took off. When I was only about three feet onto Mary's lawn, my kickstand dropped and caught. I leaned over to kick it back up, but it was as if it were stuck in the grass. I got off the bike and crouched down to loosen it. It was stuck in a hole the size of a quarter. I pulled my hand back, thinking *Snake hole!* I hated snakes.

As I quickly removed the stuck kickstand, that voice within spoke again, saying, "Call for Bobby."

I stood up and looked around. Everyone was calling him. I could hear them throughout the neighborhood. I kept hearing or feeling that voice telling me to call into the hole.

I was stunned. The hole? It was no bigger than a quarter. *How stupid,* I thought, and was about to leave. Then it felt as if something held me so I couldn't move. Again, I looked around, feeling rather ridiculous, but I crouched down again and softly said to that hole, "Bobby?"

Nothing. I was rising up when it felt as if a hand was on my shoulder, and that voice, gentle yet insistent, told me to call louder!

I was twelve, an extremely shy twelve, and this was making me feel stupid and embarrassed. Yet, I felt compelled, albeit reluctantly, to get closer to that hole and said louder, "Bobby!"

I heard a quiet sort of muffled sound from within that hole and then sobbing that quickly turned to loud crying. I almost collapsed, but I stood and screamed over and over again, "Bobby is in the hole! Bobby is in the hole!"

My voice grew hoarse.

People started appearing from everywhere. My dad and uncle finally appeared as I sat by the hole, sobbing and scared. We could all hear Bobby now, crying very loudly.

I was pulled back, along with my bike. Adults gathered around the small hole. Frantic voices wondered about the depth. Was it an old well? Was there water in it? Would it collapse if they pulled the grass back? Was Bobby hurt?

I could still hear Bobby crying.

Then, the local volunteer fire department arrived. My dad and uncle were both firemen, so it was determined that one of them should go down the hole. I later heard that grass was pulled back, rotten wood was removed, and my uncle was lowered down, tied to a rope. I have no idea how far he went down, but he came up with Bobby clinging to him.

It was determined that he'd fallen in a long-forgotten cistern that had been boarded up and covered with grass for many years. Mary didn't recall that there was a well there.

Bobby was fine, no broken bones, but maybe a few nightmares now and then.

People, as well as a local reporter who did a story on this incident, asked me how I knew to find Bobby in that well. I didn't want to tell them about the voice, so I claimed I had heard him crying.

Many years later, I began sharing about hearing the voice to a few church groups who "got it." It isn't just in Bible verses that we learn of those who hear the voice; it happens in our ordinary lives as well.

— Barbara Jackman —

83

Look Down

When my father didn't have my hand, he had my back.
~Linda Poindexter

On a typical chilly day in February, I went to visit my close friend Beverly. She had been in a hospice facility for three months. By the grace of God, she had survived stage 4 breast cancer for over eight years, but now the cancer had metastasized to her brain. Her time was drawing near.

I had visited Beverly once or twice a week since she was admitted. I never missed a week.

One of the nurses noticed and eventually asked, "You are not her sister, are you?"

I said, "No."

She stated, "Do you know why I knew?"

I said, "Because we don't look alike." I laughed.

She stated, "No. Only a very loyal friend would visit every week like you do."

Beverly's son came often, too. We made sure we visited on separate days so she would feel she had visitors throughout the week. I spent a few hours with her, always bringing her some healthy snacks that she loved.

After one visit, I drove to the cemetery to visit my parents' and grandparents' gravesites. I'd found myself going there every week since my mom's passing a year earlier. I was still struggling with her loss, and now I was anticipating the loss of Beverly as well. I always talked to my parents at the gravesite, and that gave me some comfort. After thirty minutes or so, I felt better and went home.

When I had settled in, I noticed that my diamond wedding ring was not on my finger. For a quick minute, I forgot what had happened to it. Then I remembered I had taken it off and placed it in my coat pocket when I needed to put on disposable gloves to help Beverly.

I hurried to the coat closet and reached into the right pocket. No ring! I checked the left pocket. No ring there either. Dang! I thought maybe it had fallen out of my pocket in the car, so I went to check. It was not there either. It was late, and the cemetery had already closed, so I could not go back there to look. I knew it must have been lost there. All I could do was pray that I would find it the next day.

The next morning, I went to a home-improvement store first to buy a metal detector. When I arrived at the store, I asked an employee to direct me to the metal-detector aisle. He informed me that the store did not stock any.

I left and drove to the cemetery, trying to stay positive. I arrived just as one of the cemetery staff was opening the gates. I parked in the same spot as the day before. My parents' gravesite is a few yards away from where I always park, so the walking path is very short. This made it easy to retrace my steps. As usual, I began talking to them while searching around their grave. It may sound crazy, but I asked their spirits for help in finding the ring.

I looked around their graves for about an hour before giving up. I walked back to my car, turned around to face their graves, and stayed still for a little while, leaning on the car. Then I heard a man say, "Look down."

I looked around. I didn't see anyone, but the voice sounded so familiar. I heard it say again, "Look down."

It was my dad's voice. I couldn't believe it! I hadn't heard his voice for more than nine years. That day, it was as clear as a bell.

I looked down and stared at the ground. Suddenly, I saw something sparkling in the grass only a few inches from where I stood. It was my ring.

Then, I remembered what had happened. When I arrived at the cemetery, it was much colder than I realized, so I decided to put on my gloves. When I pulled the gloves out of my pocket, the ring must have fallen out in the grass before I started walking toward the gravesite.

I cried, not only because I had found my ring but because my dad's spirit helped me find it.

Coincidence? Some might say it was just luck that I found my ring. Yet I know it was a small miracle that I found my ring at all. I would never have found it on my own as I was too busy searching in the wrong place.

My ring may just be a material object, but hearing my dad's voice brought me unspeakable joy and inner peace. He was still watching over me.

— Anneice Chapple —

84

Lord, Help Me Make It to Lordsburg

*Be not forgetful of prayer. Every time you pray, if your
prayer is sincere, there will be new feeling and new
meaning in it, which will give you fresh courage.*
~Fyodor Dostoevsky

I was driving my two young kids and my teenage nephew from
Texas to Disneyland in a twelve-year-old Oldsmobile sedan.
We made it to Las Cruces, New Mexico the first day without
incident. The next morning, while heading west on I-10, I
felt the transmission hesitate a bit. Knowing that miles of barren
desert lay between us and the next town, I felt a bit of concern. I
quickly shrugged it off, determined to take my kids to Disneyland
and comforted by the fact that the old car had just been inspected
and equipped with new hoses and filters.

About two hours later, I stopped for gas at a small, lonely facility featuring one pump and a tepee occupied by one circumspect,
uninterested attendant. I paid for the gas, took the little ones to the
restroom, found a few snacks, and got back in the car. Uplifted by my
fellow travelers all singing a boisterous "It's a Small World," I pulled
out and started up the entrance ramp to the freeway.

All of a sudden, the car wouldn't shift out of first gear. We got on
the shoulder of the interstate and plugged along at less than twenty
miles per hour. My mechanic grandpa had taught me that sometimes

one could "kick" a car into shifting by accelerating, then letting off the accelerator, and finally giving the pedal a quick stomp, or "kick." I tried this again and again. It was not working.

I passed a sign that said the next town, Lordsburg, was in forty miles. "Lord, help me make it to Lordsburg," I whispered. Things went from bad to worse when my windshield was suddenly spattered with water flying out from under the hood. *Water pump* was my first thought as "Oh, no" escaped my lips. The kids quit singing. I pulled even farther off the road and stopped.

"It will be okay," I chirped while trying not to panic at the thought of being stranded in the July heat, in the middle of nowhere, with two-year old Stephen, six-year-old Susan, and teenage Michael.

I got out and raised the hood. It looked like one of the new hoses was actually leaning on the top of the hot radiator and had a quarter-sized hole burned in it.

It was so hot. And this was before cell phones. We were surrounded by sand and tumbleweeds, and the only traffic was huge trucks barreling past us. No one was going to stop to help us.

Susan and Stephen were both crying. Trying to hide the quiver in my voice, I said, "God will help us. We must pray that God help us in some way."

In frustration, Michael angrily kicked a big rock, sending it sailing across the hot sand. Helplessly, I watched it land on something that flipped over.

"What did that rock land on?" I asked.

"I don't know, and I don't care," Michael said. "I just want to go home."

I had seen the object briefly; I knew what I thought it was.

"Go look," I said.

Michael stomped the thirty feet or so from the car and stopped. He slowly reached down, picked up the object, turned with disbelief on his face, and held up a length of radiator hose. He brought it to me. It looked new and strong. In all the miles of desert, in the exact landing spot of an angrily kicked rock, we were given a usable piece of hope. It was a miracle.

"Thank you, Jesus," I breathed.

Thankful for the gallons of water I had in the trunk, I got to work. I had no tools. I had no clamps. But again, as if guided by some inner source, I had a plan. I cut our newfound treasure lengthwise with a knife from the picnic box, centered it over the hole in the existing hose, and popped it in place to make a new exterior wall for the damaged hose. I cut a Batman pillowcase into strips and then tied them in a solid row along the length of the "patch." I poured all of the water I had into the radiator.

I said a prayer, started the car, and pulled onto the road. Trying not to think about the fragility of my makeshift patch and the forty miles ahead of us, I prayed. "Lord, help us make it to Lordsburg." I tried my "kick trick" again to no avail and then decided to hold off on it, fearing the transmission would strip out altogether. We pushed on in hushed silence. After a few moments, the confident voice of Susan broke the quiet.

"Mommy, try that kick thing again. I just asked God to make it work."

Oh, the faith of a child.

"Good girl," I said.

Trying not to think of what I would tell her if it didn't work, I accelerated, let off the accelerator, and firmly gave it the kick. The car shifted perfectly.

Tears of relief and gratitude streamed down my face as the car was filled with shouts of joy.

"We're going to Disneyland!" Stephen shouted.

I drove at a steady pace to the Lordsburg exit, where we found a gas station and service center. As I put the car in park, steam and water spewed from under the hood. All I could do was laugh. We had made it.

The miracles continued after that. The station owners put us up in their guest house, and their grandmother made us a wonderful Mexican dinner. The transmission problem turned out to be the governor valve, which cost only $40 to replace.

I kept that bandaged radiator hose tucked away for years as a reminder of the power of prayer.

— Story Keatley —

85

A Joyful Shopping Encounter

Let me tell ya. You gotta pay attention to signs.
When life reaches out with a moment like this
it's a sin if you don't reach back...
~Matthew Quick, The Silver Linings Playbook

It was a busy day and I was feeling somewhat overwhelmed, but I had a few minutes before lunchtime, so I stopped at a local market to pick up some groceries. I took a cart at the front and hurried inside the door.

As I focused on my shopping list, I heard someone call my name. When I looked up, I became aware of a woman I had not seen for several years. She had been a student of mine when I was teaching yoga.

"Wow," I said. "It's been so long!"

"Yes, it has," she agreed. "How are you?"

And that was the start of an unexpected and delightful conversation about our current lives. We talked about our children and our interests, about what we were involved in and our mutual friends.

Then, she looked at me with an unexpected softness in her eyes. She told me that I had helped her become the person she was now, and she would be forever grateful. I got teary and thanked her for telling me that. It was rare that I heard from a former student, and it was a joy to know that my teaching had had a positive effect on someone.

Other shoppers had to walk around us as our conversation continued.

Finally, we had shared all we needed to, and I was ready to pick up the groceries I had come in for.

"Our carts are empty," I said. "I guess it's time for both of us to go shopping."

She smiled and turned her cart back toward the door.

"No," she said. "I already shopped and put my packages into my car. When I came back to replace the cart outside, I found myself walking into the store instead, as if I was being guided. Then I saw you."

We looked at each other.

"It was meant to be," we said together.

We hugged and went our separate ways. I found myself breathing gently and smiling as I went through the store. Lunch would be a little late, but I didn't mind. My body could handle it. After all, my spirit had already been fed.

—Ferida Wolff—

86

This Happened

Not everything we experience can be
explained by logic or science.
~Linda Westphal

My mother is a very sensible woman. A more solid and down-to-earth Midwesterner you will not find. I have never heard her say anything that would cause me to feel she was embellishing a story to make it sensational. She is not easily flustered, is cool under pressure, and has never made me suspect she was losing her mental faculties.

With that being the case, I was recently surprised when she told me and my siblings that twenty years ago she plainly heard a voice tell her to do something, and to do it quickly. She did what the voice told her to do, and she will be forever grateful for the outcome.

Back then, my mother was the head of her department at a state university. She was younger than my father, so while he was close to retirement, she was still working. She was tenured and highly respected in her field. The university where she worked offered "cafeteria-style" benefits, and my father was self-employed, so she paid the fee to add him to her medical, dental, and vision coverage. They had never really experienced many medical issues, and had been comfortable with the higher copayments and deductibles that came with lower-cost premiums.

Like many people on cafeteria-style benefits, my mother had simply not responded to the annual enrollment e-mails and was content to let the system automatically "roll over" her coverage with the previous year's selections. This particular year, however, on the afternoon of the last day that changes could be made for the upcoming year, she had the following encounter with a commanding voice.

It was a Friday. Most students had left classrooms and labs to begin weekend activities. Faculty and staff were busy wrapping up their paperwork, cleaning off their desks, answering phone messages, and responding to e-mails. While attending to paperwork in her office, my mother heard a loud and commanding voice clearly say to her, "Get insurance."

She thought someone had stepped into her office because the voice seemed so loud and clear, but she found no one. She got out of her chair, walked to the door and looked in both directions, only to find an empty hallway. There was no one to be seen, and all the other doors were closed. She shrugged it off and went back to her paperwork.

A short time later, she heard the voice say again very clearly, and this time with urgency, "Hurry up and get insurance!"

Once again, she got up and found no one in any direction who could have been speaking to her. Her heart rate increased. She turned to her computer screen, and a few e-mails down the list was a reminder from the Human Resources Department that this was the last day when changes could be made to benefits for the upcoming year.

My mother looked at the clock and saw that there was just enough time to walk across campus to the H.R. office. She grabbed her jacket and purse, locked her office, and headed out the door. A few paces out the door, she heard the voice for the third and final time. All it said was "HURRY!"

She walked as fast as she could without losing her footing, and she got to H.R. with only ten minutes to spare. She found an unusually empty lobby and was greeted by an employee who was normally unhelpful, but today was happy to be serving the last person of her week. She asked what changes my mother wanted to make, and my mother said, "Max out every insurance option." The rep said it would cost more, but it was always better to be safe than sorry. As they were finishing up, my mother heard the distinct "click" of the lobby door being locked. It had been a close call!

Several months after my parents' new benefits went into effect, my father began to have health issues. He had hypoglycemia, heart issues, kidney failure, and other internal organ issues. Unfortunately, doctors began treating the symptoms one at a time as they were discovered, and no one, including relatives who were doctors, could find a diagnosis or effective treatment.

Dad was in and out of hospitals for the next two years. He had heart surgeries, kidney dialysis, and multiple other treatments and procedures. He took a long list of pharmaceuticals. Nothing helped.

Mom eventually found a doctor who studied the records, made additional tests, and concluded that Dad had amyloidosis, which causes the body to produce excess protein. The organs slowly become unable to deal with the excess, so they shut down one by one until nothing can be done to preserve life.

It is not clear if anything could have stopped the disease if it had been diagnosed sooner, but the medical bills up to the time of Dad's passing were astronomical. My mother has not shared the financial details, but it is certain that she could never have afforded to pay their share of the bills had she not made changes to her benefits two years prior to his passing. She is certain that she would have lost the modest house that she is now comfortably retired in.

Mom attributes the "voice" to an angel, perhaps her guardian angel, and feels nothing but gratitude for that highly unusual Friday afternoon. She shows her gratitude by helping other senior ladies in her neighborhood to keep living in their homes as long as possible. She drives them to appointments, takes them shopping, checks up on them regularly, and has them over to eat on a frequent basis. She is a remarkably helpful person.

Mom kept quiet about hearing a "voice from heaven" because people might think she was delusional. I am certain that my father would not have believed her. I don't think anyone else she knew would have believed her either.

This event was not disclosed to all of us until just a few weeks ago when Mom decided she would risk skepticism and tell us what had happened. Nothing like it had happened to her before, and nothing like it has happened since. She wanted to tell us the story so that if any of us were ever to have a similar experience, we would not make the mistake of ignoring it. I have always been skeptical when I hear claims of "hearing voices," but I don't know anyone I would trust more than her. If it ever happens to me, I'm going to listen.

— Thomas Brooks —

A Mother's Message

I would maintain that thanks are the highest form
of thought; and that gratitude is happiness
doubled by wonder.
~G.K. Chesterton

Although it's been five years since my mother died, I think of her every day. I remember her perfume, the way she threw her head back and clapped her hands when she laughed, her iced coffee on hot summer afternoons, and the love she had for her garden and the flowers that graced her house in Colorado.

My mother was of Dutch heritage. She, like her parents before her, possessed an uncanny appreciation for and relationship with nature and all things that sprout from the earth. Growing up, I remember her spending hours in the backyard of my childhood home, tilling, digging, cutting, pruning, planting, feeding, watering, and cultivating in every sense of the word a vast array of plants, bulbs, and flowers, including her traditional Dutch tulips.

She would sit on her potting stool in the middle of the garden, hands covered in well-worn gloves, with a weathered straw hat on her head, plaid shirt and shorts covered in fresh dirt, and an assortment of once white sneakers. And with her trowel in hand, and her instinctive gift for all things colorful, green and leafy, she would create landscapes bursting with color, energy and beauty that rivaled even the Old Dutch masters in their paintings of my mother's beloved Netherlands.

My mother's green thumb didn't stop at the door to the house. She would gather every extra water glass and vase from the kitchen and skillfully fill each one with an array of garden flowers, seasonal berries, decorative leaves, small green branches, and cattails and pussy willows from the creek that flowed around the perimeter of the backyard.

Yet as glorious as the yard and the house always looked, with blooms filling the outdoor and indoor spaces, her greatest passion was on the wooden windowsill above her kitchen sink. There she kept her prized African violets — nine or ten of them at a time — which disappeared one by one after her death.

A year after we lost my mother, I was home in California when a dear family member unexpectedly came to visit. Tasha had been the housekeeper for my husband's family for decades, and she remained a treasured friend. She had never been to my mother's home in Colorado, but she had met my mother on several occasions when she was visiting our home in California.

Tasha, who was a wonderful cook, would come to our home and help with dinners, lunches, barbecues and whatever else we had planned during my mother's visits. They had become good friends.

So, on this particular day, Tasha appeared at our house — sad and solemn — to pay her respects. She came bearing gifts, one of which was her fabulous Mexican chili de pollo, which was packed with traditional spices and chicken, still hot from the oven. As we all settled in to chat, catch up, and enjoy her fabulous meal, she told me she had something else for me as well.

She began by apologizing. She explained that when she was in the grocery store that morning purchasing her usual poultry, beans and chili spices, she passed through the floral section. She looked around for a few minutes and thought about bringing some flowers, but none really caught her eye, so she decided to just bring her chili.

Then, as she was about to leave the store and enter the parking lot, she said she saw one little plant sitting all by itself on a bottom shelf. She said she didn't know what it was, and she had never seen one before. It wasn't very pretty, and she didn't know if I would like it or not, but for some reason she felt compelled to buy it and bring it to me.

She reached into her bag and then brought out a little potted plant. It had dark-green, heart-shaped leaves with a furry texture sporting a touch of purple — an African violet with two tiny flowers in bloom.

Gasping, I began to tell Tasha about the little plant. I told her what it was called and explained the importance of these little plants to me and my family. I told her they were my mother's favorite flower, and I described how my mother had loved and cultivated them for years and always kept them on her kitchen windowsill in Colorado.

We were thunderstruck. As we gazed at each other in disbelief, my mother's presence at that moment became overwhelming and palpable. We could feel her in the room. It was as if she had never left us. And as Tasha and I hugged each other, laughing through our tears, we knew my mother was there with us as well, embracing us both, showering us with her love, and probably throwing her head back and clapping her hands with laughter.

The smallest things in life can teach us the biggest lessons. That little African violet taught me that while certain things in life inevitably change, some remain forever constant.

Now, I always have an African violet or two gracing the windowsill above my kitchen sink, where the small, sweet plants serve as a constant reminder that my mother is still looking out for me, watching over me, and sending me her love.

— Susan Wilking Horan —

88

The Timely Warning

I think that someone is watching out for me. God,
my guardian angel, I'm not sure who that is,
but they really work hard.
~Mattie Stepanek

I had just started working at a car dealership as an apprentice salesperson, learning the ropes from an old-timer who was getting ready to retire. I couldn't wait to get going and meet the rest of the staff.

White-collar staff was discouraged from hanging out with the blue-collar workers in the car-repair and auto-parts areas, mainly because of the liability risk associated with the possibility of being injured in the garage work zone. Instead, we were encouraged to get to know one another around the water cooler and coffeepot in the staff lounge.

My seasoned sales instructor liked to go out to a restaurant for a long, leisurely lunch, while I usually saved money by brown-bagging mine. After wolfing down a quick lunch, I would roam around the dealership, exploring all its interesting nooks and crannies, including the forbidden garage area, while almost everyone else was out for their midday meal.

On this fateful day, I was standing over the battery-charging station, where a series of car batteries were linked together by wires to charge them. In a car-sales lot with hundreds of cars sitting around, there are always dead batteries that need charging.

So, there I was, looking around and minding my own business, when I heard an agitated person shout, "GET AWAY FROM THERE!"

I spun around to see who had caught me snooping. Suddenly, an explosion right behind me knocked me off my feet. Looking up as I lay on my back on the cement floor, I could see that the garage ceiling twenty feet above me had been damaged, as bits of paint and plaster fell to the ground.

It turned out that something like a spark had caused one of the batteries to blow up, straight up through its top. Had I still been gawking down at the batteries, I wouldn't be around now to tell the story. Happily, whoever had yelled at me had probably saved my life.

By now, everyone had returned from lunch and heard about what happened. As each staff member approached me individually in the lounge where I rested throughout the afternoon, I told them my version of the events. I asked each and every one of them if they had shouted the warning. No one admitted to shouting at me. No one knew who it could have been.

To this day, my warning savior has remained a mystery. I am forever grateful that my guardian angel had my back that afternoon.

— Sergio Del Bianco —

89

Pinned Under an Excavator

Miracles, in the sense of phenomena we cannot
explain, surround us on every hand:
life itself is the miracle of miracles.
~George Bernard Shaw

I glanced at my phone. There was a text from my husband Greg: "Call me ASAP. Austin's been in an accident."

I called. Greg picked up immediately. "A firefighter called me. They've got Austin en route to Knoxville. He rolled an excavator on top of himself. All they can say is that he's got a broken ankle."

"That makes no sense!" my nurse's instincts screamed. "They don't airlift you for a broken ankle! Something's terribly wrong!"

The possibilities tumbled through my mind — head injury, brain bleed, crushed organs, collapsed lungs, amputation, and the list rolled on.

I left work and met Greg for the drive to Knoxville. I barely managed not to come completely unglued by desperately calling anyone whom I knew would pray.

The hospital told us nothing, just confirmed that a John Doe had arrived. This cranked up our anxiety exponentially.

When we arrived at the trauma unit, a doctor finally gave us details. Eleven broken bones, including both crushed scapulas, five broken ribs, eye socket and sinus cavity fractures, and both lower leg bones snapped completely in two. Both lungs collapsed, and one hemothorax. Many bruises and contusions but, miraculously, no brain damage or concussion.

As he rattled off the laundry list of injuries, Greg swayed and had to put his head between his legs. He could not bear to hear of Austin in such poor shape.

Me, I needed the details and just had to see him.

Austin was on the ventilator, in a medically induced coma, and almost unrecognizable from the swelling. He didn't know we were there, but we spoke to him, kissed him, and prayed over him.

He was alive.

Before we even arrived in Knoxville, prayer teams from our local churches kicked into gear. Word spread like wildfire, and soon friends, strangers, and people from other countries joined the prayer band.

Austin only heard much of this later. At first, he required surgery to place a rod in his leg. Chest tubes, catheters, braces, and sedation were on the menu. He'd lost too much blood and received transfusions en route. I peppered the nurse with questions, which he patiently answered. Austin's nurses were phenomenal.

Austin spent three days in the ICU, then another eight days on the floor healing, resting, pushing, and learning how to deal with his injuries and walk again. Another eight days in rehab brought him to discharge on his twentieth birthday. He walked out with a cane and arm brace.

Four months later, he's still undergoing therapy for his strength, nerve damage, and the slow healing process. We have been amazed at how well he has recovered. We know that God spared him.

Now for the backstory — because when you live in a small town, people know each other. If it weren't for the small-town network, we'd never know these details.

The accident happened an hour and a half from home. When the machine flipped, Austin got pinned underneath. Four thousand pounds crashed onto his upper back. At first, he was conscious, looking around, but unable to draw a breath or scream. He thinks he lasted five minutes, watching the other guy working on another machine, before passing out. He said he knew he was going to die; no one could see him.

A neighbor down the hill changed her routine that afternoon. Instead of sitting inside, she decided to spend fifteen minutes on her porch, scrolling her phone. When she heard the *thunk*, it didn't alarm her. However, even over the noise of the heavy equipment, she clearly heard someone calling, "Help me!"

She instantly screamed at her husband, who came running. The old man ran up the hill and found Austin. With EMS on the line, the lady stopped her husband from his plan to hook up a chain and pull off the excavator, which might have killed Austin.

The responders arrived within minutes, snapping into action. We later learned that the main paramedic is from our town. Our other boys "randomly" met him after the accident and found out he'd worked on Austin. Austin met him after his discharge, and he filled in some details.

When the paramedic arrived, he thought Austin was dead. He'd passed out by then, and as they evaluated the scene, the paramedic and his partner had to make a split-second decision. Instead of using the Jaws of Life, they joined forces with around six men to push the excavator off Austin to save time.

The paramedic was one of only two army field medics in our region. Because of a scheduling glitch, instead of a rookie EMT, the other field medic showed up — another thing that saved Austin's life. The seasoned pair had worked together in Afghanistan. They simply made eye contact, nodded, and dove in. These two placed chest tubes immediately. He told our boys their ambulance had never seen so much blood flowing over its floors.

An ambulance, helicopter, two or three resuscitations on the way when they "lost him," and then a dash through ER finally landed Austin in the trauma ICU.

The weeks that Austin endured in the ICU, hospital, rehab, and therapy were tough for him. He fought against great injuries. He became exhausted. He got frustrated. He missed out on activities but has amazed us all at the timeline in which much of his recovery has happened.

Austin ended up with nerve palsy that left his right arm and hand immobile and numb. This was from the tremendous crushing injuries he endured. They told him it might take eight months to regain function. He has fought, pushed, and rested when necessary.

At four months, he's exceeded their predictions. He still tires easily, has residual weakness with his arm, and can't stand or walk for long. However, in addition to his regular therapy, he works out at the gym with his brothers almost daily, and he presses himself to heal. Austin drives everywhere, volunteers at church projects, and always pushes to stay active.

When we look at the many details that lined up perfectly that terrible day, we know God spared him. He sent the right people at the right time, and that's no cliché. From the woman on the porch with a phone in her hand, her husband being home, the highly skilled first responders who "happened" to work that call, to the mercy of a God who sees the plans He has for a teenage boy, we see miracles. We see the miracle of people pulling together to pray for and support our son, many of whom will never meet him.

Today, when I bump into someone in town, even a person I hardly know, I'm frequently asked, "How's Austin?" I then recall God's mercy to us all in stepping in to save our boy. I give the report, whisper a grateful prayer, and always add one more request at the end.

"Thank you, Lord, for sparing Austin. You saved him for a purpose. Please reveal that plan to him."

—Laurie Spilovoy Cover—

90

Expect the Unexpected

*It was possible that a miracle was not something that
happened to you, but rather something that didn't.*
~Jodi Picoult, The Tenth Circle

My commute to work takes me from the lush Cowichan Valley through the scenic seaside village of Mill Bay and then over the Malahat Summit of 356 meters and down through Goldstream Provincial Park and on to Victoria, British Columbia. One rainy Monday morning found me southbound in my work van passing through Mill Bay and hurrying to get to work on time. As I started the climb up the Malahat highway, my "inner voice" told me, "Expect the unexpected." I've had these inner voice messages before, and usually I pay attention to them, but this was such a vague message. It didn't really make sense. I did start watching for deer or stray dogs on the road, but I'm always on the lookout for deer anyway.

The message became really insistent and repetitive. To be honest, it was becoming quite annoying, so I turned up the radio to drown it out.

By the time I got to the Malahat Summit, the music was pretty loud, and that was beginning to annoy me too, so I turned down the volume. I heard no more inner-voice messages, so I assumed whatever was going to happen had happened, and I got on with my thoughts of the day's jobs ahead.

Passing through Goldstream Provincial Park, "expect the unexpected" started up again in my head. It was so insistent that it became hard to ignore. Rounding the last curve, the highway goes from one lane to two southbound. There is a slight rise and a tree-lined curve to the right before a straight stretch.

By now, my inner voice was really irritating me. I was the lead vehicle, and with a line of cars behind me, we were all doing about 80 kilometers an hour in the rain coming into that last turn. Unexpectedly, I hit the brakes. I don't know why; I just did. The car behind me, which was starting to pass, also hit his brakes, and we all started to slow.

As we came out of the curve, an old lady with her back to us and carrying a big stick stepped out onto the highway — in my lane. She wandered from the slow lane to the fast lane and then into the oncoming traffic lane. Fortunately, the northbound cars could see her coming and had already stopped.

Now at a full stop, I could see that this old lady, who never once looked back before crossing this very busy stretch of road, was following a cow. When she and the cow got to the far side of the highway, she smacked it on the rump, and the two of them headed back across the highway again and disappeared into the trees.

I've driven that stretch of road for thirty years, and I have never seen a farm or farm animal in that area.

I said a quiet "thank you" to my inner voice and the spirit guide who looks over me.

— N. Newell —

91

From a Distance

Impossible situations can become possible miracles.
~Robert H. Schuller

I live in Detroit; most of my family is across the world in Australia. I miss all the everyday exchanges, the lazy afternoons together, the holidays, the "Can I get you anything from the supermarket?" calls. Sometimes, I must miss happy family events, and I'm not around during the tough times either. Those are the times that cement family and community, but from a distance, I can't do anything to help other than pray.

No one in my family had heard of a diaphragmatic hernia until my nephew in Sydney was born with a hole in his diaphragm. All the organs in his abdomen had moved through the hole and up into his chest, squashing his lungs, which hadn't grown at all.

As soon as he was born, he was given emergency surgery to close the hole and put all his organs where they were supposed to be.

From almost 10,000 miles away, I saw pictures and heard the grim reports that the doctors had given my brother and sister-in-law. I prayed and gave a listening ear, but what else could I do? I was busy with carpools, cooking for my family, and discussing the latest basement floodings with my Detroit neighbors, people who don't even know my family.

Hearing updates through the telephone wire made the everyday angst of what my family was living through feel very far away.

For weeks, Chaim and Danielle lived in the bubble of the ICU ward. At one point, they were standing next to the little hospital crib, looking at their baby who was swollen with medicine. Electrodes and wires were attached all over his body. The doctors were tense, just waiting around.

"Can't you do anything?" Chaim implored them.

"There's nothing else we can do," one doctor answered him frankly. "We've done everything we can. Now it's up to him. Honestly, we've seen babies who were far better off than this one die. We need to tell you: prepare for a funeral."

The doctors had given up, but Chaim and Danielle refused to accept their prognosis. The heavens were pounded with prayers from around the world, all for this new baby who seemingly had no chance.

Time is a strange thing in a hospital where every day looks the same. It felt like time was standing still, but suddenly it was Passover.

On the last day of Passover, Chaim invited four of his mates to join him for the Chabad custom of Moshiach Seudah (a hopeful and uplifting feast celebrating the imminent arrival of the Messiah) at the hospital. They walked the forty-five minutes to the hospital together. Chaim asked the nurse, "Do you mind if we sing by the baby's bedside? We won't be loud."

The nurse readily agreed, so the men pulled up some stiff, plastic chairs by the baby's crib. Careful to keep their voices low, conscious of the critically ill kids in the ward, they began to slowly sing the ancient soul-stirring Chabad melodies. Their voices blended together. These men in their holiday finery rocked to and fro in their seats, with foreheads furrowed and eyes closed, lost in the moment and their private prayers. They were ending with the very last song known as the "Alter Rebbe's Niggun," the same haunting melody that's sung during Chabad weddings, when Chaim peeked — and suddenly saw the baby's eyes flutter open.

He quickly called over a passing nurse.

"The baby's eyes opened," Chaim told her.

"That's impossible," the nurse said sadly, as she glanced over. Instantly, she did a double take. The baby's eyes were open for the first time. He had defied the odds and pulled through. It was a moment, all those men state with conviction, they will never forget.

At four months old, the baby was able to go home.

He needed therapies, of course, but soon he was walking, talking, and dressing himself — hitting milestones with breathtaking speed as time shot forward. There were appointments. School. Visits to his grandparents and cousins in Melbourne.

At age three, Mendel had an upsherin, the traditional hair-cutting ceremony. By that time, it was very clear that Mendel was out of the woods. So, around the same time, Chaim and Danielle threw a huge Seudas Hoda'ah (thanksgiving feast) to celebrate the miracle of his birth — yet another family celebration on a very long list of things I missed. One evening, the Yeshivah Centre on Flood Street housed the rollicking, wall-shaking thanksgiving party as the entire community pulled up in droves, dressed in their best clothes, and danced up a storm. Friends and family flew in from Melbourne, and kids ran around the place, shrieking with excitement, their exhilarated faces smeared with remnants of the generous nosh table or decorated with face paint. This was the same community who'd prayed for exactly this outcome.

***

As Mendel's bar mitzvah approached, I knew with conviction that I had to be there. Because of COVID, it had been the longest I'd ever gone without visiting my family. I flew from Detroit to Melbourne and enjoyed spending time with my parents, siblings, nieces, nephews and childhood friends.

I was in Melbourne for two and a half days, and then we flew to Sydney for the bar mitzvah.

Squashed among a huge crowd of ladies eagerly looking down from the women's section, with lollies clutched in our hands, we waited for the moment. And then Mendel, this miracle child, was called to the Torah with his father. He said the blessings and read from the Torah. And with that, the baby who wasn't supposed to live had done it — he'd become a man!

The men spontaneously burst into song and joyfully grabbed

each other's shoulders, weaving and dancing around the synagogue. Mendel was in the lead, holding up his arms in a victory pose, while the little kids, oblivious, scurried around them, scooping up the lollies the women had rained down.

Among the crowd of women, and some of the most emotional, were two non-Jewish women, Steph and Charlotte.

Later, when the celebratory meal was in progress, these two women clambered on top of a couple of chairs to address the crowd.

Steph introduced herself. "Charlotte and I are ICU nurses; we looked after Mendel in the hospital when he was born. We've looked after many sick babies and been privy to the journey of many families. There are some families we will never forget. Mendel was one of the sickest babies we have ever looked after, and we didn't think he would make it. We believe he lived because of the rock-solid faith of Chaim and Danielle, which they held on to and which kept them going. One of the doctors, who is a self-acclaimed atheist, told them, 'I don't know what you're doing, but whatever it is, it's working, so keep doing it!' To be here right now, to see this miracle baby reach manhood, is one of the most incredible, heartwarming moments of our lives."

Later, I asked Charlotte, "How many times have you seen the fruits of your labor at an event like this?"

She looked at me through eyes that have seen too many babies die young, too many parents robbed of the chance to raise their precious children, and the agony of countless families during the most pain-filled parts of their lives.

"This is the first time," she answered.

At the party on Sunday, the dancing was non-stop, the atmosphere electric. Everyone was dancing and jumping ecstatically. No one could sit with this type of energy pulsing in the air.

This wasn't just a bar mitzvah; it was the celebration of a miracle.

For me, it was surreal. Knowing I was leaving the next morning and who knows when I'd next have the chance to visit again, I relished the minutes, dancing like there was no tomorrow. Although I had missed all the steps that led to this incredible event and had been far away during the hardest parts of their journey, with overwhelming gratitude to God I was right there at this magical moment to help them celebrate this amazing milestone.

—Rochel Burstyn—

Chapter
10

Listen to Your Dreams

92

The Second Cup of Coffee

Death ends a life, not a relationship.
~Jack Lemmon

"I want to see you," Matt said by way of greeting when I answered the phone call. I had moved to the West Coast six months earlier when my interim job in the Midwest ended, and my son and his fiancée started planning their wedding. I decided to retire a couple of years ahead of schedule, glad for their invitation to move closer to them.

Leaving Matt was the most difficult part of the decision and transition. We had reunited as romantic partners ten years earlier, more than thirty years after my graduation from the college where we had met. He sent me an invitation to his retirement party; I went, and we restarted our special friendship as if we had not spoken for a few months, instead of a few decades.

He had multiple commitments to teaching and his grown family. I had my priorities. Amid the flurry of my packing, we said goodbye, and I knew he would visit as promised. He also had other connections in my new city.

He visited me on the West Coast in December, and I noticed that his pace had slowed when we walked, and he had to stop and catch his breath.

I had savored every moment we spent together in the past ten years. The angst of figuring out how to live a life, choose careers, and what partnerships to enter into had slid into the past. The gift of older age is that one can be more present. As empty nesters and single adults in later life, we could enjoy the long weekend mornings, a night out at a music or theater venue, or cooking a meal while listening to jazz.

We traveled regionally and internationally. I had been waiting until I retired to travel. He introduced me to his favorite places in Europe. Then we would break the bubble and return to our waning careers or family events.

I had given Matt a range of dates in our telephone conversation that would be convenient for me to host his visit. A couple of hours later, I remembered a one-weekend conflict and called and left a message on his voicemail.

I didn't hear from him for the next two days. On the third morning, I woke up, and he was lying next to me in bed.

"Oh, good, you got here," I said. He didn't say anything, but he held me and looked deeply into my eyes. He looked younger; there was no gray in his hair. I heard, although he didn't speak, "I'm so sorry. I love you so much." I rolled over to go back to sleep, with my back nestled against his hug.

When I woke up again, he was gone. I made a cup of coffee and looked around the room, expecting to see Matt, and then thinking perhaps I had dreamed. How had he gotten into my apartment? But the experience felt more real than a dream.

I opened my laptop and entered his name in the search box. His obituary, published that morning, popped up. He had died of a heart attack unexpectedly the night he called me. It might have been his last conversation.

He had kept his promise to see me. I told multiple friends this story, to save it in shared memories as real and not imagined. I did not return for a funeral. He would be eulogized by many from his past lives, and I had been a quiet companion in his last years. Besides, we had our private goodbye.

Although I was sad at his death, I was immensely comforted by his presence. Over the next weeks, I saw signs that he was lingering.

I kept them to myself except for talking to a deeply intuitive person, a chaplain I knew. The months passed, and I moved on.

I went into the kitchen upon waking one morning. One curly, black hair lay on the sink, inexplicable among the blonde and whitening hair I might shed. "Were you here, Matt?" I asked out loud. Then, I paused a moment before double-checking the wall calendar. It was the first anniversary of his death.

"Thank you for reminding me," I said. I poured hot water into the pot he had given me and set the coffee to brew. I set out an extra cup for him, so I could sit at the table with two cups ready.

— Sharon Johnson —

93

Get Ready, Daddy. I'm Coming!

Pay attention to your dreams — God's angels often
speak directly to our hearts when we are asleep.
~Eileen Elias Freeman,
The Angels' Little Instruction Book

My wife's due date was still three weeks away when Shady Cove Cabins called to confirm our reservation. Focused as we were on the baby coming, we'd forgotten all about the booking we'd made a year before.

After knocking the idea around for a few days, my wife decided that we owed it to ourselves to go as planned. Once the baby arrived, it might be quite some time before we'd have any free time to ourselves. Our midwife, Cynthia, thought it was a great idea, too, as long as my wife felt up to it. In fact, getting some relaxation could make the delivery easier.

So, I filled up the tank and packed the RV the night before so we could get an early start and drive straight through.

We were both kind of giddy that night at bedtime. We got to reminiscing about how much we enjoyed our last visit to Shady Cove. We began trading fond memories:

"Remember that pizza place with the real brick oven?

"And that little pond where thousands of ducks were nesting?

"And what about the cool general store we found out in the middle of nowhere with all those old-timey gadgets on the walls?"

Caught up in the moment, I think we both forgot that my wife was eight-plus months pregnant!

I set the alarm just in case but was awakened instead by a fantastic dream of a visitor. It was so vivid and real that it took me several seconds to decide whether it was a dream or not.

In this dream, a lovely girl of about eight or nine was floating above me, grinning. Her hair was blond and flowing as if caught in a gentle breeze provided just for her benefit. And I was certain I knew the little girl, although we'd never met before. And when she spoke, it was as if I'd heard her sweet, little voice a thousand times.

She said, "Daddy, get ready. I'm coming."

I knew my unborn daughter was speaking to me. She was telling me she was coming early!

The next morning, I found my wife getting ready for the drive and immediately inquired how she was feeling.

"I'm fine! Excited to go!" she said, stuffing a satiny nightie into her overnight bag.

"You know, if you have any doubts, we can go another time," I said.

"No, I'm fine!" she promised. "I really am! And we both know that another time may never actually come!"

Then she must have noticed something odd in my expression because she wrapped her arms around me and drew me in close, saying, "You look worried. Is there something you're not saying? Is it the baby?"

I nearly told her about my dream but suddenly felt foolish and instead confessed a half-truth, "Well, kinda, sorta. I mean…"

"Listen. Everything'll be fine! I'm not due for two weeks, and everything feels perfectly normal. I promise, I'm not having this baby anytime soon!" Then, she rolled her eyes impishly the way she does and said, "After all, who's the expectant mother here?"

"Okay." I smiled, not nearly as certain as she was.

Even as we pulled out of the driveway that morning, I kept hearing that sweet, little voice whispering in my ear, "Daddy, get ready.

I'm coming."

I honestly don't remember what we talked about on the ride up — or if we talked at all. I just kept thinking that the longer we drove, the farther away we'd be when our daughter arrived.

We got to Shady Cove Cabins by 11:00, checked in, and put away a few things. We changed shoes and headed down the road to our favorite diner. My wife had a craving for Eggs Benedict — and they had the best either of us had ever tasted. Walking in, waves of wonderful memories came flooding back as if we'd been there just the day before!

My wife headed directly to the ladies' room while I chose a booth by the window and ordered for the two of us. A minute later, I heard my name being called from across the restaurant. When I looked, I saw my wife standing by the door, motioning frantically for me to come. I could read her lips: "Come on! It's time!"

We'd been driving around with the baby bag in the back of the RV for weeks, so we headed straight to the interstate bound for home. I suggested we go to the nearest hospital — at least to have her examined — but my wife had her mind set on making it to the birthing center about ninety miles away.

I pushed the speed limit and watched the blue-and-white hospital signs flash by.

About halfway home, we stopped at a rest stop so my wife could use the restroom, and I could call ahead. Cynthia advised that we stop at the next emergency room and verify that it wasn't false labor, but I assured her that we were both certain.

"Our daughter is coming!" I told her.

"So, you're hoping for a girl?"

"It is a girl, Cynthia! I'm certain!"

By the time we reached the birthing center, everything and everybody was in place. The smell of sweet sage greeted us as we entered, Native American flute music calmed us, and the birthing pool was warm and gurgling invitingly. The stage was perfectly set for the arrival of our daughter.

No sooner had Cynthia poured my wife a cup of steaming raspberry tea and helped her slip into the water, than the contractions began.

Cynthia took a quick look.

"This baby's coming, like now!" We all gathered in close. "Get ready to catch, Daddy! This baby's wasting no time!"

Time seemed to slow down and then come to a complete stop.

Suddenly, I was holding this little girl in my arms and staring into the very eyes that woke me that morning! And even though I've heard that newborns aren't capable of intentionally smiling, I know in my heart that when I smiled at her, she smiled back. It was the very same, sweet smile I've seen a million times since!

"Well, what are we going to call her?" my wife asked excitedly.

"I don't know if you're aware of it or not, but today is the first day of summer," Cynthia said. "Seems to me this little girl went out of her way to be born specifically on this day!"

My wife and I looked at one another and nodded. "That's perfect! We'll name her Summer," my wife said.

Now, I know many fathers have special relationships with their daughters, but I have yet to hear of one that began even before birth.

Although we've never discussed our very first meeting, when I look into my daughter's eyes, I always see a glimmer of special recognition, as if some part of her knows that we first met in another time and place.

Perhaps she even knows that I was first to know she was on her way.

— James R. Coffey —

94

Love Survives

Perhaps they are not stars in the sky,
but rather openings where our loved ones
shine down to let us know they are happy.
~Inuit Proverb

My husband J. Dee died in an explosion in a Titan missile silo, along with fifty-plus other men, near Searcy, Arkansas. I was twenty-four; he was twenty-eight. The shock was overwhelming. I had never known anyone who had died and never been to a funeral, much less been to a mortuary to view a body.

One day, life just is and is good; the next day, every aspect of life has totally changed. Taking our two children, ages nine months and three years old, I went back to college at UC Davis to complete the degree that had been interrupted by falling in love and getting married. I was grieving, but I was coping.

Several months later, I awoke one morning with a Technicolor dream fresh in my mind in clear detail. I was in an old-fashioned drugstore sitting on a stool beside a tall counter with a jukebox playing "Smoke Gets in Your Eyes," a favorite song we danced to in the Student Union at Oklahoma State University. In walked my husband, dressed in Western clothes, which he seldom wore in real life. (The OSU football team was the Cowboys.) He walked directly over to me and said, "I want you to know it is okay for you to get on with life, to go out, and have fun. I know you love me; I'll always love you. Never be afraid you aren't loved."

As I woke, I had the feeling of having had a real experience, even though I was surprised at the setting of the drugstore. I smiled at the symbols of OSU in the dream. My feeling was one of comfort, thinking, *Wasn't that sweet of my husband to come and reassure me, to let me know that getting on with life wouldn't be unfaithful to his memory.* Fifty-five years later, I can still see the scene, hear the music, and feel the feelings.

I still feel loved.

Through the years, I completed my college education, remarried and divorced, raised my children, practiced my profession, and went on with life. My last husband and I married late in life. He was eighty-five; I was seventy. He died of pancreatic cancer after nine years of married life. For several years, it had been our routine to read books together, with me reading out loud and pausing frequently for us to discuss the author's points. We would alternate choosing books, but both of us chose historical and current books on topics of religion, spirituality, philosophy, and consciousness. We both were convinced of life after death, the power of the mind, extrasensory perception, the reality of intuition, and the universal power of love in the universe.

A few months after Dave died, I was taking a shower one morning, not specifically thinking of Dave but just mindlessly going through the motions. Suddenly, in front of me, up popped a big bubble with Dave's head and shoulders shining through it. The bubble was about a foot high, in full color. He looked radiant and lively, flexible and energetic, extremely different from how he looked his last several months of life. I clearly heard him say just one thing to me: "It's true, Ruth! It's really true!" He and the bubble disappeared.

Immediately, I thought, *As always, Dave kept his word. He kept his part of our agreement: Whoever dies first will come back and tell the other one what it's like.*

I knew he was alive and well in his new location.

I also received a message from a good friend of several years, Bob. He was one of those friends I enjoyed sitting around with, drinking coffee, philosophizing and talking, talking, talking. He talked nutrition like I talk nutrition; we both wrote, published, marketed and sold nutrition booklets. One of our favorite philosophical conversations consisted of me trying to convince Bob that love is the greatest power in the universe. Bob played devil's advocate, countering my ideas with a scientific fact or a conjecture leading in another direction. We had our discussions at odd hours so we could stretch a pot of coffee without making the waitresses at Denny's too impatient.

After a few years, I moved away, and we didn't keep in touch, not by letter or by telephone. One night, twenty-plus years later, and living across the country, I had one of those crystal-clear dreams with color, sound, and feelings.

In the dream, I saw Bob coming down the sidewalk and went to greet him. It was a joyful time! We picked up the conversation right where we left off, walking together down the street to a McDonald's. We went into the inflated play area where kids jump and joined them — jumping around, laughing, and having a lot of fun! After a few minutes, we sat down on the plastic bubbles. Bob looked at me directly in the eye and said, "I just came to tell you that you were right. Love is the greatest power in the universe." *Poof!* I woke up.

It was so unusual that, the next morning, I searched around, found his old telephone number, and called Bob, wondering if he still lived at the same place after twenty years. It was his voice on the answering machine, but he didn't pick up, so I left a message along with my new telephone number so he could call me back and hear about the dream.

That evening, I got a call from Bob's son. "You must be psychic," he said. "My dad died last night."

I couldn't help but smile and think, *Wasn't that nice of Bob to come back to let me know I was right?*

— Ruth L. Wallace —

One Last Goodbye

A sister is a gift to the heart, a friend to the spirit,
a golden thread to the meaning of life.
~Isadora James

"I cannot believe I am dying," Katherine said. Her eyes were bottomless wells of sadness.

"I can't either," I tearfully replied to my beautiful sister.

We were on the back deck of her cottage, surrounded by trees and wildlife. It was our respite from the real world, from the reality of her situation. Her diagnosis was terminal, but hidden deep in the middle of these woods, we sometimes felt as if death wouldn't be able to find her there.

Over the course of seven months, though, we began to see evidence of the cancer's rapid progress. As if a thief came each night and stole a little more of her, Katherine slowly lost her health and youth. She began turning into an elderly version of herself. I spent night after night with her as she entered this final chapter of her life. Being the older sister, I had always come to her rescue in times of distress, but this time, there was nothing I could do. So, I steadfastly remained by her side, and we focused on her peace, comfort, and making the most of the time she had left.

In an attempt to capture her beauty, gentle mannerisms, and graceful ways, I constantly took pictures and videos. I also sought to memorize all that cinematography couldn't capture, like the absolute peace I felt in her presence, and the perfect way she understood and loved me. How would I ever be able to live without my sister? How could I ever say goodbye to her?

On May 6, Katherine was having a particularly good day, so I decided it was a safe time to make a quick trip home. I would leave that evening, refresh my bags, spend the night with my children and husband, and quickly return to her the next morning. I told Katherine I would be back soon, leaned over and kissed her forehead, and told her I loved her. She wrapped a frail arm around me and said, "I love you, too."

The next morning, my dad called to let me know that Katherine was gone. I gasped in shock. Then and there, a part of me died, too. Sadness filled me, and so did something else: guilt. I was supposed to be there, holding her hand as she left this world and entered the next. I thought back to our last moment together. I had told her I loved her, but did she truly know how much? If I had known she would die that night, I certainly wouldn't have left. Our goodbye had not been big enough or final enough. Unrest settled in my soul, and I longed and ached for one more hug from my sister.

We had a funeral for Katherine, and I went through the first weeks without her in a swirling fog of emptiness and numbness. I missed her terribly and thought about her constantly. So many questions circled in my mind. Where was she? Was she healthy and at peace? What did her eyes see at this very moment? Then one night, several weeks after her death, I had a dream that would finally bring me peace.

In my dream, I found myself in a quiet room. Everything was white and serene, illuminated with only the flickering glow of candles. In the dim light, I looked in front of me to find Katherine standing in the middle of the room. Silent and still, radiant and perfect, she was ethereal. Her dark hair was long and thick, and her body was strong again. My sister opened her arms, and I ran to her, collapsing in them. Her embrace was warm, and I erupted into tears. Sobbing uncontrollably, I cried, "I miss you, Katherine. I miss you so much. Please come back. Please!" I begged. I was hysterical, but Katherine remained completely calm, her arms wrapped around me tightly in a blanket of comfort, never speaking a word.

Eventually, I took a step back and looked into my sister's eyes. She still didn't speak, but her luminous eyes said everything. They were no longer sad and defeated but full of peace and knowingness. The soft expression on her face was one I had seen a million times before. It was how she looked when she was with her children, when all was right in the world, when her heart was content and full.

I woke up the next morning feeling as if I had just been with my sister. After years of looking out for Katherine, I was certain that now she was looking out for me. Maybe Katherine hadn't wanted to say goodbye when she was sick and frail, and perhaps this final encounter was exactly how she wanted to say goodbye. I would remember her the way she was in my dream: happy, healthy, and whole. With tears still spilling down my cheeks, I smiled. I had gotten the final goodbye hug that I so desperately needed.

— Rachel Chustz —

96

Finding the Courage to Take Action

Life is funny... We never know what's in store for us,
and time brings on what is meant to be.
~April Mae Monterrosa

He was smiling broadly, walking toward me. His bright, sky-blue shirt matched the color of his eyes. He looked at least twenty years younger, healthy, and just as I remembered him so long ago. I loved him then but even more now. He reached out to take my hand and said, "Make a decision, even if it's wrong." And then he was gone.

I woke abruptly, filled with a brief and unexpected contentment. It was the first time in a few months I had seen my husband in my dreams. He had passed away after a hard fight with a rare and untreatable cancer.

The dream played in my mind for days. What did it mean? What did he want me to do? He had been a decisive person, usually choosing action over inaction. I had heard him use that phrase before.

He looked so much better than I did. I was thin and haggard. Friends asked if I was eating. I had cried an ocean full of tears, and my spark for life had been snuffed out.

Make a decision, even if it's wrong.

I felt the need to meet others coping with the loss of a loved one and joined a grief support group. We hugged, cried, and bonded quickly. There was an unspoken understanding.

I also enrolled in an online class focused on teaching ways to increase the sense of wellbeing in your life. One exercise was to write three thank-you notes to people from the past whose friendship or advice added to the enrichment of my life. This required considerable effort but was very rewarding. The homework helped me remember how fortunate I was to have such close relationships in the past.

Another assignment was to start each day thinking about five things from the previous day that made me feel grateful. Some days, it was hard to find two things, let alone five! On many days, I used the same items as the day before and the day before that. Something had to actually change in my life if I was going to achieve the goal of having five different items to be grateful for each day.

Make a decision, even if it's wrong.

As a married couple, I was part of "we and us" for many years, but now it was only "I and me." I needed to learn how to be single again. Although most of my friends were married, I started accepting their invitations, even though I would be the third or fifth wheel. The kindness of my friends to include me made it easier. The days became brighter, and I was feeling more optimistic.

A good friend encouraged me to join an internet dating site. As a widow, she had been dating awhile and recommended one particular site. It would be fun to have a new friend to do things with again, but was I really ready for the dating scene after all these years? Months passed as I wrestled with myself on what to do.

Make a decision, even if it's wrong.

What did I have to lose? I wanted more joy and love in my life. I took the plunge and joined a dating site. I heard from men younger and older, those who played golf, and couch potatoes who preferred their TVs over everything. It was frustrating, interesting, and even fun at times. If we started to message each other, it was almost like having a blind date without actually getting together.

I gingerly put my toe in the water and found the courage to meet men for coffee or lunch. I even progressed to dinner with a few of them. None of them worked out, so I moved on and tried again.

One day, I received a message asking if I had grown up in a nearby, small town. I didn't recognize the man's picture and decided not to respond. Surprisingly, though, I did grow up in that town! Sensing my hesitation, he wrote again a few days later, giving me his full name and sharing that we had danced together in the seventh grade. The seventh grade? We were only thirteen at the time.

Stunned, I recognized his unique name immediately but had no recollection of knowing him at all. I was taking ballet classes in the seventh grade when my dance teacher decided to conduct a cotillion ballroom dance and etiquette class, open to all seventh-grade girls and boys in the area. Every Friday night for six weeks, about twenty-five kids got together for the dance class. My new mystery man remembered dancing with me several times; I only remembered learning the dance steps!

We went to different schools and never dated. We both remembered saying hello at a friend's party one night when we were in our early twenties. That was the last time I saw him. We each went our separate ways, leading our own lives. Little did we know that, forty-five years later, a dating site would bring us back together again.

He invited me to lunch. How could I say no? He recognized my picture and remembered me after all these years. I felt nervous and exhilarated at the same time. We connected in special ways over lunch because of our hometown and discovered we even had some mutual friends.

We progressed to dinner and then to another. We attended concerts, joined a couples' dance class, and had fun doing simple things. I was starting to feel more like myself again. It had been a long time.

My husband's unexpected gift nudged me to get back on my feet. Choosing action over inaction helped me to become more positive and gave me courage to embrace the unknown. My seventh-grade dance partner and I have been together for eighteen months. Who knows what the future will bring, but I hope he is a part of it!

— Barbara Dorman Bower —

97

Absolutely, No Parking

Follow your intuition, listening to your dreams,
your inner voice to guide you.
~Katori Hall

S
omewhere around 3:00 AM, I jolted awake, breathing hard. I'd had a nightmare. In my dream, I had been walking down a busy city sidewalk when I heard footsteps behind me. Although the sun was shining, and people were out and about, a terrible sense of panic washed over me. I immediately knew I was being followed and was in grave danger.

I quickened my pace, trying to get back to the safety of my car, only to hear the footsteps behind me closing in. I turned just in time to feel the cool blade of a knife slide against my neck and came face-to-face with two unknown assailants. One looped his arm around my waist and pressed me against the side of a skyscraper, as if we were tourists or a couple simply admiring our surroundings, while his accomplice sliced my purse strap free and stripped it from my shoulder.

"You have survived an armed robbery. You're okay," my brain whispered. "Don't move a muscle. The thieves have what they wanted and will move on."

But the pit of my stomach knew better as the pair exchanged a bone-chilling glance between each other. The purse was about to be the least of my worries. I opened my mouth to scream for help before jolting awake.

Back in familiar surroundings, I strained my ears to listen for any suspicious noises before I dared to move a muscle in my bed. But after several long minutes, I was met only with the peaceful whoosh of my ceiling fan. I flipped on every light in the house, checked every closet, and whipped open the shower curtain before my breathing finally calmed down.

"Where on earth had that dream come from?" I wondered, before it instantly clicked. I was meeting a friend for lunch later that day at a swanky steakhouse in downtown Anchorage. Normally, I would rather wrestle a bear than drive in downtown traffic, but she had just received news of a wonderful job promotion and wanted to celebrate. I'd moved on to another job myself, and it had been several weeks since we'd caught up. Although I wasn't eager to fight traffic, I was excited to see my friend.

Of course, that was the source of my stress, I reasoned. I was anxious about driving and the roulette of finding street parking, and it had manifested as a nightmare. I would simply leave earlier, I rationalized, and give myself plenty of time to find a spot. I tossed and turned and did my best to fall back asleep, despite the gnawing concern that lingered in my stomach.

I'd allotted myself an extra forty-five minutes to beat lunch traffic and exhaled a sigh of relief upon spotting an empty parallel-parking spot just down the block from our intended restaurant. I eased my little, two-door Jeep Wrangler into the spot and popped out to pay the street parking meter. There were eleven minutes remaining on the meter, but no matter how many times I hit cancel or slid my credit card into the reader, the meter timer would not reset. Since I had time to spare, I decided I would simply wait for the timer to count down to zero, then surely it would reset and I could load two hours onto it. If a traffic cop happened upon my car, I could easily explain that I was waiting and wouldn't have to worry about a ticket, or worse, a tow.

It was a rare warm April morning. The sun was shining—a true blessing after a long Alaskan winter. Although there were no pedestrians directly near me, I was within fifty feet or so of the main avenue and felt at ease. Even though I was on a one-way side street, I was still visible from the busy main road.

Suddenly, every hair on my body stood straight up, as if a bolt of electricity had just surged through me. "Run!" my brain screamed. "Run! Run! RUN!" I didn't hesitate and shot back into my Jeep before slamming the door shut and locking the doors. I felt as if my very life were at stake, with an unshakable urge that I needed to move right then.

I whipped out of the parking spot and gunned it down the side street, where I'd make a right-hand turn and loop back onto the main avenue. Luck was on my side. The traffic light at the end of the block turned green just before I reached it, and I wouldn't have to come to a stop.

As I made my right turn, my heart leapt into my throat. The two assailants I had seen in my dream were just rounding the corner, and they would have reached the street meter I had been waiting at in seconds. I felt my jaw drop in shock as I passed them and then horror as they locked eyes with me as I zipped by. I glanced in my rearview mirror and saw that one of them — the one who had worn that same, unmistakable red jacket and sliced my purse strap from my shoulder — had turned to watch me drive away.

I drove several blocks north before looping back around to the restaurant and approaching from the opposite direction. My would-be assailants were nowhere in sight, and as I reached the restaurant, a street parking spot opened directly in front of its main doors. I parked and craned my neck before daring to open the vehicle door, but the dubious pair was gone.

I am not sure who was looking out for me that day, maybe a guardian angel or a warning from one of my beloved relatives who've since passed on. Had I been able to pay the first parking meter, I would have sauntered slowly to the restaurant, enjoying the warm April sunshine to kill time, and those assailants would have ended up right behind me, just as they had in my dream.

But I will be forever grateful that somehow, someway, I had a protector guiding me to safety and finding a way to slip a dire warning into my dreams before stalling that parking meter.

To this day, when I stop to enjoy the warm sunshine on my face, I make sure to take a thorough look around before closing my eyes to soak in the wonder, and gratitude, of simply being alive.

— Kristi Adams —

98

My Mother's Earring

A dream which is not interpreted is like
a letter which is not read.
~The Talmud

The year I turned forty-six, my ninety-two-year-old mother entered hospice care. Initially, she rebounded, and my sister and I were stunned that she was doing so well. For a time, we were convinced that we had made the wrong decision. But within a span of two weeks, her decline became apparent, and we were eventually called to her bedside one night to say our goodbyes.

Our mother suffered a small stroke that night, and although she was alert, she could barely speak. Sometime around 2:00 AM, she looked me in the eyes, and then her eyes began scanning the room. I could tell that she was looking at something, but I could not figure out what she was trying to tell me.

I asked, "Are you afraid?" She shook her head, but she was obviously absorbed in whatever she was sensing. Eventually, I asked her what she was looking at.

"Angels," she whispered. As the sun rose that morning, my mother did not.

Grief is such a devastating emotion, like a knife to the chest initially, and later like a one-hundred-pound weight laid upon my chest. It impeded my breathing and left my mind a muddled mess. Few memories of the first six months stuck with me, and I got in the habit of just putting one foot in front of the other so that I could make it through the day. At times, compartmentalizing worked, but then again, standing in the grocery store checkout line buying carrots and milk, I would be suddenly overwhelmed with such a profound feeling of loss that I would bolt from the store. I was still in this state two years later after experiencing yet another devastating loss when my husband passed from cardiac arrest at the age of fifty-four.

In a desperate moment, I called my closest girlfriend and invited her on a trip to Mexico. I had brought a book with me about angels, still taking comfort from my mother's last word. I spent my time reading the stories and drifting back to thoughts of better days and better times. My grief was thick and raw, and with it the guilt that came from trying to forget my sorrow or to steal a moment of happiness or peace.

Within a few hours, we found ourselves at our resort in Playa del Carmen. We adapted to the resort routine very quickly. Each morning, we donned the satin robes provided as a part of our stay. We sat on the hotel-room balcony enjoying strong black coffee and pastries delivered by room service. We gazed at the ocean, listened to the birds calling from the trees, and watched the palm trees swaying amidst the beautifully groomed grounds.

Each evening, we took turns soaking in the massive bathtub. We added scented oils or bubble bath for a bit of luxury and then took extra time to fix our hair. We put on tropical sundresses, and then set out for a culinary adventure at one of the resort's specialty restaurants.

But my favorite activity of the day was the time that we spent on the beach. We started with lunch at the cafe overlooking the beach, replete with white tablecloths, bottled water in crystal glasses and shrimp cocktails. We indulged in white wine, avocado salad, and tiramisu for dessert. As we dined, we gazed out of the cafe's magnificent windows and watched the tide roll in, only to then see it pulled away again as if by some magical magnetic force.

Our lunch completed, we adjourned to the beach where we gathered ourselves under a colorful umbrella and set up beach lounge chairs onto which we placed our fluffy, blue-and-white-striped beach towels. This was our routine.

On the third day, we had almost completed this process and I, having made ready my lounger, pulled my sundress over my head in preparation for an interlude of relaxation and reading. As I pulled the dress over my head, it caught on one of my mother's diamond studs.

After a fifteen-minute search for the missing earring, I called off our efforts and gave up, resigning myself to the fact that my mother's earring was hopelessly lost. That entire beach was covered in sparkling sand and it was impossible to find a diamond amidst all the shininess. I plopped down onto my lounger, angel book in hand. The sea was moving in and out, making a delightfully soothing sound. The sun was warm, the sand was warmer, and the sea breeze caressed my face and blew through my hair. I could see the bluest of skies above, interrupted only by the cumulus clouds on the horizon and seabirds that soared above us. Three chapters into my reading, I set my book on my chest, allowed my eyes to close, and began to doze.

At just that moment between awake and asleep, I was shocked back into consciousness by a huge visual image of my diamond earring. My eyes were closed, but the image was so vivid that I instantly snapped to attention. When I opened my eyes, the image was gone, but in its place was a thought, intuition, or message telling me to move my lounge chair. Without thinking, I stood and lugged the lounger four feet to the left and two feet backward. My friend said, "What on earth are you doing?"

Now, feeling that I had done what I needed to do, I straightened my beach towel on the lounger, sat down sideways, and dropped my gaze back down to the dazzling grains of sparkling sand by my feet. In a stunning event of serendipity, or maybe with some help from the angels, I was looking right at the diamond earring.

— J. Lynn Benkelman —

99

Big Ol' Bear

To understand the intricacies of life, study the antics
of your dreams.
~*Michael Bassey Johnson*, The Oneironaut's Diary

Native American culture teaches us that nature has a way of communicating and guiding us. We just need to stop and pay attention. Looking at the sky tells us about the weather. The movement of the trees tells us which way the wind is going, and our animal totems bring us messages. That belief was confirmed when it came to stories about my biological father.

When I was six years old, my parents split up, and my father disappeared. Mom took my sister and me to another state. There were no visits, phone calls or letters. Mom never wanted to talk about him. He was just gone.

I was always curious about this guy no one wanted to mention. What kind of person was he? Did I look like him? Did I act like him? Did we have anything in common?

The one piece of information we did get from my mom was that he was Native American. I became fascinated with their culture and my heritage.

In my studies, I learned about animal totems. A totem is a spirit guide that you feel a special connection with who accompanies you through life. I have always felt my special connection with bears.

One night when I was in my thirties, I had a dream related to my dad. In the dream, I was walking down the dirt trail leading to my favorite beach in Coos Bay, Oregon. As I reached the sand, I noticed a large, brown bear sitting next to a small campfire. That may sound a little strange, but because the bear is my totem, I was not surprised to see him.

"Have a seat," he told me as I kicked off my shoes and wiggled my toes in the sand. "I know your dad."

"You do?" I walked over to the fire and leaned forward to warm my hands. "I never really got to meet him."

He smiled as he answered, "Oh, you will."

"I doubt that I would even recognize him."

"Aww, but that is where you are wrong. Follow your heart, and you will find him. And he will not be hard to recognize. He looks just like a big ol' bear."

I startled awake then and knew exactly what I needed to do. When I was a kid, I had no idea where to find my dad, but in my thirties we were entering the age of the internet and search engines. I did not know much about him, only his full name. That was enough to get started, so I sat down at the keyboard and typed his name into the search engine.

Sitting back and holding my breath in anticipation, I watched as the computer blinked and whirred. My maiden name is not very common, so I was stunned to see a list of twenty names appear on the screen, complete with telephone numbers.

Of course, back in those days, everyone still had landline telephones, and there were directories where you could look up anyone's phone number. I stared at that screen for what seemed like hours and finally reached for my telephone.

The first number on the list was disconnected. I dialed the second number, but it just rang and rang as my heart pounded faster. Finally, I hung up and called the third number.

A deep, baritone voice answered the phone. He sounded kind, so I decided to take a shot. But he lived in Colorado, which was a long way from our home in southern Oregon.

"Hello, I am looking for someone with the same name as yours."

The words rushed out of my mouth before I could lose my nerve. "May I ask you a personal question?"

"Sure," he replied.

I had decided ahead of time to ask an easy, telltale question that would let me know if I was speaking to my biological father. So, I took a deep breath and continued, "May I ask where you grew up?"

He chuckled in his deep voice. "Well, few people have ever heard of it, but I grew up in a little town in southern Oregon by the name of Medford."

I gasped. He must have heard my shock because his tone changed. "Who is this?" he asked, sounding a little nervous now.

"My name is Tisha." Now my voice sounded a little strange all of a sudden.

"Tisha Railene?"

"Yes," I whispered. This time, he gasped.

The line got quiet, and for a moment I thought he had hung up. Then I heard a quiet sob. His voice dropped to almost a whisper. "You know, when you were a little girl, I used to call you Angel." I did know that.

Through the tears, we talked for hours, catching up on thirty lost years. I told him about growing up on a farm, going to college, and raising three kids. I also let him know that his other daughter lived near me and had raised two boys of her own.

He told me he was Native American and involved in the culture as a medicine man. He knew the language and the crafts, attended powwows, and had a totem. His totem was a red-tailed hawk. He also looked to nature for messages. He told me he loved to karaoke and dance, just like me. By the end of our conversation, he was making plans to fly out for a visit.

On Christmas morning of that year, my sister and I were standing at the airport terminal with a news-media team from the local newspaper who had heard about the reunion. Clare picked at a few split ends in her hair, and I chewed my fingernails as we waited for the flight board to announce the arrival of his flight.

"How are we even going to recognize this guy?" Clare asked as the passengers began to file off the plane.

Moments later, we spotted him, the last passenger to leave the plane. There was no mistaking him. A tall Native American man with a long, gray braid paused to tease one of the flight attendants before turning to walk toward the building. As he turned, we caught sight of a sign he was wearing around his neck. In sparkling, blue letters about four inches tall was the word "DAD."

"That's him," I pointed. "He told me on the phone that we could not miss him, and he is right. He looks like a big ol' bear."

—Tea Railene Coiner—

Dot Matrix Dreams

Truth and dreams are twins.
~Austin O'Malley

In the world of sports or the military, initiation challenges can be rites of passage, a way to prove oneself worthy of being part of the team. For my husband in the military, his challenge was to snort an oyster — a quirky initiation that became part of the unit's lore. The surprising part? He actually did it. The guys still talk about their shock at his willingness to embrace the peculiar tradition. My husband loved that kind of thing; he had a quiet sense of humor and loved pulling one over on a worthy opponent.

After thirty-two years of marriage, I unexpectedly found myself a widow. His heart stopped while riding in the passenger seat on I-95 just outside Baltimore following a Father's Day outing to Camden Yards.

Two months after his passing, I was buried in boxes and grief. One night, exhausted after cleaning out our storage unit, I fell into a deep sleep. Sometime in the night he came to me in a dream. During our late night conversations we had decided whoever went first would try to reach the other through dreams.

My dreams are always vivid, filled with details that surprise those who hear about them. When I awoke after this one, I wondered if it was a dream because it felt so real. His smile and laughter lingered, and I felt held and comforted even when I was awake.

In this particular dream, our family was leaving a military base, a scenario we had lived through multiple times in reality. Our children played in the yard as I finished cleaning our home. They bid farewell to friends while I finished packing the car. My husband, in his office, prepared to transfer responsibilities. Unbeknownst to me, he was also setting a challenge for his successor, one that was more sophisticated than snorting an oyster.

His challenge wasn't just a passing fancy; it was a clever riddle, a tradition to determine rank and gauge the wit of fellow officers. In my dream, I completed my tasks, packed up the kids and drove to his office and waited. Eventually, we sought my husband, watching him through his outside office window meticulously crafting a bulletin board, a puzzle awaiting the next occupant of his office.

The board, adorned with orange paper (a nod to his love for the Baltimore Orioles), displayed his dot matrix image on the left side, while the right side formed a cityscape silhouette with black and gray squares. His mischievous grin spoke volumes about the hidden clues within those squares.

I awoke, feeling his warmth and laughter lingering. Throughout the day, I smiled wistfully, wishing I could see him and talk with him again. I opened one of the boxes from our storage unit, chucking this, keeping that, lingering over something I never knew, or remembering something we had shared. I stopped short as I grabbed a folded picture — a dot matrix printout of his face. It was the same image from my dream, a photo I had never seen before.

My husband had stashed that box in the back of our storage unit seven years earlier, and I don't know where it was before that. The dot matrix photo of himself was dated as being printed nearly one year before I met him. It was buried in a box of childhood school papers, calendars from that time, photographs, and old letters — all of which I had never seen.

How could it be?

Mike's surprise left me pondering. Was this his way of sending a message, assuring me that he had a glimpse of my future, and showing me he was watching from beyond? Was he leaving me clues to unfold? Or, perhaps, he was reminding me that he walks beside me, aware of my life's happenings. Skepticism might suggest it's a mere coincidence, a creation of my subconscious. But the timing of finding the dot matrix printout couldn't have been any sweeter.

I don't know where heaven is, or where my husband resides in the vast universe, but I believe he leaves me breadcrumbs, reassuring me that I am not alone.

— Kristine Benevento —

Taking Mom's Travel Advice

In every moment, the Universe is whispering to you.
You're constantly surrounded by signs, coincidences,
and synchronicities, all aimed at propelling
you in the direction of your destiny.
~Denise Linn

I had almost missed my flight, barely getting to the gate before they closed it. Breathlessly, I entered the plane from the gateway, sure that the only seat left would be at the back of the plane. I was surprised when I saw two empty seats in the very front row.

I sat down in one of the seats and began buckling my seatbelt when I heard commotion at the plane door. The flight attendant was motioning for someone to hurry aboard.

"Mom?" I said, surprised to see her entering the plane. She smiled and quickly sat in the empty seat next to me, shoving her large purse behind her legs. She had always carried large purses when she was alive, so it made sense she brought one into my dream.

I wasn't sure where this flight was headed as we looked out the window at the puffy clouds below us. Mom told me she loved to travel over the oceans to the beaches and told me I should take every opportunity I had to do the same. "You must go," she said. "Take your dream vacation. Don't put it off." She held my hand as she had done in our prayer time years ago and she smiled at me.

The morning alarm roused me from this dream before I could respond to her. It was time to get ready for work. As I drove to the office, I smiled at my mom's appearance in my dream, but shook my head at the notion of taking a dream vacation. My family did not have the money or time to fit that in. We hoped to take my teenage daughter to Hawaii one of the two summers she had left with us before heading to college, but I couldn't see any way that would happen.

When I got to work on that cool spring day in 2019, I logged into my computer. An e-mail popped up from the airline where my husband and I accumulate a lot of travel points through work trips. I'd often thought how this dream vacation would be possible if only this airline had flights to Hawaii, but they didn't. Up until this morning, that is, when they were announcing new flights to Hawaii! My heart raced. I thought of my dream. I called my husband immediately even though he was on a business trip, and I didn't really know his schedule. As luck would have it, he was on a break.

First, I told him about my dream and what my mom had said, then I told him about the airline announcement. He, like me, saw it as a sign that we needed to jump on this opportunity. He did not hesitate for a moment and began looking into flights. I texted my adult daughter who had long wished with me that we could go to Hawaii. The three of us talked and texted until we found flights that would allow us and my younger daughter to take the trip of a lifetime that summer.

Truly though, had I seen the e-mail without Mom's dream advice, I don't think I would have pursued the trip. There were so many other costs involved such as hotels, meals, car rental, and activities. Without the dream, I likely would have shrugged my shoulders and ignored the airline announcement. But the irony of Mom telling me only the night before to take my dream vacation was the driving force to make the trip fit into our budget. And somehow, we did.

The summer of 2019, on the anniversary of Mom's departure to heaven, instead of sitting in my home sadly reminiscing her passing, my family walked from our beach hotel in Maui to board a sailboat we had booked for a sunset dinner. Looking to the horizon as the golden sun sunk below the Pacific Ocean, coloring the sky in pastel pink and orange, I felt an overwhelming peace come over me.

It took another year for me to also realize how perfectly timed Mom's advice had been. Had we waited until the summer of 2020, the trip would not have happened because of travel restrictions due to the pandemic. I'm thankful she joined me on that flight in my dream to make sure we didn't put off taking the real-life trip of our dreams.

— Lisa Marlin —

Meet Our
Contributors

Kristi Adams has enjoyed sharing her stories in numerous magazines and publications, including seventeen books in the *Chicken Soup for the Soul* series. As a military spouse, and veteran, Kristi especially loves writing stories filled with courage, adventure, and a dash of wonder. Read more at www.kristiadamsmedia.com.

Patti Alexander received a Bachelor of Science degree in biology from the University of North Carolina at Chapel Hill in 2006 and currently works as a Medical Technologist. She is the mom of three amazing kids. In addition to spending time with her family, she loves to read and hopes to one day write her own book.

Mary Ellen Angelscribe is author of *Expect Miracles* and *A Christmas Filled with Miracles*. Her heartwarming pet newspaper column on Facebook at www.facebook.com/PetTipsandTales ran for twenty years. This is her eleventh story in the *Chicken Soup for the Soul* series. Her swimming cats appeared on Must Love Cats ("Kitty Paddle") and Anderson Cooper. E-mail her at angelscribe@msn.com.

Sarah Asermily is a multi-genre author with an affinity for character-driven stories. She is a Rochester, NY native, where she lives with her husband and two sons. Her first novel, *Until the Sun Forgets to Rise*, is available at most major retailers.

One of the greatest gifts **Elizabeth A. Atwater** has ever been given was when she was taught to read in first grade. She immediately fell in love with the written word and has had a book in her hand since. The love of writing soon followed. Decades later, reading and writing consume a lot of her time.

Betts Baker is a freelance writer living in Colorado. When not writing for businesses, she helps craft family legacy memoirs and writes nonfiction stories and essays. She enjoys gardening, reading, and exploring the Colorado outdoors with her husband, their children and grandchildren.

Anne E. Beall is an award-winning author whose books have been featured in *People* magazine, *Chicago Tribune*, *Toronto Sun*, and she's been interviewed by NBC, NPR, and WGN. She has also been published in several literary journals. Beall received her PhD in Social Psychology from Yale University.

Kristine Benevento, a recent widow and mother to two adult sons, called diverse corners of the Air Force world her home. With a bachelor's degree and an associate degree, she seeks to inspire. Moonlight Graham is her feline companion.

J. Lynn Benkelman has been a psychotherapist for over thirty years working with children, adults, and families. She is currently working with kids and teens on a non-profit ranch doing equine assisted therapy. J. Lynn loves to garden, write, work with her flighted parrot and dogs, and loves spending time in the mountains of Colorado.

Laura Bentz received her Bachelor of Arts in History and English from Southwestern University of Lakeland, FL in 1977. She is a retired educator, living now in Flint, TX and is a member of the East Texas Writers Guild. She published a book titled *The Land of Efacia*.

Since publishing her first story in *Chicken Soup for the Soul: Laughter Is the Best Medicine*, **Karen Blair** was inspired to write about her experiences in small business while receiving her master's from San Diego State University. Her efforts resulted in a self-published book, *Chasing Chickens*, and can be found at chasingchickens.com.

Barbara Dorman Bower is a CPA and retired from the financial services industry. She has contributed stories to three previous titles in the *Chicken Soup for the Soul* series. She enjoys having time to explore her creative side and travels as often as possible.

Joanna McGee Bradford, a retired risk manager, makes her home in a Chicago suburb. She has published personal experience stories, devotions, and a romance novel. Her son, Marcus, now resides with his Father in Heaven. She enjoys reading, exercising and dining with friends. Learn more at www.joannabradford.com.

Thomas Brooks received his M.Ed. from Ashland University and is a retired communications technician and technical educator. He is married to a science and math teacher and has two adult children. Thomas enjoys carving, making and flying kites, fixing things, singing bass in local choruses, and writing when time allows.

Merry Broughal retired from her job after nineteen years to devote her time to running a non-profit organization in Kenya. She also hopes to get back to writing short pieces and devotionals. She loves spending time with family, especially her four grandchildren. Traveling to Kenya visiting friends and family is another favorite.

Jill Burns lives in the mountains of West Virginia with her wonderful family. She's a retired piano teacher and performer. She enjoys writing, music, gardening, nature, and spending time with her grandchildren.

Rochel Burstyn is a busy mother, author, and freelance writer. She enjoys Jazzercise, back massages and has an intense passion for dairy chocolate.

Sarina Byron is a widely published writer, Yale Writers' Workshop alumni and non-profit leader. Published in over seven magazines, she has been invited to speak at a "Big Tech" firm. Featured by *Voyage Tampa*, *Canvas Rebel*, and *Bold Journey* magazines, Sarina is working on her first book.

Anneice Chapple's writing skills were first noticed in the fifth grade. She has since written SOPs and Work Instructions. On a personal writing level, she has kept journals for over three decades about her son and important everyday matters. She has continued this tradition of writing about her toddler grandson and his escapades.

Pastor Wanda Christy-Shaner is a retired minister, missionary, and gospel singer. She spends her spare time writing and doing photography. She is married and has four fuzzy furballs to keep her company.

Rachel Chustz attended college at Louisiana State University, where she earned her bachelor's and master's degrees. Rachel was an elementary school teacher until the birth of her first child. Rachel and her husband, Michael, now have three children. Rachel enjoys traveling with her family, writing, reading, and art.

Tess Clarkson, a former dancer (Broadway's *Riverdance*) and lawyer based in New York, now lives in Missouri with her husband and dogs. She's a writer, yoga teacher, astrologer, and end-of-life doula. She's written for *The Washington Post*, *HuffPost*, and more, and is a past contributor to the *Chicken Soup for the Soul* series. Learn more at www.TessClarkson.com.

Christina Ryan Claypool is an award-winning journalist who has been featured on *Joyce Meyer Ministries* and CBN's *The 700 Club*. She is a graduate of Bluffton University and Mt. Vernon Nazarene University. She enjoys spending time with family, an inspiring film or book, and good coffee. Learn more at www.christinaryanclaypool.com.

James R. Coffey holds degrees in Liberal Arts, Psychology and Anthropology from USF. His work appears regularly in numerous publications, including *Journal of Compressed Creative Arts*, *Close to the Bone*, *AntipodeanSF*, *History Defines*, *Mystic Owl*, *Salvo Magazine*, and also in *Chicken Soup for the Soul: Well That Was Funny*.

Tea Railene Coiner received her Associate of Science degree from Rogue Community College in 1985 before working in customer service and the hospitality industry. Tea enjoys photography, spending time in nature, and, of course, writing. E-mail her at tea.railene@gmail.com.

Cj Cole lives on the Eastern Shore of Delmarva with her new rescue pup Sampson Red Feather. A third-generation tribal storyteller, Cj has been a radio morning drive DJ and weekly advice columnist, as well as a women's traditional dancer.

Laurie Spilovoy Cover lives with her family in beautiful East Tennessee. She has three amazing sons and a wonderful husband. She blogs and vlogs about off grid homesteading experiences, enjoys life as a crazy cat lady, and loves to dabble in herbs, flowers, crochet, writing, and thrifting vintage treasures.

Priscilla Dann-Courtney is a clinical psychologist and writer living in Boulder, CO. Her work has appeared in a number of national magazines and newspapers. Her book, *Room to Grow*, is a collection of her essays. Yoga, cycling, writing, baking, family and friends light up her world.

Elton A. Dean is an educator, author, and retired soldier. He owns Big Paw Publishing and recently released his children's book, *A Yeti Like Freddie: Talking to Kids About Autism*.

Sergio Del Bianco has a background in fine arts and psychology. He is an artist and a writer, interested in the intersection of art, psychology, and the humanities. He resides in Europe with his spouse and growing family of rescue animals. E-mail him at sergiodelbianco@yahoo.com or through X @DelBianco97.

Barbara D. Duffey is a retired R.N. after fifty-five years of nursing. She obtained a Bachelor of Arts degree in English in 1979, from the University of Baltimore. She loves writing and has written five books available on Amazon. She's currently writing a young adult novel.

C. Durand is an amateur writer who has lived in New York, Ohio, California, and Alaska, and has been forced to adjust accordingly. She is constantly impressed by the mercy of God reaching down to bless her life. She loves reading, writing, and playing softball, and she can often be found walking in the rain.

After spending two decades working in the European luxury fashion industry, **Tara Flowers** now spends her days raising her teen son and managing her consulting business, Le Papillon Marketing.

Jacqueline Ford holds both a Bachelor of Arts and a master's in social work. She has committed over three decades to the CT Department of Children and Families. From North Haven, CT, she resides with her devoted husband, John, and their daughters, Alexandra and Rebecca. She loves animals, philanthropy work, and boating.

Karleen Forwell spends her days raising her family, tending to her garden, and making wine. She enjoys writing stories of her life, as she had a wandering soul when she was young and met many interesting people and had many unusual adventures. The majority of her writings are darker books under her pen name.

Dawn Smith Gondeck travels the U.S. full-time. She has rheumatoid arthritis but loves to stay positive while connecting to others who struggle. She loves to hear from readers on Instagram at RandombitsRV.

Mónica Moran González is committed to sharing with people stories of the gifts and challenges of caring for loved ones with dementia. She has a special interest in writing about dementia and spirituality, especially in terms of faith in God, oneself, one another, and the community.

Maureen Ryan Griffin has loved words since her *Cat in the Hat* days and leads writing workshops and retreats. Her books include *Spinning Words into Gold, Tag, I'm It!* and *How Do I Say Goodbye?: A Companion in Grieving, Healing, and Gratitude*. She lives with her husband, Richard, in Charlotte, NC. E-mail her at info@WordPlayNow.com.

An educator for over forty years, **Deborah Guilbeault** now dabbles in all things artistic and historical. She raised two fine sons and now enjoys retirement. She is heavily involved in community theatre as a director, choreographer, and performer. She enjoys pickleball, golf, travel, genealogy, and social time with long-standing friends.

Sarah Criswell Guldenschuh is a retired Licensed Professional Counselor and the widow of a genuine American hero who was U.S. Navy, Ret. She lives in the mountains of Southeast Oklahoma, where she strives to maintain her reputation as a reclusive, cantankerous, weird old widow woman.

Hana Haatainen-Caye, a resident of Pittsburgh, PA, was a full-time writer, editor, voice-over talent, and speaker until her stroke in 2021. Her book *Vinegar Fridays* is available on Amazon and her work can be found in countless magazines and anthologies. Her children's books were featured on the digital platform iStoryBooks. E-mail her at speechless@comcast.net.

As someone with a lifelong passion for the written word, **Shelby Harrell** has worked as a writer in several capacities. She graduated from Manchester University in 2018 with a Bachelor of Science in Communication Studies and a minor in Journalism. She is currently writing her first novel.

Christy Heitger-Ewing lives in Indiana with her husband, two sons, and four felines. She's an empath and over-thinker who loves hugging and hates cooking. She enjoys writing, running, and practicing yoga. She's passionate about advocating for mental health awareness. Visit her author website at christyheitger-ewing.com.

Nancy K. S. Hochman is a mostly retired English teacher and tutor, who is still actively writing news, features and spiritual essays for numerous print and online publications. She is currently writing several books on heroes and miracles since.

Susan Wilking Horan is a wellness advocate, attorney, and businesswoman. She lives in California where she runs Fleischer Studios, a family-owned company, with her husband. She is a best-selling author, a three-time cancer survivor and an outspoken proponent for the rights, wellbeing and empowerment of women everywhere.

Storyteller **Cindy Horgash** has previously contributed to the *Chicken Soup for the Soul* series. She believes the world would be a much better place if everyone shared their stories, one at a time. Cindy is a member of the SCBWI, the Northwest Indiana Storytelling Guild, and Write-On Hoosiers, Inc.

Christy Hoss is the author of *The Rubber Band*, a children's novel series and *My Question for Jesus* picture book. She's a former elementary art teacher, now retired, and she teaches swimming part-time. She resides with her husband in Eastern Tennessee and together they have three grown children.

Barbara Jackman is a retired pastor/chaplain. She had been a school librarian for twenty years prior to entering seminary. In retirement she and her two cats enjoy living in a senior co-op overlooking a pond with geese, attending theatre productions, concerts, and is a member of Memoirs, a local writing group.

Michelle Jackson is a psychologist, artist, and author living in the Southwest. She enjoys helping people and sharing the human experience through the art of the written word.

Sharon Johnson is a retired healthcare administrator. She is a grandmother who frequently walks by the river. She has had poems, essays, and short stories published in *The Timberline Review*, *The Memoirist*, *Women's World*, and other places. Her blog, "Common-Sage," can be found at www.common-sage.com.

Erin Kani has had numerous interactions with the spirit world throughout her life. She lived in a haunted house, managed a historical house, and got married within that house while a beautiful, spectral woman played the piano during the ceremony. Erin is currently researching spirituality for her next project.

S.R. Karfelt is married with two children, two grandchildren, and two part-time dogs. She writes magical realism and memoir. When she's not sneaking off to write somewhere with a moat, she lives in the Soaring Capital of the World in Big Flats, New York.

Story Keatley is a writer of essays, short stories, songs, and poems with a focus on creative non-fiction. Her work ranges from humorous to thought-provoking. She is working on her first book, *Erin's Magic*, that follows the life of a beloved special needs child. Story lives in Texas with her husband, Jon. She loves dogs, cooking, and guitar.

Jennifer Kennedy is a features writer for *Costello Communications*, specializing in profiles for their digital and print magazines. She is a regular contributor to the *Chicken Soup for the Soul* series and *Guideposts* magazines. She lives in Philadelphia with her husband, sons, and rescue dogs. Contact her on X @JenKennedy2.

Rick Kurtis is an international author with thirty-seven books published so far. He is just a simple farm boy from a small town in southern Wisconsin. His books have received some 5-star reviews, and he is delighted to continue writing.

In 2018, **Debbie LaChusa** retired and relocated from her lifelong home in San Diego, CA to the Western North Carolina mountains where she lives with her husband and two Golden Retrievers in a home they've nicknamed "The Treehouse." She enjoys writing, hiking, and visiting hospice patients with her therapy dog Hope.

Marie Largeant received her Bachelor of Arts, with honors, from Long Island University and owns her own environmental consulting firm. Marie lives in New York, enjoys hand quilting, and loves to write funny stories centered around her family, much to their chagrin.

Lisa Marlin's essays have appeared in newspapers, magazines, and books, including the *Chicken Soup for the Soul* series and *Laugh Out Loud*, a humor anthology from the Erma Bombeck Writers' Workshop. She credits her family as her greatest source of joy, worry, and writing prompts. She lives in Colorado and posts at lisamarlin.com.

Nan McKernon is a writer and communications strategist in corporate behavioral health as well as an Academic Director for the Great Books summer program at Amherst College. She earned a B.A. in Communications from Simmons College and an MFA from Western CT State University in Creative Writing. She lives in Charleston, SC with her family.

Dee Dee McNeil has been a published singer/songwriter and freelance journalist for six decades. Her music has been recorded by icons such as the Four Tops, Gladys Knight, Diana Ross, Nancy Wilson, and Edwin Starr. Her original music is on albums at CDbaby.com. She currently contributes to LAjazzscene.buzz and Makingascene.org.

Shannon Shelton Miller received her bachelor's degree from Michigan State University and her master's degree from Northwestern University. She lives in Southwest Ohio with her two preteen sons and works as a writer and editor. Shannon enjoys distance running, volunteering, the arts, and, of course, writing.

N. Newell, a longtime skeptic, discovered his own psychic ability at the age of forty-seven. Since then, he has helped several people with messages from the spirit world. He considers himself a reluctant psychic.

Nanette Norgate is a Canadian-born author and freelance writer. She is a two-time *Writer's Digest* award-winner and contributing author to the *Chicken Soup for the Soul* series. The upcoming release of her first picture book in her newest children's series is expected out later this year. Learn more at nanettenorgate.com.

Freddy B. Nunez has a master's degree in education from Southern New Hampshire University. He has three children with his wife Carrie and two dogs. Freddy teaches special education at the middle-school level. He enjoys reading and drawing and loves movies. He plans to write a science-fiction novel for teens.

Susan Allen Panzica brings an eternal perspective to earthly matters through writing, speaking, and teaching. She is the author of *Mary Had A Little Lamb*, a children's Christmas story, and *The Quest*, a modern-day fairy tale. Susan is also an advocate, the founder of Justice Network, which raises awareness about human trafficking.

Suzanne Garner Payne has had the privilege of being a daughter, a wife, a mother of two sons, and a teacher for thirty years. She earned her Bachelor of Science in Intermediate Education from East Carolina University and her Master of Education in Reading and Language Arts from the University of North Carolina at Chapel Hill.

Since retiring from the practice of plastic surgery, **Judith Jackson Petry** has been able to engage in her passion for writing. Her goal is to connect with other humans on a soul level of understanding where words evoke universal feelings. She lives in Vermont on a peaceful hilltop with her husband, two llamas and a partly feral cat.

Erin Pfeifer-Andrin lives in Madison, CT with her husband John and three children. She has an MSSW from Columbia University and is an LCSW in private practice. She enjoys cooking, traveling, and going to museums. Her cousin, Julianne, lives in California with her two boys. They have enjoyed bonding over this experience.

Kendra Phillips is a stay-at-home mom of two young daughters. In her spare time, she enjoys blogging and has worked as an editor for several online publications. Kendra loves writing stories that are filled with heart and humor. She is currently working on her first novel.

Cheryl Potts loves gardening and RVing with her husband Richard and their cattle dog, Kattie. Her primary writing interest is historical fiction and she is eager for the release of her debut novel, *The Castles of Ann Lynch*, available to readers soon. She was born, raised and currently lives in Northern California.

Debbie Prather is a people-loving introvert and has a weakness for powerful, redemptive stories. Her essay "When God Whispers" about her family's adoption experience is included in the national bestselling book, *So God Made a Mother*. She shares her reflections about faith, family, mothering, and marriage at 742iloveyou.com.

Melinda Pritzel is a graduate of Avila University, Kansas City, MO. She enjoys photography and uses her photography skills, together with her love of animals and humor, to create greeting cards. You can find her cards at greetingcarduniverse.com/yowzers.

Toya Qualls-Barnette holds a B.A. in Communications/Public Relations from Pepperdine University, Malibu. Originally from Los Angeles, she resides in Northern California with her husband and two sons. Toya enjoys travel, music, and writing inspirational stories. Her fictional memoir will be published in late 2025-2026.

Shirlene Joan Raymann has a master's degree in psychology. She has been practicing psychology for thirty-five years. She loves spirituality, and connection to the divine is an integral part of her life. She is committed to living her best life and continues to say "yes" to opportunities coming on her path. Her sons are her biggest joy.

Ruth Rogers is a former public television producer, writer, and on-air host. Now a career coach, she empowers others to listen to their hearts and follow their dreams. She is a person of faith and a life-long learner. She and her husband have two grown children, five grandchildren, and live in the Midwest.

Patricia Rossi is an avid writer. Many of her essays, academic articles and poems have been published in literary and scholarly journals, newspapers, and magazines. In her spare time, she volunteers, serving on a number of local non-profit boards and facilitating "writing to heal" workshops for cancer survivors.

Judy Salcewicz is a poet, playwright, and story writer. She lives, writes, and gardens in New Jersey. Judy feels lucky to be part of the *Chicken Soup for the Soul* series. She is a cancer survivor who hopes others find inspiration in her life stories.

Kristen Schad received her Bachelor of Science degree from SUNY Cortland. She worked in Human Services for years before moving to the Eastern Shore of Virginia in 2020. She has two children and a granddaughter. Kristen enjoys photography, travel, camping and gardening. She is now a high school career coach.

Claudia Irene Scott is a freelance writer, feature newspaper columnist and women's magazines contributor. A retired educator and native New Englander, she lives in Florida with her husband of fifty-one years. Her passions are visiting art museums and formal gardens, and reading history and mythology. E-mail her at Cipscott@comcast.net.

Patricia Senkiw-Rudowsky earned a B.A. degree from Kean University in 1983. She spent her adult life working as a prevention educator using her creativity as a tool to convey lessons. She is retired now and writing about the many inspirational moments she has been blessed to experience. E-mail her at Storyteller1012@aol.com.

Judy Bailey Sennett is a retired school counselor living a charmed life with her two cats, Amos and Frankie, in suburban Philadelphia, PA. She enjoys singing, gardening, book club discussions, playing with her grandchildren, and writing about the wisdom she has gained from a lifetime of rewarding experiences.

Billie Holladay Skelley received her bachelor's and master's degrees from the University of Wisconsin. A retired clinical nurse specialist, she is the mother of four and grandmother of three. Billie enjoys writing, and her work crosses several genres. She spends her non-writing time reading, gardening, and traveling.

Maureen Slater is a wife, mother, grandmother, and a retired nurse. She has three married children and eight adorable grandchildren. She loves to write short stories and poems.

Karen Storey is an award-winning writer and has been featured on the "Bestseller Experiment". Her stories have won places in several global competitions. Born in New York, she lives in England with her husband, whose surname Storey was the perfect wedding gift, along with a Zoom–crashing cat and a dog who barks at the sky.

Jennifer Stults grew up in a suburb of Portland, OR. She has one daughter and a very supportive extended family. When tragedy struck, she found writing to be her only way out. She has written and self-published a book about her grief entitled *Carry on Castle* which is available online.

Deborah Tainsh is a published author of poetry, short stories, a children's book, an anthology of military family stories, and a personal memoir regarding the death of an Army son in the Iraq war and the grief journey that followed. She is the widow of a retired U.S. Marine and Mom to Phillip. E-mail her at deborahtainsh@msn.com.

Jodi Renee Thomas started as a performance art/fashion designer. In her late thirties she took a chance at writing. She has spoken on women's rights, produced successful plays, and been a proud member of the Chicken Soup for the Soul family for almost a decade. She lives happily in Florida with her husband and dogs, who like to help her type.

Christine Trollinger is a retired insurance agent. She is a widow and has three children, three grandchildren, and three great-grandchildren.

Christine enjoys writing, family and her friends. Over the past twenty years, she has been published in several books in the *Chicken Soup for the Soul* series.

Diane Young Uniman is a lawyer turned writer and motivational speaker. Her writing won numerous awards including IAN's Book of the Year, LA Short Film & Script Festival's Best Comedy Script, Beverly Hills Film Festival, and was featured at Lincoln Center and Off-Broadway. She's blogger Princess Diane von Brainisfried.

Molly Mulrooney Wade is a mother, a Catholic, a writer, and lives in constant pursuit of joy. God has blessed her in a million ways, and she strives to return the favor every day.

Beverly F. Walker is currently living in Knoxville, TN. Besides writing, she enjoys crafting and a little gardening. She is counting her blessings in her senior years and hoping to stay healthy!

Ruth L. Wallace, PhD practiced clinical dietetics in the field of mental health in Kansas, California and Arizona. She has enjoyed publishing two non-fiction books and flying The Green Apple hot air balloon. Ruth has three children and is now retired, living in Arizona.

Melinda White is a freelance photographer who lives in Ekron, KY with her husband and three children. She has a B.A. in English from Freed-Hardeman University and has worked for several newspapers as a reporter and photographer. She loves to write stories and is always reading.

Ferida Wolff is the author of nineteen children's books and three books for adults as well as the contributor to more than two dozen books in the *Chicken Soup for the Soul* series.

Elisa Yager has been out of school for a very long time. Since then, she has raised two great children, enjoyed a rewarding career in Human Resources and Safety and is looking forward to retirement in the near future. Her hobbies include refurnishing furniture and working on her historical fiction novel.

Linda Zelik is a retired occupational therapist, mother and grand-mother. After the tragic loss of her son, she published *From Despair to Hope: Survival Guide for Bereaved Parents* to help others in their grief. Linda is a volunteer puppy raiser for Canine Companions, a provider of free assistance dogs for the disabled.

Kristine Ziegler lives in Southern California.

Luanne Tovey Zuccari lives in Western New York and is a retired public relations and news writer and Coordinator of her county's MADD chapter. She has two children and eight wonderful grandchildren. She was recently inducted into the local school district Wall of Fame for community/school service.

Meet Amy Newmark

Amy Newmark is the bestselling author, editor-in-chief, and publisher of the *Chicken Soup for the Soul* book series. Since 2008, she has published 200 new books, most of them national bestsellers in the U.S. and Canada, more than doubling the number of Chicken Soup for the Soul titles in print today. She is also the author of *Simply Happy*, a crash course in Chicken Soup for the Soul advice and wisdom that is filled with easy-to-implement, practical tips for enjoying a better life.

Amy is credited with revitalizing the Chicken Soup for the Soul brand, which has been a publishing industry phenomenon since the first book came out in 1993. By compiling inspirational and aspirational true stories curated from ordinary people who have had extraordinary experiences, Amy has kept the thirty-one-year-old Chicken Soup for the Soul brand fresh and relevant.

Amy graduated *magna cum laude* from Harvard University where she majored in Portuguese and minored in French. She then embarked on a three-decade career as a Wall Street analyst, a hedge fund manager, and a corporate executive in the technology field. She is a Chartered Financial Analyst.

Her return to literary pursuits was inevitable, as her honors thesis in college involved traveling throughout Brazil's impoverished northeast region, collecting stories from regular people. She is delighted to have come full circle in her writing career — from collecting stories "from the people" in Brazil as a twenty-year-old to, three decades later, collecting stories "from the people" for Chicken Soup for the Soul.

When Amy and her husband Bill, the CEO of Chicken Soup for the Soul, are not working, they are visiting their four grown children and their spouses, and their five grandchildren.

Follow Amy on X and Instagram @amynewmark. Listen to her free podcast — Chicken Soup for the Soul with Amy Newmark — on Apple, Google, or by using your favorite podcast app on your phone. You can also find a selection of her stories on Medium.

Thank You

We owe huge thanks to all our contributors and fans. We received thousands of submissions for this popular topic, and we spent months reading all of them. Laura Dean, Maureen Peltier, Kristiana Pastir and D'ette Corona read all of them and narrowed down the selection for Publisher and Editor-in-Chief Amy Newmark. Susan Heim did the first round of editing, and then D'ette chose the perfect quotations to put at the beginning of each story and Amy edited the stories and shaped the final manuscript.

As we finished our work, D'ette continued to be Amy's right-hand woman in working with all our wonderful writers. Barbara LoMonaco, Kristiana Pastir and Elaine Kimbler jumped in to proof, proof, proof. And yes, there will always be typos anyway, so please feel free to let us know about them at webmaster@chickensoupforthesoul.com, and we will correct them in future printings.

The whole publishing team deserves a hand, including our Vice President of Marketing Maureen Peltier, our Vice President of Production & COO Victor Cataldo, and our graphic designer Daniel Zaccari, who turned our manuscript into this beautiful, inspirational book.

Sharing Happiness, Inspiration, and Hope

Real people sharing real stories, every day, all over the world. In 2007, *USA Today* named *Chicken Soup for the Soul* one of the five most memorable books in the last quarter-century. With over 110 million books sold to date in the U.S. and Canada alone, more than 300 titles in print, and translations into nearly fifty languages, "chicken soup for the soul®" is one of the world's best-known phrases.

Today, thirty-one years after we first began sharing happiness, inspiration and hope through our books, we continue to delight our readers with ten to twelve new titles each year but have also evolved beyond the bookshelves with super premium pet food, a podcast, adult coloring books, and licensed products that include word-search puzzle books and books for babies and preschoolers. We are busy "changing your life one story at a time®" Thanks for reading!

Share with Us

We have all had Chicken Soup for the Soul moments in our lives. If you would like to share your story, go to chickensoup.com and click on Books and then Submit Your Story. You will find our writing guidelines there, along with a list of topics we're working on.

You may be able to help another reader and become a published author at the same time! Some of our past contributors have even launched writing and speaking careers from the publication of their stories in our books.

We only accept story submissions via our website. They are no longer accepted via postal mail or fax. And they are not accepted via e-mail.

To contact us regarding other matters, please send an e-mail to the webmaster@chickensoupforthesoul.com, or write us at:

Chicken Soup for the Soul
P.O. Box 700
Cos Cob, CT 06807-0700

One more note from your friends at Chicken Soup for the Soul: Occasionally, we receive an unsolicited book manuscript from one of our readers, and we would like to respectfully inform you that we do not accept unsolicited manuscripts, and we must discard the ones that are sent to us.

Angels and Miracles

101 Inspirational Stories about Hope, Answered Prayers, and Divine Intervention

Amy Newmark

Paperback: 978-1-61159-964-0
eBook: 978-1-61159-263-4

More angels and miracles...

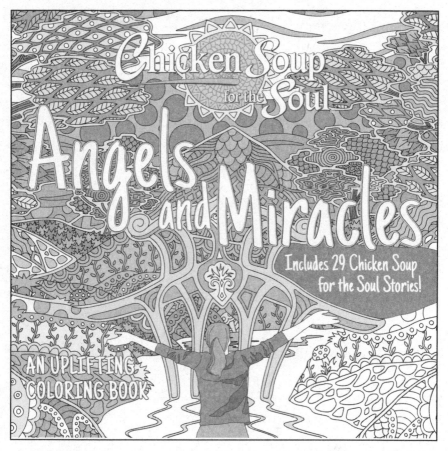

Paperback: 978-1-61159-106-4

to read and color!

Changing your world one story at a time®
www.chickensoup.com